SEMESTERTICKET
ABSCHAFFEN
MACH WAS
DAGEGEN!

di::angewandte

Massive Attack

edition: 'ʌngewʌndtə
Book Series of the University of Applied Arts Vienna
Edited by Gerald Bast, Rector

Massive Attack

IOA Sliver Lecture Series:
Selected Friends and Enemies

Edited by Wolf D. Prix & Kristy Balliet

Birkhäuser Basel

Massive Attack
IOA Sliver Lecture Series:
Selected Friends and Enemies

Editors
Wolf D. Prix, Kristy Balliet

Managing Editor
Alexandra Graupner,
Roswitha Janowski-Fritsch

Assistant Editor
Angelika Zelisko

Contributing Editors
Kristy Balliet, Justin Diles, Caroline Ecker, Alexandra Graupner, Roswitha Janowski-Fritsch, Anja Jonkhans, Robert Neumayr, Güvenc Özel

Copy editing
Matthew Weiner

Translator
Janima Nam, Camilla Nielsen

Transcriptions
Susanna Ernst, Sille Pihlak, Daniel Rhomberg

Photography
Katharina Kohlroser, Csenge Lanszki,
Reiner Zettl

Design
Atelier Dreibholz London/Vienna,
Paulus M. Dreibholz and Ana Luísa Martelo

Print
Paul Gerin GmbH

Head of Institute
Klaus Bollinger, Institute of Architecture,
University of Applied Arts Vienna, Austria

Library of Congress Cataloging-in-Publication data. A CIP catalog record for this book has been applied for at the Library of Congress.

Bibliographic information published by the German National Library. The German National Library lists this publication in the Deutsche Nationalbibliografie; detailed bibliographic data are available on the Internet at http://dnb.dnb.de.

This work is subject to copyright. All rights are reserved, whether the whole or part of the material is concerned, specifically the rights of translation, reprinting, re-use of illustrations, recitation, broadcasting, reproduction on microfilms or in other ways, and storage in databases.

For any kind of use, permission of the copyright owner must be obtained.

© 2015 Birkhäuser Verlag GmbH, Basel
P.O. Box 44, 4009 Basel, Switzerland
Part of Walter de Gruyter GmbH, Berlin/
Boston

Printed in Austria on acid-free paper produced from chlorine-free pulp. TCF ∞

ISBN 978-3-99043-458-1

www.birkhauser.com

CONTENTS

Reality Architecture

Foreword by Sylvia Lavin

As in television, so in architecture: reality is in. Architectural discourse has been taken over by a new kind of realism as professional practice protocols of budgets, ventilation systems, clients and real estate now occupy the places of architectural attention filled not long ago by the idealities of diagrams, 9-square grids, media matters and critical theory. And if the Pritzker Prize is not yet akin to *American Idol* or *Keeping Up with the Kardashians*, the spectacle of the real is just as present on data-covered architectural "boards" as it is in the hellish kitchens on BBC.

The irony is that all this convergence produces not reality but rather so many different realities that the very concept comes undone, revealed as but an effect of how it is produced. While the reality of TV is a place born of exaggerated histrionics, the reality of architecture is filled with sober charts and the parading of facts. Similarly, if the turn to reality in TV began as a way of reducing production costs (no writers, no actors' fees, no residuals required for participants in *Big Brother*), the turn to reality for architecture is meant to suggest not a base interest in finding ways to make more money but rather the opposite, an elevated interest in serving the social good (and a supposed corollary self-disinterest on the part of the architect). There is no pretense of contributing to the social good amongst the *Housewives of New Jersey*. And if *Bridezilla* offers only the faintest hint that her reality is actually real, architects seem impressively convinced by theirs.

The Lecture Series is the name given by architecture schools to their reality programming. Each school, or rather network channel, hosts its own seasonal series—the Angewandte's is called SLIVER—the logo is sometimes shown as sLIVEr—with individual episodes in the form of lectures that come and go. Well, they are supposed to come and go, a succession of oral performances, their very evanescence permitting them to offer a touch of color to the flow of architecture's everyday life and a soupçon of realism for the education of young architects. The Lecture Series has transcended its traditional role as a mere supplement to other more familiar and respectable architectural formats, like books or buildings or curricula, to constitute a genre of discourse and a category of architectural design in its own terms. So important has the lecture series become to schools of architecture that every school must have one, and often not just one, but an evening series, a lunch time series, coffee klatsches and pecha kucha nights.

Yet despite (or because of) this achievement and potential, lecture series, like reality TV itself, have expanded beyond simple ubiquity to enter the realm of extreme proliferation. Just as reality TV began as a reformatting of the documentary film, the architectural lecture series initially offered the murmur of an inquisitive accompaniment whispering prods and provocations to the major melody of the field. Lectures were where the reality of practice could give way to the idealities of reflection and critique. Now, in contrast, they seem driven fully to mimic Reality TV with each speaker goaded into screaming "I've got talent!" to a mystified panel of judges. In such cases, the lecture series functions less as an entertainment event and more as a costly branding tool of the architectural academy. Hosting a lecture series in these instances is a good excuse to produce a media blitz linking the name of an institution to the names of famous architects, not so famous architects, once famous architects, up and coming architects or the next best thing. It's hard not to imagine that sooner rather than later some dean or other will have the good sense to save all those travel costs and honoraria fees and just send out a Web Blast listing a bunch of events without bothering or ever intending to have a lecture series at all. One can read this tendency toward the not quite beyond good and evil without ever going to a single lecture. And I mean read in the most old-fashioned sense of the term since architectural programs have, given their otherwise traditional penchant to showcase their use of new technologies and mediums, an unexpected attachment to "the poster." What makes the attachment odd (and perhaps sentimental) is the fact that many other formats are certainly more efficient or at least more agile in disseminating the content of any given lecture, the facts pertaining to a series, and even in producing the rub-off effects of fame or stature by association (between school and lecturer). Indeed, the persistent use of the poster is increasingly anachronistic, a vaguely nostalgic evocation of the good old days of the Russian Revolution when posters plastered city walls, subversive and irrepressible signs of political protest. The question now is not only if those days have faded from view but whether or not their potential legacy is degraded by endless school corridors decorated with advertisements that speak through their production value above all of an institution's budgetary strength. I'm not sure if the number of colors or special cutting used in producing the posters is meant directly to indicate the number of CNC drill bits or 3-D printers available to the students, but there is some correlation of resources that is implied. And as if their material costs weren't evidence enough, their graphic design has developed an arms race quality—bigger, shinier, more composite, more folded—turning Neutra's *Survival by Design* into *Survivor! by Design*. This dynamic not only reveals the poster's primary embeddedness in fiscal rather than political or disciplinary forces, but indicates the degree to which the poster is more a weapon in the increasingly fierce economic competition between schools than an instrument for or against the state (of architecture and its pedagogies).

If lecture series are an excuse to produce a poster, and if posters are the tradition of paper architecture reincarnated as a branding tool, what impact on or relation to the lectures themselves does this packaging have? ituned, podcasted and YouTubed within an inch of their lives, differences in their content or particular form of delivery notwithstanding, lectures can no longer claim the light touch of ephemerality. Whatever Walter Benjamin thought the photograph was going to do to aura, the Internet has so proliferated the sights and sounds of just about everything that the relationship between reproduction and aura has started a boomerang phenomenon wherein the conflation of multiple channels of audio and visual information (the image of the architect, the images of her work, images of work already seen in magazines, images held back from magazines and shown only in lectures, etc.) constitutes a new *ding an sich* with its own vastly magnified aura. No matter how much more sense it makes to watch the latest show and tell of recent work by this or that architect from the comfort of your own computer, audiences are lured by the sweet enticements of "liveness." Or rather to the stage where conflicting notions of "liveness" are worked out. If neo-realism has so overtaken the field that architects have ceased to understand that when they are talking to a client, presenting in a board room or "dialoging" with a community review panel they are performing a part, the theatrics of lectures, for which the poster serves as a kind of preliminary proscenium, the red curtain of anticipation, forces even the most dyed-in-the-wool worshippers of reality architecture to understand that they are part of a show. In fact, *The Lecture Series* show is the best place to see the field grappling with the stupefying contradictions between its zealous attachment to the real and its intoxication with the virtualities of media, mediations and money.

Pushed in part by packaging to become Reality TV, *The Lecture Series* in turn is changing the terms of both reality and our experiences of it. *Sliver: The Series* is a specific example of how architecture participates in the cultural regime of the reality entertainment industry. And while I am fairly positive that none of the curators of Sliver know this film, I think of *Sliver: The Series* as a remake of a film made when film rather than reality TV was in. Sliver, the 1993 movie, is about architecture and its shaping of the culture of voyeurism and exhibitionism, cultural habits that were still considered perversions in the1990s but that by now through reality TV and social networking are just the lubricants to social engagements of any kind. The film's title refers to a thin infill high-rise apartment building in NY, a typology produced by the real estate boom of that era. Over the course of the movie, real relationships between neighbors turn into manias fed by one-way security systems, video monitors and other visual apparatus until the inevitable mayhem ensues caused by the confusion between CCTV that looks real and some other kind of realness. It should come as no surprise that Diller + Scofidio were consultants on the film, although the relationship was short lived.

If *Sliver: The Movie* was engaged with the issues that concerned architects in the 1990s, like surveillance and security, *Sliver: The Series* engages issues that concern architects today, such as color and material. And while for some these phenomena and others like them script a discourse of neo-positivist realism, *Sliver: The Series* instead scripts a reality spectacle. A nicely crafted Freudian slip, a combination tongue twister rebus and logo, *sLIVEr* oscillates verbally and visually between Silver and Live, performing like a gestalt figure/ground drawing that never settles down into a single term. This indeterminacy is the best thing about *The Lecture Series* and the most productive aspect of its allegiance with reality TV. No matter how faithful to facts and figures even some progressive architects think they are, fiction becomes paramount in the lecture. As such, lectures that appear to serve as reinforcements to the real undermine the false positivisms of architectural realism instead.

Does it matter who lectured in this series or that one? What they said and how they said it? Yes, but not in structural terms. Despite heartfelt claims to the contrary, there isn't that much difference between one school's lecture programming and another, particularly over the long run. The series may have begun as a means of distinguishing one school from another and of feeding architecture's cult of celebrity, but there is an overall leveling effect that produces sameness instead. Does anyone remember who won the first season of *Big Brother* or who lectured where last year? Yes, there is significance in who was invited to the Angewandte and who was not—apparently it was both friends and enemies, tribes on both sides of the *Bully Beat Down* fence. But these differences emerge only after very close readings of each episode, an exercise in discrimination that is at odds with the spectacle of seriality itself. This is especially evident in *Sliver*, a series over the multi-semester course of which the list of speakers kept getting longer and longer and longer. As I was reading the list, without ever getting to the end, I began to think that everyone who calls themselves an architect had been invited to speak and that a few more who don't call themselves architects were included for good measure. And then I started to assume that students had had to drop out of school in order to attend all these lectures. Perhaps they just moved into the lecture hall to watch a literally endless series of episodes of "reality architecture." In my fantasy, watching architecture on the IoA channel became the reality of becoming an architect, which then turned the school into a live-on set where life itself was taken over by the false event. Or rather by what architecture does best, which is to produce an endless version of reality, bent to its own will. The intersection between architecture and the real used to be exemplified in films such as Andy Warhol's *Empire*, a single almost interminable shot of the Empire State building, a moving picture that caught the building live on film doing nothing. Warhol used the cultural expectations of architectural slowness and stillness to raise questions about what constitutes life, liveness and their unfolding, what kinds of events rise to the occasion of the meaningful. Now Reality TV has taken up this problem where everyday architecture is often the setting not for life but for the interminable staging of an increasingly deadening reality. Reality TV now needs architecture and its uncanny success in faking the real to bring some life back into its spectacle.

Architecture has what might be called historic expertise in managing the real, so it was inevitable that sooner or later Reality Architecture would present itself as an important opportunity to rethink the terrain of architectural design. And *The Lecture Series* is the perfect showcase for this rethinking: the ideologically taciturn architect, the architect with little to say, who wants silently to say that the work speaks for itself, who wishes to claim for architecture pure instrumentality and base economic metrics, this silent architect may be a star in real life but is a poor choice of star for Reality Architecture. The exigencies of neo-professionalism, the realities of practice and sustainability equations, don't make a good show unless they are well stage-managed and given adequate special effects. But of course this makeover transforms them instantly into performance rather than fact and in so doing gives even the taciturn architect a new lease on life. So if *The Lecture Series* at first appears to be a shift away from what was called the linguistic turn and towards the exigencies of capital and production, its effects turn out to be counter counter-revolutionary instead. An endless streaming of talk, cheap talk, recorded talk, chatter and any number of words, utterances, images and stuff even only tangentially related to architecture, on the face of it, by its very indeterminate, multiplicitous nature, serves to undercut architecture's attachment to the false idol of the real. Reality Architecture may be the final holdout against total capitulation to architecture as a service industry feeding the "experience economy of reality," and in this resistance, in this tiny sliver wherein other realities may yet be produced, architecture can still hope to do some real good.

Selected Friends and Enemies

Introduction by Wolf D. Prix

"Selected friends and enemies" is a title with a long story but I will keep it very short. Back in 1968, when we opened our first office in Vienna, we asked ourselves, "Who should we invite?" Our office was a big loft; therefore, if we only invited our friends, the office would have still been quite empty ...
So we decided not just to invite friends but also selected enemies. Actually, it was a great success. Lots of people came and said, "I am your enemy—can I have a glass of wine?"

The same happened when inviting people to this lecture series. A lot of them said, "I will be there, but count me towards your enemies."

At this point, I explicitly want to thank Kristy Balliet and Alexandra Graupner for organizing the IOA Sliver Lecture and Gallery Series since 2008.

Hans Hollein. It is a great pleasure for me to have Hans Hollein here as the first lecturer, as the keynote speaker so to say of our two semester lecture series.
There is a special reason behind my pleasure; after all it was he who brought me to this place, to this university. As you might know, Professor Hollein shaped an institute—precisely and decisively through his long-lasting teaching activity—with an outstanding international reputation. We owe this to him, amongst other things. Architects today can be described in various ways. They are either betrayers, defaming the architectural profession like enemies, or renegades, who betray their dreams right after school and pave the way for the so-called practical constraints. Those are the personalities we have to beware of. The partisans or rather the resistance fighters neither betray nor recant their ideals. Over and over they transgress the boundaries of their own understanding in order to prove that architecture is more than just fulfillment of an economic or functional constraint.

Reality doesn't create us, but we create reality.

Lectures

Hans Hollein / Eva Schlegel /
Kivi Sotamaa / Kristin Feireiss /
Erwin Wurm / Aaron Betsky /
Patrik Schumacher / Zaha Hadid /
Peter Cook / Peter Noever /
Hitoshi Abe / Nicolai Ouroussoff /
Gerhard Matzig / Thom Mayne /
Eric Owen Moss / Marie-Therese
Harnoncourt / Greg Lynn /
Brennan Buck / Winy Maas /
Brett Steele / Hani Rashid /
Michael Rotondi / Carme Pinós /
Wolf D. Prix

Hans Hollein

Works and Ideas

Edited by Kristy Balliet

1 Tomb of Eurysaces the Baker, Rome, 1960

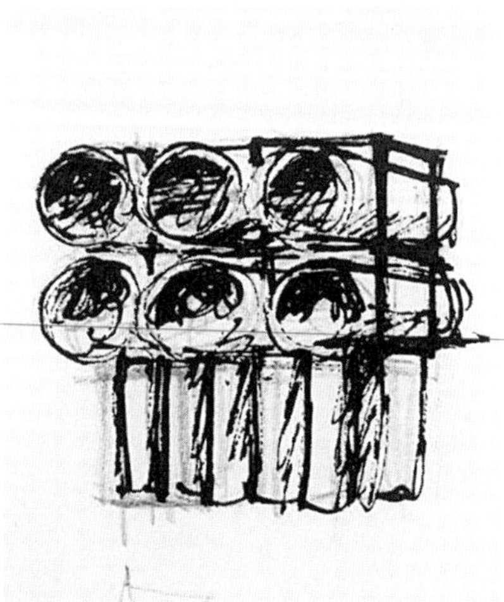

2 Baker's Tomb Inspired Sketch, Hans Hollein, 1960

Thank you for your introduction, Wolf [D. Prix]. I am honored to talk here today and we will see how long it lasts. Sometimes my lectures last very long. [laughter]

It was the early 1950s, and I wanted to get out into the world. Europe ...

SPAIN

I hitchhiked to Spain. The railroad still had four classes, one, two, three, four. So below "Holzklasse" there was an even lower one. But you could have a pass that allowed you to travel anywhere in Spain. So that was ideal for me, I was there for two months. I saw Barcelona, churches, *trojas*, a variety of things. I went to Santiago de Compostela. At that time no pilgrims came to Santiago, only a few. Today it's a fashion to go to Santiago de Compostela. So for me, this encounter was very important.

ROME

It was also interesting to go to Rome. When I came to Rome of course I saw many of the things you have to see. But I was very interested in this building, which I thought was a very condensed architecture. (fig.1) It's the baker's tomb, the hollow circles had to do with baking and the others were pilaster or columns. So for me this was a very important encounter, also because it was already partly destroyed. And I tried to translate this into a language of the twentieth century. I made my version of the baker's tomb. It gave me an idea: you have to have columns and you have to have tubes. (fig.2)

CANTILEVERS

Later on, I extended this vocabulary—my own vocabulary—and I had a building, which was cantilevering out into the space. (fig.3) You have a space underneath. I also thought about what typologies may be important for the development of building in architecture. And for me, I started to have some kind of hill, something above the level of the earth. Or you had parts going into the earth. These are the first things I thought were important in architecture and in building.

And that you can go on, you can go in a kind of geometry, you can rise up the little hill and further on you go on and on and this was for instance clock towers and other kinds of towers, but they were also then becoming skyscrapers. So that was around the nineteenth century and I became interested in the extension into space and the cantilever. So this went on. It was the architecture of the 1920s, 1930s, 1950s. And also next was that you could rise into oblique shapes. So basically, you had something sticking out, radiating out; you had an enclosure, and what at that time was called tensions through juxtapositions.

CHICAGO/UNITED STATES

In 1958 there was a very important change in my life because I received a fellowship for the United States, the Harkness Fellowship. The fellowship indicated that you could study where you wanted, that you could travel. I said, "I want to study in Chicago with Mies van der Rohe." They gave me a car and I had seven dollars a day. I had to take care of my meals and gasoline. Gasoline fortunately was cheap. So finally, I had covered at the end of my fellowship 100,000 kilometers, crisscrossing the United States and a little part of Mexico.

When I arrived in Chicago, of course I looked at the skyscrapers and the Illinois Institute of Technology (IIT), but I also tried to ... I was interested very much at the time in Frank Lloyd Wright (FLW). I knew FLW of course and have seen books of FLW. I liked his architecture very much. But it was a completely different thing when I saw FLW's buildings in reality. I decided to dive deeper into his work and at the end I had practically seen all FLW's buildings in the United States, even the big styles in Alabama and so on. I thought, I want to talk to FLW, so I took the telephone and tried to get FLW's studio in Wisconsin. And I said, "Here is Mr. Hollein and I would like to meet the master." And within a week I got a message: You are invited to dinner with FLW. To encounter this person was of course a very important thing. On the other hand, it was very interesting. I was one of three guests at the time. The guests introduced themselves. And I came into the studio and up there was a painting—a painting by Klimt. At that time in New York, you could have Klimt drawings for 10 dollars. FLW was wonderful, the first person in years who knew that this was Klimt. FLW had been in Vienna—it's a famous story—with the wife of his client. He came to Europe and then there was the Wasmuth portfolio. This was always very interesting for me because he had to leave the United States and draw the drawings for the Wasmuth portfolio ... I hope you know it. This was a little lengthy thing, but it was something to tell you, I think that you are students and starting architects, so this was a very important encounter.

MIES VAN DER ROHE

I was a student of Mies van der Rohe and these were some first sketches of skyscrapers I made as a student there. I dove deeper into the discussion of the skyscraper because Chicago was the center of the involvement of the skyscraper. I tried to make slight modulations of the Miesian skyscraper. I did many sketches. But then I thought I wanted a little

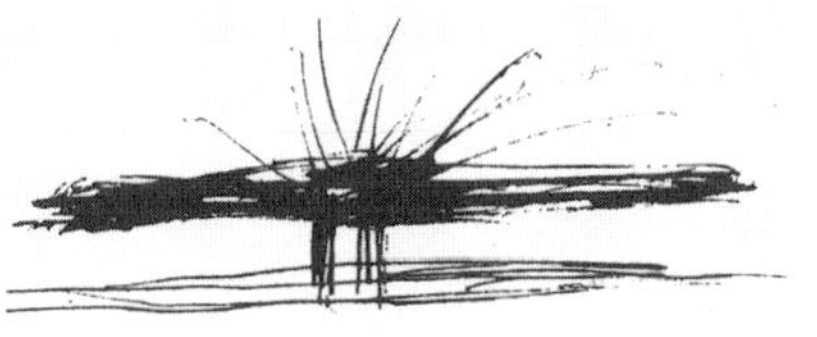

3 Cantilever Building Sketch, 1958

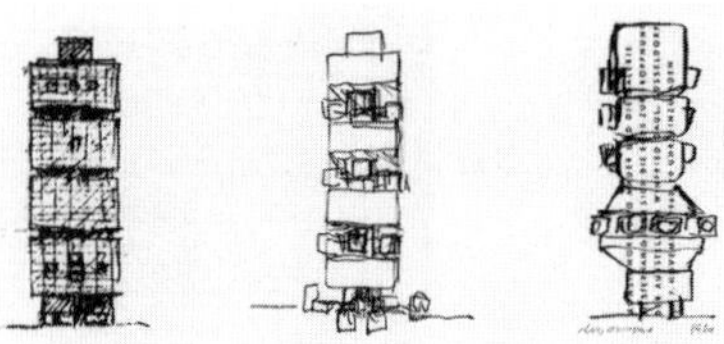

4 Skyscraper Sketch, Chicago, from left to right: 1958, 1959, 1960

5 Skyscraper Sketches, Chicago, 1958

6 *Potjomkin* sculpture, University of California Berkeley, 1960

difference. And the difference looked… But remember this skyscraper (fig.4) and so I said: What is a skyscraper? And this is a skyscraper, and this is a skyscraper… I drew a lot of skyscrapers. (fig.5) I also made a skyscraper on the basis of Panama and the Panama Canal. The skyscraper cuts through the Panama Canal.

CALIFORNIA, HOVERING CITIES

I went to Berkeley and I did my master's, and there I also started with skyscrapers, models and then a city. I made an exhibition in Berkeley and this was a hanging sculpture I called *Potjomkin*. (fig.6) This was not thought to be a building but something in the air. But was this a city or just a building? You could sit in this model. I graduated and went on with what I had in my pocket about cities, hovering cities. The city I had envisioned at the Berkeley project above Vienna. (fig.7) This is a cultural building. That's another hovering element.

I had an idea to say this former plan equals the section. You could turn this building in all directions in space. You could go up and down into the earth. I was interested in aircraft carriers because aircraft carriers are a city. (fig.8) At that time, 7,000 people lived in an aircraft carrier and they had every necessity they needed for survival. You had hospitals; you had storage for crops and whatever. So I said, "Why don't we put a 7000-person aircraft carrier as a city into a landscape?" This is the landscape in Austria, in Lower Austria. So that was the idea, to have a building with a skyscraper. Of course, I also thought what other objects you could transfer into buildings: giant cars or a Rolls Royce grille in Manhattan (fig.9) or another high-rise or a monument for the victims of the Holocaust.

FIRST BUILDING, CANDLE SHOP

I show you now my first real building, by me. I mean, I had worked on very big buildings in other architects' offices, but this

7 Collage Over Vienna, 1960, Collection Centre Georges Pompidou, Paris

8 Aircraft Carrier in the Landscape, 1964, Collection MoMA Museum of Modern Art, New York, Philip Johnson Fund, 1967

was my first building. It was a candle shop, a very strange thing to have a candle shop. It was 60 square meters. And I decided to make out of it an architectural manifesto. I wanted new materials, and I took aluminum. And I had ideas set to see it, to have showcases. (fig.10) There are two parts: in the first space you have some candles exhibited and in the next one was actually storage, but it was storage you could walk into and select. That for me, space-wise is this very small building. I wanted to open it up into the infinite.

NEXT CHAPTER

Again, I had small exhibitions in architecture, I had them in art. I don't need to tell now a long story. I was asked by the director of the new museum in Mönchengladbach—that was a city at that time very well known for soccer, but not at all for culture. So they absolutely wanted a museum and the director of the museum had made exhibitions of my work both in architecture and in art, so he suggested me. And so then I had the opportunity to make this building and this museum, which was the most sort of completely new idea about museums. (fig.11) This was a building which was also a walk-on building. A part of the building is subterranean. There is this hill and you can walk down these undulating walls, which go over into the old city walls. And you have one of these Greek temples, which is the entrance to the building. Mönchengladbach Museum was a very important step forward because I received the Pritzker Prize.

MUSEUMS

A museum in Tehran, in an old building from the Qajar period. I was asked to make a Museum of Glass and Ceramics. The building was considered by the University of Munich, that the loads of the population were serious. But I wanted to keep the opening and windows. So I built into the building an additional structure to stabilize, but I otherwise left the building and just repaired it. And here you have glass, 2,500 years old. And here some of these showcases you have half a million lux of light on the glass because this glass is 2,500 years old, and glass this old you cannot see anymore. (fig.12) It looks more like ceramic or something. There were some places which were destroyed so we made a contemporary interior.

PILLS AND INFLATABLES

And this is … I thought it would be … I developed an office, where I could have an office and come with an airplane, inflate it …

9 Rolls Royce Grill on Wallstreet, 1966

10 Retti Candle Shop, Vienna, 1964–1965

11 Städtisches Museum Abteiberg Mönchengladbach, 1972–1982

12 Museum of Glass and Ceramics Tehran, 1977–1978

13 Mobile Office, 1969, Collection Generali Foundation Vienna

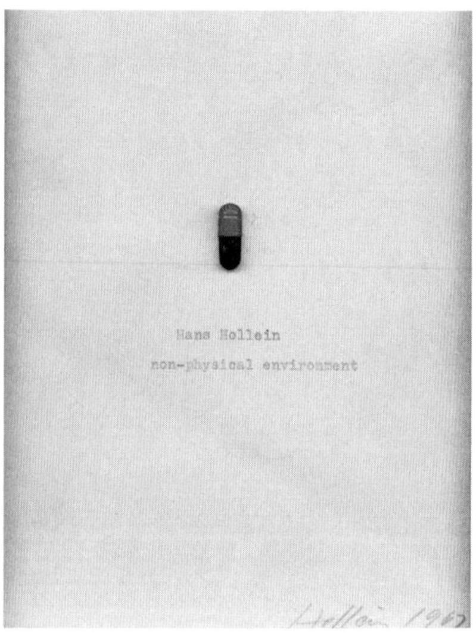

14 Hans Hollein, Non-Physical Environment Pill, 1969

Today you would need not just a drawing board. (fig.13) And this brought me to the idea of a size where you could survive and work also. I developed a telephone object that you could sit there, work there and finally you can use it as a coffin. And the other was the non-physical environment. (fig.14) A pill, from which you can get whatever you want, in terms of let's say also architecture. And starting from the idea of how you treat claustrophobia or agoraphobia with certain drugs, that you could also get elements for ... let's say the Hagia Sophia as a building. Today it is very outdated, but at that time was a project of mine—how you extend the university in Vienna. Inflatables had a number of possibilities.

VENICE BIENNALE

This is Strada Novissima in Venice at the rope factory. I was invited to do façades in this long corridor. I decided not to make façades, but I decided to take up the motive of the already existing columns and in between have a variety of other columns. Some you can read easily: Adolf Loos, and another column from Vitra. The strange thing is that it has now—in the Centre Pompidou is an exhibition not only about this, but about things like that. (fig.15) So we have the most contacts now, asking for this, we don't know why.

UNDERGROUND

Back again into questions of the underground. And this is my winning project for Volcania in France. (fig.16) The building, 50 percent above and 50 percent below. These were some first ideas, collages I made. (fig.17) Here you see the extinguished volcanoes at 1,000-meter altitude. And you have a museum, which is more than 50 percent below. You walk down a walk, there are volcanic stones. You have this metaphorical volcano with the inside of this golden lining and a restaurant on top. So you walk down and ... This is stainless steel and titanium gold color as a metaphor of the volcano. And here you dig down deep into the earth.

Finally, this goes back to one of the projects I made in Chicago,

1958. [reference fig.4] And this is a project in China, in Shenzhen. (fig.18) It is a city which came up in the last 30 years. It was a village 30 years ago and has now seven million people. And Shenzhen wants to have the most important stock exchange in the world, and there was a competition for that. I didn't participate because I didn't know about it. Rem Koolhaas won this competition. That is Rem Koolhaas and the stock exchange. And this is our building for two banks, Chinese Bank and ... It goes back to the idea, which I worked on in Chicago in 1958, that you have open and closed elements in the skyscraper. And we are starting construction this December.

And with this I end my lecture. Thank you!

15 *Strada Novissima, The Presence of the Past*, 1980, Venice Biennale, 1980

16 Vulcania, European Center of Volcanism, St. Ours-les-Roches, France, 1994–2002

17 Vulcania Museum Sketch, 1994, Hans Hollein

18 SBF Tower Shenzen, China (rendering), 2009

Eva Schlegel

On Failure

Edited by Robert Neumayr

1 Untitled, 1985, Super8 film on ventilator, diameter 60 cm

Eva Schlegel is one of those Austrian artists who pushed the envelope of the narrow borderlines of the Austrian mind. I met her about 20 years ago in Los Angeles at an Art Fair where she was presented as an emerging young artist. She was dressed in a black leather suit, black hair and black eyelashes. A girl all in black at the Austrian Embassy reception. She was sitting there yelling at the waiters for another glass of champagne and we both pulled the tails of a waiter's long suit, so that he stopped and suddenly the tray, full of glasses, fell on the floor. That was the beginning of our cooperation.

I once proclaimed that architecture could be the art of the twenty-first century. Therefore it contradicts the functional dictatorship of capitalistic economics and liberates space. Eva's concept to disintegrate space, through glass-mirrors and blurred glass, is the more radical approach. But we, as architects, can learn from it.

Saint-Exupéry, the poet, said, "If you want to build a ship, don't send out the men to gather the wood, but teach them a desire for the wildness of the sea." The dream of flying, to overcome gravity, one of the themes of Eva Schlegel's current exhibition in the MAK, is also a key theme in architecture. In order to define new architecture, architects have to push across the border lines of science, technology, sociology and philosophy. In the Bible Eve seduced Adam to try an apple. Eva Schlegel seduces us to taste the flavor of art.
— Introduction by Wolf D. Prix

"Progress and catastrophe are the opposite faces of the same coin."
— Hannah Arendt

It is a great pleasure for me to talk here tonight. I am doing an experiment myself this evening by not showing you my work but by concentrating, instead, on the process of doing, of developing, experimenting and creation—which, to a certain extent, includes failure, and being stranded.

Failure in the artistic process is something you are confronted with sooner or later. On the one hand, you try to put a particular abstract idea into a form. On the other hand, you realize often enough that it's not possible, that you need temporary—sometimes total—failure in order to reach a certain point, to achieve a form. We have to acknowledge that failure is a convention defined by society, but it is not static. It is changing. What is claimed to be a failure sometimes turns out to be a success. The history of science in particular shows us that when correctly posed, new and open questions, questions that cannot be answered at a given moment, ultimately produce a result and lead to new solutions. Failure refers to the state or condition of not meeting a desirable or intended objective, and may be viewed as the opposite of success.

As I am here at the University of Applied Arts, confronted by a lot of students, I think it might be interesting to mention that I studied here myself, and to tell you something I experienced as a student: I must confess, I suffered a lot. I suffered in different ways. All of my colleagues seemed to know exactly what art was, except me. (But to tell you the truth, only a few of them are still working in the field of art.) It was the time of late conceptual art and the beginning of the emerging wild new painting. On the other hand, whenever I visited galleries or museums I found myself in front of perfectly arranged installations. The work was contextualized and everything was in relation to everything else, telling stories. But at the same time this excluded the recipient in a way, not letting him or her participate in the process and only confronting him or her with results. At the time, our professor Oswald Oberhuber had invited Mario Merz, a leading artist of the Italian Arte Povera movement. He told us about the artistic process, about being alone in the studio and about being confronted with all of your doubts. He told us that when he tried to develop an idea or find the right media for it, when he tried to find the right language or a suitable form for his idea, he often failed. And so he had to try again and again, although sometimes he totally failed. This opened up a new perspective for me, since he emphasized the process itself as the most important thing in art.

The first photo in a way includes a process: my graduation. What you see here is a Super 8 film of a fan. It is motionless, starts to turn, rotates at high speed and then slows down and comes to a standstill again. The film is looped, and I projected it directly onto the real fan. The blades move so fast they create a layer you can project onto. I have always been very interested in immaterial space. I was interested in crossing the boundaries and in finding an element onto which I could project something, one that seemed to float in the air. I connected the fan to a circuit breaker to slow it down—you could see its blades increasingly interrupting the film, then it sped up again and enabled the film image to be seen. (fig.1) Here you can see the installation again, but this time accompanied by freestanding glass plates that were painted in white on one side in different layers. I was interested in how I could create a painting without color, and whether white

2 Untitled, 1985, graphite on plaster, pigment on plaster, 30 × 20 cm each

was a color in its own right—one that could only be seen through light. I painted in layers: there were five layers of white on top of each other with some spaces, some gaps in a layer of white. When looked at from the direction of the light you only saw white walls. Seen against the light, the images appeared.

Based on this experience, I tried mounting the glass plates on the wall to display them as art objects. But they looked very ugly, and that upset me. I had intended to create an illusion of space without color, floating on the wall in which three-dimensional space could be perceived. But I totally failed. I then went on to do the opposite, to concentrate on volume, mass and darkness. I made these huge panels, paraphrasing painting, covering them completely in matte black, suggesting they were very deep and dark. I combined these with other pieces whose surfaces I covered with graphite using pencils, which brought out the traces of the hand that were fixed in a surface of plaster. (fig.2)

At that time—I had to earn some money, of course—I was working at a depot for hazardous waste material where people could dispose of oil-based paints, medication, batteries and other poisonous stuff, but also of photo negatives because the silver could be recovered from them. So I got this convoluted set of negatives, and I found myself sitting there and looking at all of them. The photographs had been taken between 1900 and 1940. I realized that not only has perception changed over time, but even the approach to the process of taking a photo is different now. Today we use digital photography, everyone takes pictures and everyone is a photographer. Back then there were only very few images that could be considered failures because the act of taking a photo took much more time and required concentration. The photographer had to think more about light, composition, the foreground, the background and the situation itself.

What also struck me was the fact that I did not know anything about these photos. I did not know where

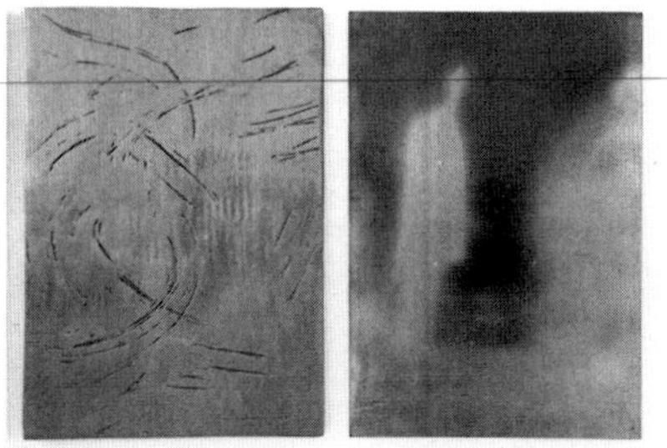

3 Untitled, 1989, graphite on plaster, silkscreen on lead, 140 × 100 cm

4 Untitled, 1991, Installation view Kunsthaus Aarau, graphite on plaster, silkscreen on lead, 140 × 100 cm each

they were taken, who took them or who was in them. They were totally anonymous so I decided to search through the photos concentrating on the failures, using them as a cultural reservoir, choosing interesting ones with associative links to Western art history.

What you see here is a very rare photo that I found. It is blurred, even though at that time one would have concentrated on the distance, i.e. on the focal point. (fig.3) And as for this one, another question became more important to me: is there something that we would call a "cultural code," something that unifies us all—being educated in approximately the same (Western) context—in our associations, reading a certain meaning, understanding it similarly? Using these images I then decided to print them in negative because they stay more abstract and harder to read, whereas if you look at old photos directly you view them sentimentally. Time immediately brings a judgmental distance between you and the work.
I combined the graphite panels I mentioned earlier with the negatives printed on lead panels of the same size, and installed them like film scenes. (fig.4) There are photos in black on the dark gray lead, with very little contrast. When you walk past an image it appears in the back of your brain and is then replaced by the next abstract panel of graphite, which is also gray on black. Leaving the gallery space, you found yourself confronted by these very light, white images—found photographs silkscreened onto glass—and I suddenly realized that I had solved the problem that had driven me to desperation years before. I could make spaces that you can recognize, an illusion of space that was only generated in white, floating in front of the white wall. Moreover, the effect they had was like a physical after-image as opposed to the heavy dark pieces.

At a certain point the works grew bigger and bigger, and this seemed to be the only possible development. It did not interest me anymore, if this was the case.
I wanted to develop something

new. I wanted to concentrate on immaterial spaces. So I started to arrange glass shapes, and tried to create complex spaces that you cannot decode ... this time I really failed.

So after a year of experimentation taking photos of these constructions, I thought I would like to get rid of all the sentimental elements in these images and leave out all the painterly qualities, which had increased. What was left was the blurred text, a text that you could not read. At the same time I started to read Derrida's *Of Grammatology*, about texts and the origin of text. (Derrida's goal was to show that writing is not simply a reproduction of speech but that the way in which thoughts are recorded in writing strongly affects the nature of knowledge.)

I created a form for the ideas on blurred text: The panels with different motifs silkscreened onto glass are man-sized. Sometimes they are installed and organized like a loose book, you can walk around the panel but you cannot read anything. (fig.5) I used different texts, various structures of text, all sorts of fonts and different languages, which can be recognized—but the primary content remains concealed. The question that arose was: What is left if I obliterate the primary information of the text? Is it perceived as an image, or is it text? And interestingly enough, you will always "read" this result as text and not as an image.

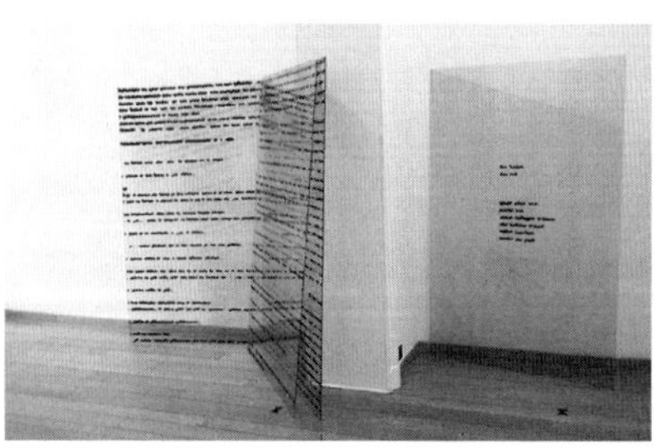

5 Untitled, 1993, silkscreen on glass, 180 × 113.5 cm

But I wanted to move on. I made an edition of 1,000 books in which I compiled all the different text motifs in one volume. It is a book where you cannot read anything, which is particularly disturbing in this case as reading creates intimacy between you and the book. Reading creates spaces inside of you, and here there is only distortion and error. Everything is blurred, there is not a single word to read, except for the number: each book is numbered, from 1 to 1,000. (fig.6) Engaging with the distortion of text myself, it was interesting to see who else had been working on this subject. *Die Verbesserung von Mitteleuropa* by Oswald Wiener, published in 1969, is very impressive. Apart from Mallarmé, he was one of the first to deconstruct the classical novel of the nineteenth century by striking out many of the words and dissolving parts of the book. There is another book I'd like to mention: *House of Leaves* by Mark Danielewski, published in 2000. It is a book about an uncanny house and a guy who is very attached to it, and goes mad and dies. When a second family moves into the house, the author introduces footnotes, and at one point the footnotes take over. The main text starts to change as different typefaces and subtitles are introduced. Danielewski organizes the book in two parallel stories—also in formal terms—and then starts to break and disperse it, creating new spaces within the book. He treats text as two-dimensional but also as an architectural "image." He mirrors the text, fragments and dissolves it. He strikes it out. He turns it, twists it, and then he makes it really unreadable. This is a book you cannot read to the end because it dissolves itself, the story

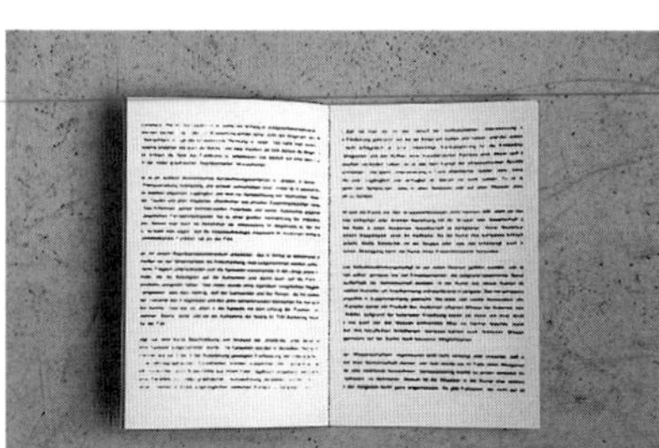

6 Untitled, 1993, 1,000 books with blurred texts, 17 × 10 cm each

gets lost. It is a really weird but wonderful story, depicted in fonts.

Failure in art is a very common thing, it is almost an intrinsic element of art.

Lucio Fontana actually drilled into the canvas, personally cut the canvas. Before he turned it into a form of expression, we would have considered this to be ruining a piece of art. He takes the act of destruction and creates art. As I mentioned before, failure is a notion based on convention. It is possible to redefine it.

But now back to my first installation. This is from an exhibition planned for the MAK in Vienna. The fan has matured and grown. It is now an airplane propeller with a diameter of 3.8 meters, and there are to be three of them. It rotates very fast to create an invisible layer onto which things can be projected. The films will show people flying as well as other things that fly or fall: birds, balloons (which are shot down by a hunter) and even Newton's apple. (fig.7) What interested me in flying and falling is that it marks the borderline between success and failure. Flying is a longstanding dream of mankind: either in our minds, or as an expression of the wish to literally overcome gravity.

The impulse for this field of research was a film about parabolic flight, simulating space without gravity. An airplane climbs up to 10,000 meters and then descends rapidly to 3,000 meters. It takes 23 seconds, and during this time you are not exposed to gravity. You float in space. Normally five to six

7 Untitled, 2010, installation view MAK Vienna, video projection on rotors, 380 cm

cycles of parabolic flights follow each other in quick succession (so participants have to be very fit and healthy).

When researching the history of flight one soon hits upon Leonardo da Vinci and the flying machines he invented. Then at the turn of the twentieth century comes Eadweard Muybridge's photographic analysis of birds in flight. What is remarkable is the documentation in photographs of Otto Lilienthal's first successful gliding flight (i.e. unpowered) at the end of the nineteenth century. But in fact about a thousand years earlier, a mathematician, physician and astronomer at the Umayyad court in Córdoba, Abbas Ibn Firnas, had been the first to successfully fly with a glider (according to the chronicles of the Moroccan historian Al-Maqqari). When he landed he injured himself quite badly but survived, and thought that the flight's failure was because there was no tailfin. And his conclusion was correct, over a thousand years ago. Then there was the first successful flight by the Wright brothers in 1903, which lasted 12 seconds and covered 40 meters.

So this is the story we know, the story of success. But what interested me in art was the *idea* of flying, the idea of getting somewhere you are not supposed to be. Yves Klein took the well-known photo *Jump into the Void* by jumping into thin air from a window. At the end of the 1950s Klein opened an exhibition where he dealt with the void in a different way. He showed an empty, white gallery space. But was *The Void* the void? The questions immediately arose: What do we see? What is there? It is a space? It has walls, a carpet, a ceiling, so it is not a void.

8 Untitled, 2007, silkscreen on lead, 30 × 40 cm

Five years ago I was asked to make a portrait by a property developer. Being a developer as the last crisis showed is a dangerous and risky job. So I decided to quote Yves Klein somehow, but not to collage the result like he did, rather to produce a straight photo. I asked the client to jump seven meters from his diving board into the lake and took the photo from below. (fig.8) As you have to practice to achieve a good shot, he had to jump several times wearing different suits.

Really important for me in this context was the work of Bas Jan Ader, born in 1944. He addressed the issue of "failing" as his key theme, very unpretentiously, very casually, but very impressively. I will show you one of his works, a black-and-white film of him on a chair, falling from the roof of a house in Los Angeles. When he was 33 he completed his last work, *In Search of the Miraculous*, where he planned to sail across the Atlantic from west to east in a small boat. He vanished, disappeared; his boat was found off the coast of Ireland a year later.

This is the second part of my exhibition at the MAK: another installation that also engages with falling, floating and flying. Eight hundred weather balloons are arranged like an amorphous sculpture. (fig.9) They are designed to go up in the air, burst because of the low air pressure and to send photos down to earth. The attached camera comes down on a small parachute. Using the weather balloons (with a diameter of 120 to 200 cm), I also take advantage of small webcams installed in this exhibition. Everyone is filmed when they enter the space. The images are transferred to a video beamer that projects them through a round mask, shaped like a balloon, onto the floor next to the visitor in question. So you can see yourself standing next to you, from above, then the projection moves until it touches a wall and bursts. This work here has nothing to do with failure, but with limitation. And this is the end of my lecture because it also has to do with death. It is a temporary death. People dissolve.

Thank you.

9 Untitled, 2010, installation view MAK, Vienna, 800 balloons

Kivi Sotamaa

Sensation

Edited by Kristy Balliet

1 *Spanish Dancer*, 21st Century Museum of Contemporary Art, 2004, Kanazawa, Japan

Kivi is an international architect and designer based in Helsinki and Los Angeles. The late New York Times architecture critic Herbert Muschamp stated that Sotamaa is developing a vocabulary that draws on and expands surrealist ideas into architecture. His work is not just about the technology—the new, the digital—but about the continuity of ideas that are integral to modern art. In addition to heading Sotamaa Design, Kivi is the director of ADD LAB, Aalto Digital Design Laboratory and Associate Professor at UCLA Department of Architecture and Urban Design. Previously he has held positions at Ohio State University and the University of Applied Arts, Vienna.

Kivi augments his deep architectural training with curiosity and desire for calculated risks. The ambitions of the designs are choreographed and eloquent. The work evokes multiple sensations, relying on color, pattern, light, shadow and movement.

— Introduction by Kristy Balliet

First of all, thanks for inviting me, I hope I'm one of the friends. After seven years in the United States, I have just moved back to Finland. I've spent seven years developing ideas around my work. It has been great for my intellectual development as an architect. I think Wolf [D. Prix] said at one point that during your career you go through stages: pioneering, settlement and then professionalism. I have gone through pioneering, that was the eight years prior to moving to the United States. Settling and intellectual development was in the US. And now I hope this is the beginning of professionalism.

BECOMING ARCHITECTURE

I thought I'd speak more about the ideas that I've developed over the last seven years through my projects and through references to some other work. I've developed a discourse around sensation and effects, and their relationship to architectural techniques.

SPANISH DANCER

I will start with a red project and I will finish with another red project.

First, a pavilion for the opening exhibition in 2004 for SANAA's

21st Century Museum for Contemporary Art in Kanazawa, Japan. (fig.1) It is a round museum with minimalist partitioned spaces and we were asked to design a pavilion that allowed people to escape within the museum. We produced an architectural pavilion and installation that generated a kind of vortex or butterfly formation—a turbulent red erotic sexy creature, nested in this beautiful minimalist bento box turned museum. When you approach it, you can't see in it. You have to fight your way through the red wings and eventually you find yourself in a modern day Zen garden of cushy white balls. Towards the outside there are organic sounds—a kind of pulse—and in the middle there are crystalline sounds, as if glass were falling from the sky. The lighting is deep red towards the outside and bright white towards the middle. Everything in this project is geared towards the production of a very particular effect, a particular sensation: the embracing centrifugal form, the pleated fabric that is painted red, and the associations that the work makes to a Flamenco dancer's dress. In short, all the architectural devices that I had at my disposal—the organization, form, color, representation, sound, ambient elements, lighting—were coordinated towards the production of a particular sensation. In my work there is a kind of minimalism; I try to produce maximum effect with minimal means.

SENSATION

What I want to talk about today is sensation. Why does sensation matter? I think this is key to our relationship to architecture. Architectural and material things are not irrelevant or superficial; they are inherently important to our development as individuals and as a society. We need objects, architecture, and the environment in order to evolve and explore new places as individuals and as a species.

Sensations generate immediate lived experiences at the expense of intellectual "depth," but in so doing they break through clichés.

Sensations are immediate and bodily. They are not anti-intellectual, but they appear to happen before the intellectual effect occurs. There is a common misconception that sensation is something that happens at the expense of intellectual depth. Sensate effects and atmosphere—that's when architecture is most powerful. However, the specific sensations matter a great deal, and too many architects and designers are trained to simply fulfill their client's wishes, to provide the "right" atmosphere for the "right" event. It is far more interesting to be a critical or projective cultural actor and suggest unusual sensations, which allow all of us to explore new and unexpected roles and ways of being in the world.

Just as opinion and convention prevent the genesis of thought, cliché prevents the genesis of sensation. The enemy of a sensation is cliché.

What's interesting is that projects that produce sensations always break through clichés. This here [the image of a chair is being shown] is a cliché of a chair, right? I don't have to think twice about it. I understand it's a chair. It has four legs, a seat and so on. It will never really get my attention; it will never produce

2 *Extraterrain*

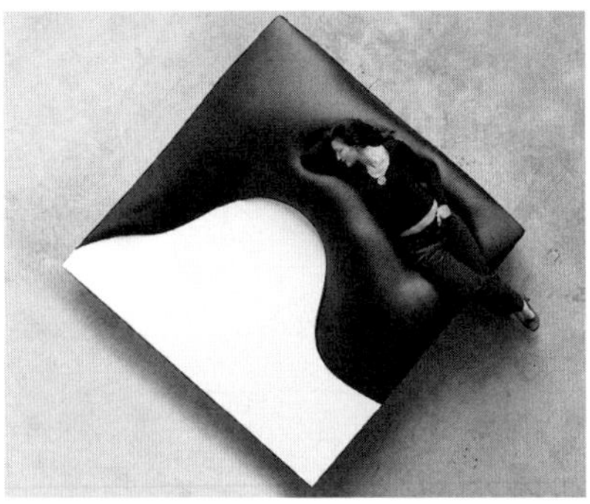

3 *Orca*

a particular sensation. If you're interested in creating sensations for your audience, you by necessity need to break the clichés; otherwise, they get in your way. In 1995, I designed a piece of furniture that was intended not to be recognizable as furniture. (fig.2) It doesn't have legs, any parts, or make typological references to furniture. It looks like it's a landscape of pain rather than pleasure. It's hard, it has edges. The only way you're going to figure out what to do with it is to play with it in order to explore the sensations it creates.

WHAT KIND OF SENSATIONS?
My critique of the contemporary field is that people are so driven by technical research that they are not interested in or in control of the effects they produce. In other words, the technique drives the work and the effects are a side product. As a designer I am somebody who goes out in the field and enters into a specific situation with a specific client and intervenes as a conscious critical/projective cultural actor. You need to be in control of what you create, in control of your effects! It's like every hard rock band: they all know how to play a love song when needed. A lot of people, maybe because of the obsession with the technique or the complexity of the technique and the attention that it requires, produce a singular effect regardless of the situation. I believe you have to be able to produce particular effects for particular audiences. While the previous design was intentionally provocative and aggressive, a similarly scaled piece of furniture called the Orca is soft, has friendly figurative line work associated with the killer whale, and changes shape in response to people's weight—everything is geared towards the production of tenderness. (fig.3)

NUANCES OF SENSATIONS
What does it mean in terms of form, structure, materiality, process and representation?

1. FORM
We start with form, and this is very subjective. In our work I use dynamic forms mainly because they produce effects of movement that you can relate to with your body rather than your mind (if such a separation makes any sense at all). We look very carefully at scales of forms, their associations, and the sensibility of forms for the effects that they create.

Dynamic forms create sensations of movement that escape the "intellect" and appeal directly to the body.

An obvious precedent for this kind of work is the Baroque. The opposite in history has to do with the Renaissance. If the Renaissance was about the pleasure of the line as a profile and the articulation of the relationship between the building and the ground or the relationship between a part and the whole, the Baroque is about defining gravity, producing an overall sensibility through massing and shadow that overwhelms the attention focusing on a part. You can see these effects in the work of Gaudí or Gehry, also in Coop Himmelb(l)au's work, and in some of Alvar Aalto's work. Finland has a history of this type of design (Eero Saarinen and Tapio Wirkkala, for example). That's where I see our work belonging in terms of its architectural and historical legacy.

In all these projects, which vary in scale including ceramics, furniture and buildings, we pay particular attention to the nature of the line work. The line work of high-tech British architecture, the Renaissance or Neoclassical architecture involves careful articulation of the part and takes pleasure in articulating structure. In our work, we are interested in line work that produces a sensation of movement, creases that emerge from the surface and then disappear like the lines of a sketch. They do not have a precise end or beginning, just implied movement, direction and flow. In all of these projects—the New York Times capsule, the Töölö Football Stadium and Mantaray ceramics—you see the employment of this formal language towards different nuanced effects. (fig.4, 5, 6)

One project where we explored form and its effects on different scales was entitled "Formation," for the Fondazione Trussardi in Milan. This architectural scale installation was nested with objects ranging from the scale of the body to the size of something that you would hold in your hand. The idea was to produce an atmospheric landscape that changes through ambient means, sound and light, filled with objects that are not clearly coded and explained in terms of their use. Instead, the people are invited to use their bodies to play with them, to explore the possibilities.

2. STRUCTURE

Structurally, most buildings are designed as if gravity were the only force. Buildings clearly articulate a hierarchy of parts and structure. The pleasure of the architecture clearly lies in the beauty and articulation of structure. We are always more interested in structure that is illegible or produces effects beyond structure. (fig.7, 8). For the Helsinki Cultural Capital we built an "architectural structure" as an experiment: it consisted of six steel structures extending from the most public space in Helsinki to an area of underground cultural life. These structures served as bridges, audience stands and sculptural elements. All of these elements were intentionally staged such that you would not be able to decipher whether they were architecture, finished or unfinished construction, art, infrastructure, etc. (fig.9) They both challenged and empowered people to define their own relationships to the environment.

3. MATERIALITY

In Finland in particular there is this notion of an authentic materiality—for example, the true nature of wood. Ask a brick what it wants to be and so on. In terms of sensation, it isn't a sensation for a brick to be a brick or for marble to be marble. It is, however, a sensation to make marble look like fabric. It's particularly interesting because while you know that it's marble, it appears to be fabric. It causes an oscillation between what you know and what you perceive, a sustained sensation.

Although I appreciate works like Zumthor's baths, I think they are in some ways antithetical to what we're trying to do. His project is about a local stone and an architectural language that enforces the massive presence of

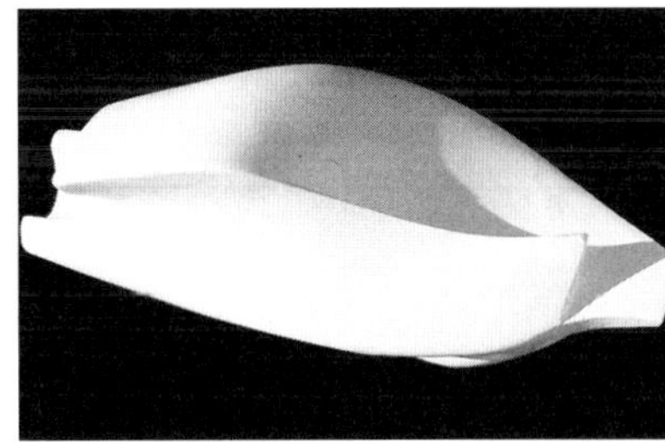

4 *aDrift*, New York Times Capsule Competition, 1999

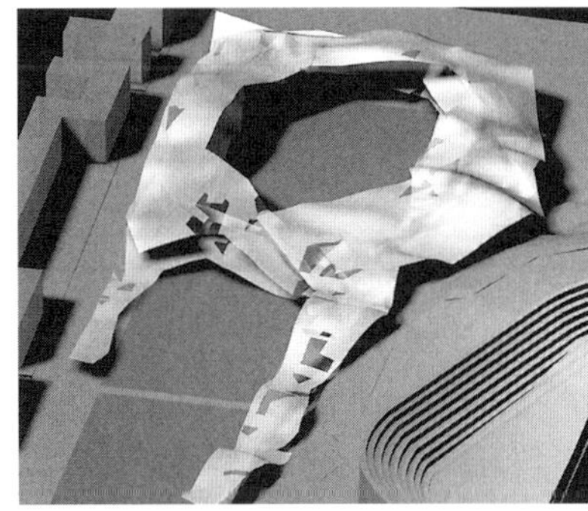

5 Töölö Stadium, Helsinki Finland

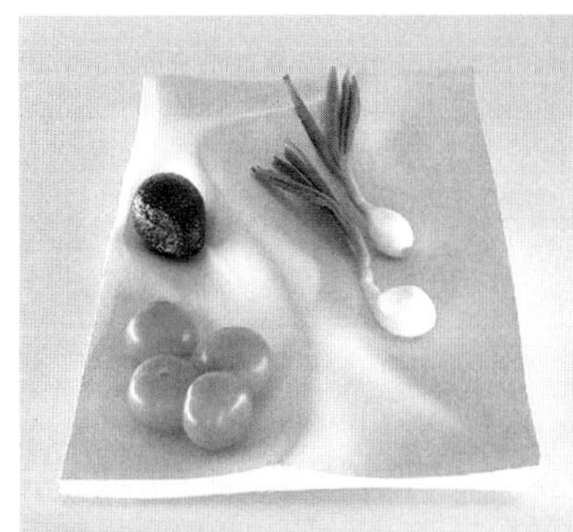

6 *Mantaray*

7 *Ahead*

8 *TerraCultura*, 1997, Jyväskylä

9 *Intencities*, 2000, Helsinki, Finland

the stone. It's all about the truth and authenticity of the material, of the true nature of the place. In contrast, if you take Herzog de Meuron's Dominus Winery in Napa, with stones stacked between two fences as façade in order to produce the effect of fabric—now that's a sensation. Stone overcomes its true material constraints to create an effect not commonly associated with it: ephemerality and lightness.

The political differences between these two attitudes towards materiality are striking, and the latter is much more aligned with values of my generation. When we work with a material we don't strive to produce completely synthetic material effects, we don't want to hide the material entirely. We look for the material's capacity to produce new and unexpected effects, as is the case with these glass sculptures we did with Ernesto Neto. (fig.10) We use new techniques to make old materials do unexpected things.

4. ORGANIZATION

Architectural projects are always made of many parts, many systems that have to be orchestrated. In most cases, the architect establishes a hierarchy between the systems, one system performing one task, another doing another job. Sometimes in a postmodern fashion designers play up the contradictions and the collisions between systems in order to produce some sort of architectural pleasure.

The problem from the vantage point of sensation is that the moment you recognize hierarchies, the moment you perceive a sustained hierarchy between systems—floors, windows, floors each having a different color, form and material, for example—the moment you see one instance of this kind of building you know the entire thing. There might be formal changes, but you always know what's going to happen since the hierarchies don't change.

Our PS1 entry is a simple example of the opposite strategy, where hierarchical relationships are undermined and things flow with and against one another. The ruled surfaces of the installation are perforated, which creates surface patterns and pointillist shadows, which are picked up by colored stones on the ground. The pattern drifts from one surface to another surface and changes in its material manifestation. (fig.11) One system, the particle, is used to orchestrate a number of different architectural elements. Minimal means for maximum effect.

5. PROCESS

Most architecture, at least in Northern Europe, is designed with BIM software like ArchiCAD or Revit that relies on typological notions of components and a Cartesian environment. You have columns, floors, walls and windows. There is a fundamental difference between that environment and the topological environment in animation software that Greg [Lynn] first and foremost has spoken about. The topological environment is based on curves, not on Cartesian geometry or typological notions. There is a big difference between the ways most of you in the audience design and how most in the field of architecture operate. One of the biggest clichés in architecture is typology, the convention between a form and its cultural signification. When you work with typology in the design process you can play with it as a language in a kind of postmodern sense, but in most cases the embedded conventions get in the way of creativity and result in dumb legibility and zero sensation.

Evidence of process is the enemy of sensation.

There's also a challenge when it comes to topological digital design processes that rely on the use of a transforming primitive that accumulates or builds up into an architectural whole. More often than not the overall formation becomes an index of the generative process, a legible register of the design process. However, in some rare cases, these digital processes are capable of producing a degree of complexity that one might argue results in constellations too complex to decipher, creating a simultaneous sensation of underlying logic and material effect—the

10 *Frozen*

11 *Flowers*, PS1/MoMA, 2006

experience of the sublime, to be precise.

6. REPRESENTATION

Representation is the most difficult and the most sophisticated issue to deal with in terms of effects, regardless of whether you are a designer, artist or architect. On one extreme you have abstraction, and on the other there is illustration, and in the middle something between the two: the Figure, a term and concept borrowed from Gilles Deleuze.

ABSTRACTION

Examples of people who successfully work on sensation within abstraction are Mark Rothko, Anish Kapoor, Olafur Eliasson and James Turrell. Most of their work relies on color and material effect to create strong sensations of flatness and depth, surface and infinite space, mood and atmosphere.

ILLUSTRATION

There are artists who explicitly use illustration—literal references to other things. Jeff Koons's *Balloon Flower* and *Puppy* are good examples. These works rely on the strategic use of an obvious reference in order to overcome any attempt to "read" the sculpture or to decipher its true materiality. The reference to a child's toy coupled with the glossy material effect makes the sculpture seem fun, cheap, easy and weightless, yet technologically it is very difficult to make, weighs tons and it costs a lot. All of the formal and material effects are enhanced because of the representational content.

THE FIGURE

What I'm interested in is something Gilles Deleuze called the Figure in his book *The Logic of Sensation*. It means something that is suspended in between abstraction and illustration. What is interesting about the Figure is that it causes an oscillation that is capable of maintaining a sensation over time. It refuses to settle into either abstraction or illustration. Abstraction is comfortable. Representation, things that clearly resemble something else, are also comfortable. The Figure is uncomfortable and intriguing. It produces unsettled associations.

The Guggenheim Bilbao has been called the artichoke, the Spanish Armada, the onion and a number of other things, most famously Marilyn Monroe in her billowing dress over the subway vent by Herbert Muschamp. It is a perfect example of a building that is not abstract, nor does it represent anything. It stages associations, and continues to invite interpretations, never settling into one particular category. I believe that if people call your project many names, then you have a good one.

The last thing that I would like to show is the other red project—a sculpture we just completed in Helsinki. It's called *Sirocco*. Sirocco is the name of a hot turbulent Saharan wind. This project is made of 431 steel profiles that are cut at different angles and assembled to produce two centrifugal spaces that you can move through. (fig.12)

CHECKLIST:

Form: It's dynamic, the scale and formal effects engage your

12 *Sirocco*, 2010, Helsinki, Finland

body. Some spaces are very tight and intense, others are more expansive. The surfaces are variably inclined and destabilize and embrace you as you move in the space.

Structure: All the structure is underground, there's nothing to read in terms of structure.

Materiality: The profiles are painted in 10 different reds that are distributed throughout the surfaces in different quantities in order to create impressionistic optical effects which overwhelm the fact that the profiles are simply a steel profile.

Organization: *Sirocco* is both one and many at the same time. The smallest element is a singular profile that aligns with others and forms surfaces that flow and wrap around one another to create a sequence of spaces and eventually two interlinked vortices. The relationship between the part and whole is fluid and without hierarchy.

Process: Although the constellation is first algorithmically designed and then parametrically modeled for construction, it is impossible to find any index of process.

Representation: Sirocco may be the name of a wind but it has many affiliations—flowers, wind, movement, Chinese ribbon dancers, *Les Parapluies de Cherbourg* and so on. It tries to find the wonderful place between abstraction and illustration.

To conclude: What I have discussed tonight may simply be my recipe for beauty, who knows. We are trying to figure out how to make something as difficult and mundane as architecture appear immediate and magical in order to seduce people into new places, to cast them in new roles.

Kristin Feireiss

The Architect between Superman and Supervisor

Edited by Alexandra Graupner
(This lecture has been translated from German)

As we all know, architecture is very difficult... not only in terms of design, but also in reality. Architecture carries weight. Anything that carries weight always requires money, and where money is concerned, politics comes into play. So you could say that political dealings constitute the invisible side of architecture. There is a lot about a building that remains hidden from the viewer. But it's exactly within these concealed areas where architecture is determined. Every architect must operate within these fields: aesthetics, politics, the economy and communication.

This is where Kristin Feireiss comes into play. She supports and promotes, and is sometimes called the King- and/or Queenmaker. It is thanks to her personality that seemingly inert wheels located in the heads of decision makers as well as architects are set into motion. Kristin Feireiss makes the impossible possible. As the founder of the first gallery of architecture in Europe, the Aedes Gallery, and as director of the NAI in Rotterdam, she has influenced the development of architecture that is representative of its time. She encourages architects to develop strategies for allowing architecture to function as a kind of three-dimensional map for experiencing our world.
—Introduction by Wolf D. Prix

Ladies and gentlemen, dear friends, students and Wolf [D. Prix]:

First of all, I am very pleased to speak here today and I am assuming—as far as I can tell from the list of speakers—that I belong to the minority in the Sliver Lecture series of those who have neither studied nor practiced architecture but whose lives have still revolved around architecture for more than 30 years, especially around that particular species of "architect people" who perform this job.

My experience has been—at the risk of sounding banal—that architecture begins with the personalities of those who give it its content and form, as well as their talents, visions, family and social environments, their passions, their inclinations and disinclinations, their allies and opponents, always considering their ability in the larger context, and above all trying as much as possible to expand their network of relationships and to strengthen that network in the course of their current personal history—a web that is teeming with delicate threads that can hardly withstand the resulting tension. This multi-layered web is the secret to and basis of this profession: one that is vulnerable and open to question, but deeply rewarding, in terms of one's own professional development, as well as in terms of the architecture that emerges from it and which, when it is more than just a formal contribution, is a reflection and impression of these complex processes.

THE ARCHITECT BETWEEN SUPERMAN AND SUPERVISOR

I have very happily taken up these threads and will therefore not talk about architectural constructions, but rather about those who create them, in light of the question of which new challenges architects will be facing (or are already facing) as a result of current global developments, which consequences they have on the profession and whether these challenges will consequently lead to a new definition of the job description. In any case, it is a balancing act between Superman and supervisor. In the following, it is obvious that I am dealing first and foremost with the supervisor. The role of the Superman is clearly outlined.

In order for these two types not to oppose each other (which I will try to clarify) they require communication as well as networking.

So the question is: "How much communication is needed in architecture?"

With the establishment of the Aedes Architecture Forum—the first private institution that turned architecture itself into a theme for exhibitions—I have devoted (often stubbornly and in a questioning manner) the most important part of my professional life to conveying what architecture means.

ARCHITECTURAL COMMUNICATION

With the term "architectural communication," or "moderation," one can best circumscribe what is involved in conveying the meaning of architecture: communication about the mediums of exhibitions, workshops, symposia, discussions, exhibition catalogs and publications—communication among different disciplines and with partners from all over the world, communication among the experts and the public and lastly, and above all, communication among teachers and students.

Because I am convinced that the subject of architectural communication is becoming increasingly important while at the same time few have the ability to do so. Because I am often saddened when an architect once again fails to present his or her good design—I'm not referring to those that are not good—with competence and poise and thus convincingly so. And because I am observing, through my involvement with the next generation of architects, that young architects are only marginally, if at all, prepared through their studies to face the changing profession and the resulting challenges.

ARCHITECTURAL EDUCATION

In Germany and its neighboring countries—I couldn't determine the current status in Austria—academic unemployment of architects is at its highest. According to estimates of the BDA, one third of the architectural firms in Germany are about to fold.

What happened—and I speak now of the rule and not the exception—in the time between the start of one's studies and the first years of employment, which has turned once-motivated enthusiastic freshmen into discouraged employees in large firms and has increasingly made those who have ventured to be self-employed go on welfare? Let's try to explain this. One cause is surely the changing circumstances: university professors, worn down and defeated by the struggle between numbers, bureaucracy and provincial politics (of which they actually want no part) are left with barely enough energy for the basics—that is, their students and content.

Another cause: the general lack of communication in the field of architecture. The *Süddeutsche Zeitung* stated: "Anyone who has experienced having an idea for a thesis and, as a consequence, the helpless, non-explanatory jabbering of budding architects—and the feeble comments of the examiner—

knows why society and architects talk so often at cross purposes."

Is this due to the students or the education? We have to assume it's the latter. I am convinced that, in the future, it will not be possible for the teaching of professional communication to be ignored in architectural curricula.

But this requires a growing interest in and basic knowledge of other disciplines based on the belief that complex design and construction processes can only be completed in an interdisciplinary partnership. The architect and dedicated professor Konrad Wohlhage, who died a few years ago, established another area that is almost entirely omitted at universities: the development and promotion of "conceptual intelligence." He had the view that, in dealing with the task at hand, the fulfillment of the room schedule should not be the focus. Instead, it should be the questioning of theoretical, sociopolitical, philosophical and sociological aspects. With "conceptual thinking," which leads to experimentation and innovation, unconventional solutions are always a risk. Just as there are situations for every architect in their daily professional life for which risk-taking is asked, one wants to implement one's beliefs and ideas. This can also be learned to a certain extent.

This provides enough reasons to promote the strengthening of the personality in university education, as well as the will to form one's own identity and to define a clear position. To do this, one not only needs one's own formal and individual identity, but also the courage to defend one's ideas and concepts against builders and politicians. But the architect can only then take over the responsibility if he or she has developed an awareness of his or her role in society.

ARCHITECTURAL MEDIATION

The global network of Aedes has taught us that the intensification of subjects in architecture and urbanism has identified architecture as a central part of the local culture of a society and its identity formation on the one hand, but on the other hand has also shown that it recurs with, converges with and faces issues on a global scale. For example, the panel discussion on the Aedes exhibition "Interdisciplinary Creative Arts from China," featuring Chinese innovators such as the architect Yung Ho Chang, showed that the issue of liberating architecture from its relation to buildings and communicating them as a process is just as difficult in China as it is in Germany or any other country in the world.

What does the student or architect get from such panel discussions, architecture exhibitions, etc.?

It helps them put the architecture, and therefore the work of the architect, into a broader, interdisciplinary and intercultural context.

- They can thereby contribute to building bridges between experts and the public; and/or:
- They can mediate the current state of the architectural debate by facing up to new global trends!

Dealing with these matters includes an expansion of the term design beyond just the design of pure buildings and forms to the design of processes, space development and political contemplation.

It's about opening up a critical space that understands design as a part of the complexity of current societal processes. Aesthetic realization, but also communication, like the didactic instructions to the general public, forms the key components. The question of the public perception of architecture is thereby newly posed.

As a privately organized institute that works for the public, we are very aware of economic and social developments that affect the nature of design, as well as of how design—through taking action—plays a part in shaping the social space.

That is why I think it especially important, at a time of global corporations and a social order oriented towards consumption, maximizing profits and individualism, to continually question how politics and architecture interact. Architects relating to the orientation and development of their work in the future must also ask themselves these questions:

- How can architecture situate itself within the complexity of contemporary social life?
- How can architects take on an active role in the field of social transformation?

FROM THE MODERATOR AND SUPERVISOR

But what do the concepts of moderator and supervisor mean for the architect? Do they mean a license for a compliant opportunism? Hardly. Instead, I imagine moderation as a tool that helps to overcome ideologically entrenched dichotomies and also helps provide depth to the inevitable pragmatism.

But then moderation is always part of the production of a *sensus communis*, a social realm of political debate as opposed to anti-reflexive rhetoric. Moderation can directly help to structure the political, as defined by Arendt: the freedom to deal with differences within a community.

However, a moderation that is not only accustomed to power but that is, even worse, confused in that it pretends to turn the relationship upside down, only strengthens the effect and weakens the power of judgment. Moderation is in this way a deeply Kantian matter: meaningless and freeform. Moderation can help form openness by creating constructive situations, gathering teammates and thereby allowing target ranges to stay undefined to a certain extent.

Moderation cannot however rely on its form already being its object. And for the architect as a moderator, this means that she can only be ethical in that she does not shrink from her position, but rather exposes and introduces it as an opportunity for her own transformation: to put oneself to the test, to change and to present one's profile in the open process.

I hope this much is clear: I do not understand architectural communication as an instrumentalized selling tool. Against the background of increasing de-politicization, as a main characteristic of today's society and therefore also of today's art, communication is one of the keys to the question about new ways of exchange as well as the creation of political platforms for public discourse.

Globalization, the instability of local markets, intolerance towards difference and problems of abstract work have all raised new ontological issues regarding architecture as a design discipline: *What could be the challenge for the new generation of architects and what defines current architecture as ethical?*

In this context, it is important to take a closer look at the practical ethics of contemporary architecture, as well as the codes of professional dealings with one another. I am aware that I am treading here on dangerous ground, but I would like to anyway because I believe the future of architecture and the architectural profession are closely associated with this question.

The relationship between ethics and design is traditionally reduced to individual responsibility, with little or no attention paid to the circumstances of the specific situation under which architecture works as design. I think the complexity of ethics could be examined by referring to Alain Badiou's theory. Badiou reminds us that ethics, once limited to the relationships between people but now generated by ecological crises, will be extended to the human realm. Here one can already detect connections between design and environmental themes, lines starting with design leading to questions of sustainability and new codes of conduct.

This is the point where I would like to bring up and reactivate the thoughts of Moholy-Nagy: that design is not a profession but rather an attitude towards the world in which we live. It is most certainly also always about the "more," as formulated by Theodor W. Adorno, my professor at the

Johann Wolfgang Goethe University in Frankfurt more than 30 years ago. The "more" according to Adorno goes beyond the practical use of a building, and is defined as the "artistic" or the "unique."

Right next to our showrooms at the Aedes Network Campus Berlin—part of our network of international and interdisciplinary academic partners, which opened at the Pfefferberg in 2008—there will be an attempt to plumb the depths of this more. In this urban laboratory, the issues raised have been explored in design units for more than two years with great success and international resonance, and their content has been developed for creative strategies relating to sustainable practices in the development of present and future realms of living.

What would you like to convey to the students? My answer was and still is: I would encourage them to practice their profession as architects with openness, tolerance, curiosity, with a readiness to experiment and take risks—uncomfortably, responsibly, and aggressively—and to find their position and defend it with the authority of their personality. In times of change, one can generate new strength in oneself and in others.

Given that experience has shown that new, future-oriented concepts in the design of the urban environment are rarely fruitful, the growing generation of architects requires an independent sociopolitical position more than ever before so their appetites for the future are unspoiled by the hard-to-digest, generic gruel that comes out of the kitchen of reactionary know-it-alls, and that they instead meet the new challenges head on. This quote from the French philosopher Vladimir Jankélévitch applies to all creative people, particularly to the architects: "At the beginning, it's always an adventure."

Erwin Wurm

Gulp

Edited by Roswitha Janowski-Fritsch

1 *Untitled*, 1997, oil paint

2 *59 positions*, 1992, c-print

The title "Selected Friends and Enemies" may be misleading. Everyone believes that the selected friends are my friends or the selected enemies are my enemies. Completely wrong! I wanted to invite not only architects but also surrounding people like artists, critics or theorists to show that our school has a certain attitude. And against this attitude we have enemies or friends. I would like to show that architecture is not an isolated discipline. I know there is a lot of discussion about architecture as a discipline, which is not depending on art or philosophy or whatever. I think that is not correct. And in order to prove that, we chose artists, theorists and other non-architecture people.

I met Erwin Wurm not personally in a gallery, but in an object. This object was a house and it said: I'm a house. *And then I figured out, Erwin wants to be a house and therefore he said: "I'm a house." I thought this a very similar surrealistic approach to our school's thinking. We became friends and last year we did a lecture together in London about surrealism in architecture. To introduce Erwin Wurm in this school would be to bring water to the Danube.*

The other thing that I have to explain, everyone invited says, "Ok Wolf. I'm your enemy, not your friend." It is much easier to be an enemy than a friend. My friend Erwin Wurm, please!
—Introduction by Wolf D. Prix

Some years ago I tried to make the exam test to the art school in Salzburg becasue I wanted to become a painter. But unfortunately they didn't accept me in the painting class, so they put me in the sculpture class. At that time that meant a big drama for me because my whole life until that was totally concentrated on the idea of painting. Painting attitude was totally filling me out and made my life and my world. And all of a sudden it got stopped from outside and it had this strong effect of changing something what comes from outside. So I took it as a chance! After half a year of depression, I realized what was necessary to research the notion of sculptures: What does it mean to make sculpture at that time? What does it mean anyway to work in 3D, in a sculptural way? What does it mean to make sculptures in the late 1970s? I started to research a lot, and after certain years of researching and trying things out, I still had the memory of me as a painter. Since I wanted to go on with this, I tried to find a way to combine those two things, sculpture and painting. This is the first work which directly goes to the center of this idea of what is in between painting and sculpture. So we get the little balls made of oil paints and it is more or less like if somebody would have scratched off the surface of a painting and made a ball with it. (fig.1) So I transformed the painting, which is normally used in two-dimensional ways and made a sculpture out of it.

Now I go back to the beginning, which was interesting for me declining in a way the possibility of sculptural possibilities of cultural ideas, from two- to three-dimensional mass, volume, emptiness, fullness, time also. (fig.2) So different values, different issues were very important for me.

When you think about Roman or Greek sculpture, bronze casts or brass casts, you see a person or a horse standing in front of you—big sizes—but they always consist only of very thin cast material. Mostly the really good casts are only one millimeter thin. And the real space underneath is hollow, empty, missing. So the sculpture is more defined by the skin. I tried to go on with this idea and tried to ask myself questions: What is another skin? What's the next skin above us? And of course it is the clothes. And one of the next skins would be the house. So for that reason, I was more or less floating slowly to these house ideas, which came up later.

This first idea about sculpture was the notion about sculpture. The second one was an economical and social reason. After finishing my studies I found myself in the situation that I had no money at all and wanted to become an artist. I did not want to get any jobs to make my living. So I thought I have to start with very low costs, and use low materials. Therefore I started to work with materials that other people threw away, for example wood. Close by was a wood shop where they made furniture and I was able to use their wood, so I started to make classical figures with it. The next step was to change the studio to another place. There I found a factory, which produced cans. So the next material was clear: I used all these cans. When you have a can, you can put volume in it, you can put a mass in it, like water. Then you have the mass. But the mass is defined again by a skin, by a very thin layer of something, material or plastic. And then I came to these clothing pieces. (fig.3) And clothes are in a way a second skin. I started to transform this and to make experiments with friends. They are normal sweaters. I wanted to show the movement when you have someone in a piece of clothing and I ask them to stand quiet for 20 seconds, so you still see this

3 Gasteiger+Reiter, 2011 photo Elfie Semotan/Wallpaper

Erwin Wurm
Gulp

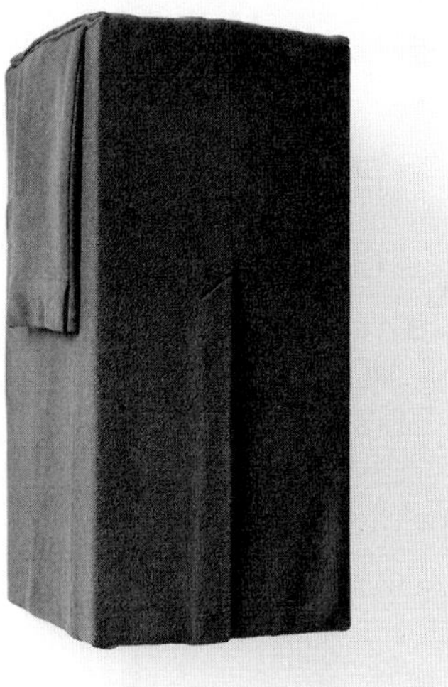

4 Untitled, 1989, coat, wood

5 Untitled, 1989, coat, wood

6 *One Minute Sculpture*, 1997, c-print

person moving a little bit. It was important for me to show the public that there's someone under it and that it's not stuffed by whatever material. This brought me directly to the video. From the very beginning until today, I was interested to work on a very wide range of ideas on materials and issues. I started to work with real 3D sculptures, with video and later on with photography. I realized that those images are quite interesting and I did not even need the video to realize this work, I could even go directly and picture these images by the camera. Later on I made also drawings and books.

In the mid- to late 1980s, I was asking all these questions: how can I combine the daily life of the art world with the idea of sculpture and the idea of psychology and philosophy? So I started to make these objects which are related to pedestals. I made these pedestals for clothes. (fig.4, 5) I made this special pedestal, which fits exactly for a coat, so the coat was covering the pedestal.

At the very beginning when I made these sculptures, these sweater-pieces with people who were just performing for a few seconds, I realized that my pieces have a beginning—like every art piece—but they also have an ending, which became very important for me. That means that sculpture lived, was existing for a very short period of time. Through these years this time became shorter and at a certain moment I decided to call these "one-minute-sculptures." (fig.6) I wanted to create a brand-mark in a way; something very interesting happened. All of a sudden, those works received an enormous amount of visibility all over the world. Many people came—fashion designers, pop groups, lots of architects, media people—who got inspired by these pieces. And they also wanted to transfer and use them. I had a show at the Kunstverein Bremen, which doesn't exist anymore. I went there 10 days in advance, and used all the materials that I found there in the office. I asked the people who worked there, also Horst Griese, the director, if they could be my models. (fig.7) The "one-minute-sculptures" became performative sculptures as an invitation to the public. I mostly made drawings connected with objects. And the people were invited to realize the pieces after my instructions.

But then I thought, it's not enough to concentrate only on the art world, galleries and museums. I would like to step out of it and create things outside for the public. I was always very much interested in the public space. Today I work a lot for the public space, but not as usually sculptors do: they make sculptures for streets, places, houses, etc. I'm much more interested in public space, which is created by the media, like magazines, newspapers, MTV, video and so on.

I had a show in Cabourg, in the north of France. I asked an institution if they could advertise in a newspaper or different daily magazines, to find people to join me as volunteers to be my models. Seven people called from different social levels. It was amazing; they didn't get paid, and at that time nobody knew my work. It was really obvious that they got intrigued by something, I didn't know what it was. Slowly I realized they wanted something from me and I wanted something from them. For example a bank manager, he came and said: "I have this idea, I would like to make this picture and is it possible to do it this way?" That meant I did not follow my idea, but I started to accept ideas from the public I was working with. In a way, they influenced also the work because it became very psychological, philosophical, dependent on a certain social group, on a city, an apartment or the personal history, the family, etc. I really wanted to create a work where the public can participate.

A few years later, in 2008, the city of Vienna asked several artists if they would make proposals for outdoor sculptures for the European Football Championship in Vienna. I thought it would be a good idea and offered them this little car. (fig.8)

The task was to find someone who would drive in this car through the city, and always drive to the stadiums where all these important games like England against Germany took place. It was quite a risk, but it worked very well.

"The Fat House," another big step in between the fat car. I only made three objects fat in my whole career. (fig.9) They were internationally very focused on and came out of a very basic idea. Again, I wanted to combine daily life and sculpture. And as a sculptor, when you make a clay sculpture, you add volume or you take volume away. When you gain weight or lose weight, you also add volume or take volume away. So you could also say to gain or lose weight is a sculptural work. And through this I had the possibility to address certain ideas, certain social issues, which were so important in our time, like obesity, or the rich become slimmer because they are more conscious about healthy food and train well. The poor become more obese because they eat all the junk food.

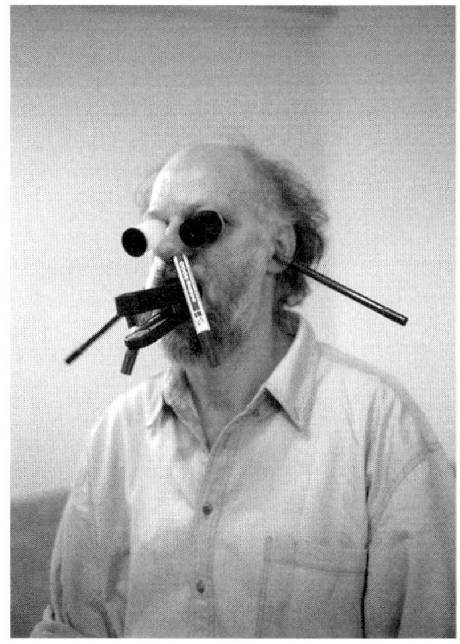

7 *One Minute Sculpture*, 1997, c-print

8 *Geste mobil*, 2008, mixed media

9 *Fat House*, 2011, iron, wood, polystyrene, aluminium, electric installation, video on DVD

10 *Fat Convertible*, 2005, mixed media sculpture

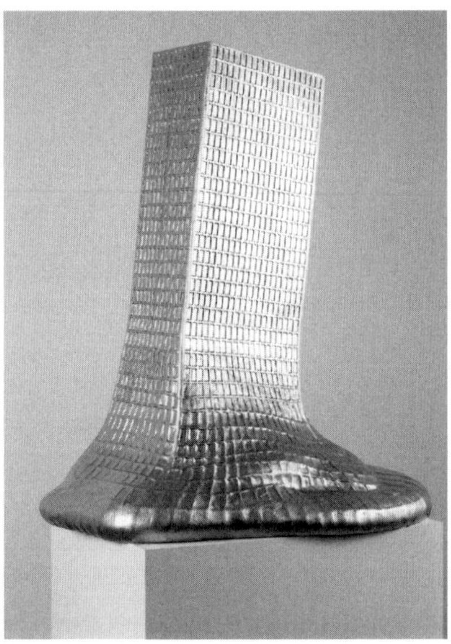

11 *Mies van der Rohe—melting*, 2005, resin, paint

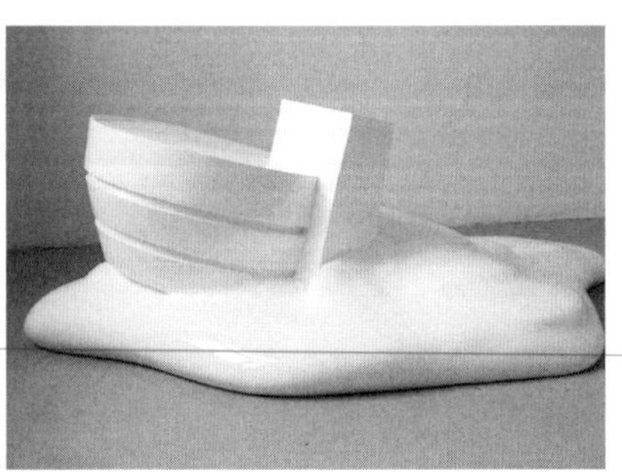

12 *Guggenheim—melting*, 2005, resin, paint

So all of a sudden this was a possibility to let all these big questions into my work. After a certain time I made the fat car, which is in a way a combination between a car and a person. It's actually a combination of two systems: the technical and the biological. (fig.10) The combination created something else and suddenly it was a car with a face. That was also the reason why I made a video animation where the car was talking. The house was talking later because it also had all of a sudden a face. And the house was addressing questions like: "Am I a house or am I a sculpture? What happens if I am a house? What happens if I am a sculpture? Or if I am both? What then? Then who will buy me? Will I be bought by an art collector or will I be bought by the person who wants to live in there?" So there was all of a sudden an interesting system to ask philosophical questions about this piece of art and architecture.

This was then when you make a form fat in a way or obese, it expands the form. The form becomes less defined and more expanded, more floating out. The next step was to let it melt! Which is even the next step of deforming a form.

I was also very interested in icons, another big issue at our time. Here you see Mies van der Rohe melting. (fig.11) And the next one was Guggenheim melting. (fig.12) I thought if I would like to do the Guggenheim, it should look like a vanilla ice cream, or kind of vanilla. So I had this idea of softness, spreading out of the melting totally. I'm from Styria and I remember that my mother always told me: "If you want to become an adult, you have to eat bread and butter every day because then you'll become big and strong and you can build a house someday in the future." So I thought this was an interesting aspect and I combined it and made a house and bread and butter together, as a kind of reminescence to that time. (fig.13)

After the first five years I had more or less expressed my vocabulary. I tried to go on with different

13 *Butterbrot II*, 2005, aluminium, paint

14 *Telekinetically bent VW-Van*, 2006, mixed media, e-mail correspondence

materials in different sets of ideas at the same time. So there were the 3D sculptures on one side and the videos on the other side, the photography, the drawings, the text works and performatives and also these sweater pieces. I thought, "It would be still interesting to bend." (fig.14)

To bend a bus, to strech a sweater over a painting, over a canvas; painting came back. So it still was there and the color was always important for me. So I was more or less dressing the canvases for a time. And then I started to make sweaters for the canvas. (fig.15) So I took a very big canvas to put this big yellow sweater, three meters long and all of a sudden it transformed very easily into something abstract. It also transformed very easily into for example landscape paintings. If you look at this it could also be for example a landscape and the sun, or something else.

I thought it would be nice to make sweaters for architecture. I was invited to make an installation in this house of John Hejduk, this famous American architect from the 1950s, who built this famous house [Wall House] in Holland. It was very important for me because as a boy and young man I was very influenced by comic strips and later on by science fiction as well. I still found it very interesting to have this guy as a starter of my work and in a way to look at the world from this perspective. This house of Hejduk looked like the house of Donald Duck or the houses of Walt Disney. I made the ceiling with a big stretched sweater piece on the ceiling and the arms are hanging down. The wall is also covered with midwear, the heating and the telephone as well.

In 2006, I was invited to do a show for the MUMOK in Vienna. (fig.16) I had this idea to realize a "House Attack": one of those houses that are standing around everywhere and growing like a cancer. It was the first time, when houses didn't need an architect anymore or

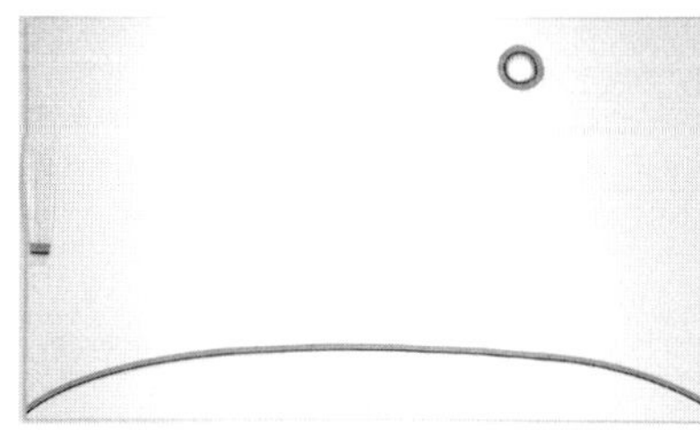

15 *Mentally Yellow (Apex of the Sun)*, 2008, canvas, wool

16 *House Attack*, 2006, c-print

Erwin Wurm
Gulp

17 *Adorno as Oliver Hardy in the Bohemian Girl (1936) and the burden of desperation,* 2006, acrylic

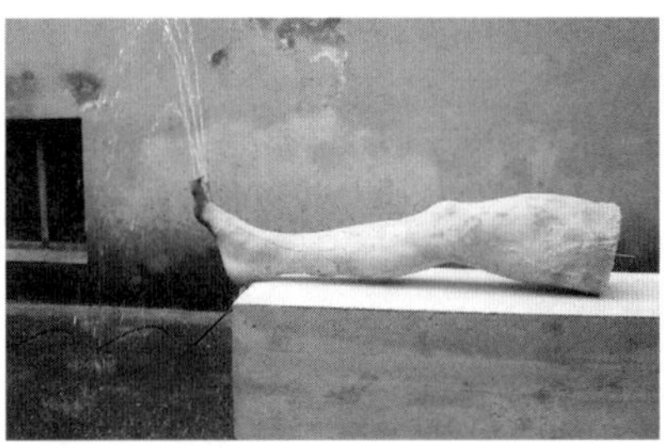
18 *Fountain for Arthur Rimbaud*, 2007, concrete, water pump

19 *Big Gulp, Series: Philisophers*, 2009, bronze, patina

craftsmen. It was a pure industrial-built house, horrible in every sense. It was in a way an answer of a certain society to architecture and art. Thanks to Edelbert Köb, it could be realized.

This is Mr. Adorno from another series, that is related to philosophers again. (fig.17) There is a very famous movie by Stan Laurel and Oliver Hardy, which is called *The Bohemian Girl*, from 1936. It plays in a torture chamber. All of a sudden they're both getting tortured. One gets squeezed very long when he walks out one or three meters tall and the other one gets pressed more or less and walks out pressed. And I made this piece with Adorno, so it's called "Adorno as Oliver Hardy in the Bohemian movie under the burden of depression."

Adorno was the one who was very important in the 1950s up to 1970s, 1980s for the art world. And he was the one who said: "After the Holocaust poems are impossible." And I think this is totally bullshit because especially after a dramatic thing like the Holocaust, poems are a necessity and very important. And he also said: "Humor and cynicism have no place in the art." And I think this is also a big mistake.

That is another fountain related to Arthur Rimbaud, this genius writer, who actually ended his writings, when he was 21 years old. (fig.18) He wrote all his fantastic poems before he was 21 and then he became a weapons dealer. And he lost his leg and always when he was reminded and asked, "Don't you write, again? Do you go back to your writings?" he answered that it's totally bullshit and crap and that he doesn't want to be connected with this. This was an interesting person and an interesting aspect, that someone is able to deny what he did, which was great, fantastic, and so dramatic. This is the reason why I made it.

Last year I tried to relate some pieces to the early 1980s when I made these videos with the sweaters and pullover pieces. At that time I used a video to transform the piece to get it out of this very short thing and to try to transform it. I was always looking for a way to realize it in 3D. Since several years scanning and the milling machine exists. It was interesting because all of the sudden you turn on the switch, and out comes a leg. (fig.19) I must say I stopped it again because it's such an easy method. I remember in the early 1970s, everybody bought a video camera and made these games with it. Just later on when it became more advanced it became really good. All of a sudden, we have a big flood of scultpures, very easy and very quick. And many of them would be very bad.

The last piece that I want to show you is called *Narrow House*. And I thought it would be very interesting to realize a piece that I wanted to do for a long time. I wanted to show a house of the 1970s again, one of those typical houses, which are built everywhere even now. (fig.20) I also wanted to show the inside of the house, so the only house I know from inside is my parents' house.

All the things from the inside, the furniture, the floor plan, the organization of the rooms, are reminiscent of my parents' house. So for example, the bathroom is 40 cm wide and everything is squeezed. The house is only one meter and all the interior is squeezed in relation to this one meter. So the bathtub, the hand wash, the toilet seat is like 6 to 7 cm and the kitchen for example is 50 cm. The living room was 80 cm. Suddenly it becomes very psychedelic. Even the pattern of the wallpaper is squeezed.

But what is important: this is one meter, but it looks wider. It was not possible to show the attraction. When you go to this house, you feel very squeezed and claustrophobic in a way. It was not possible to show this through the photography. Actually you have to go into this house and you have to be there to experience it.

Thank you very much!

20 *Narrow House*, 2010, mixed media

Aaron Betsky

Do Burning Whales Leap to Kiss the Sky? Architecture in the Blue of Sprawl

Edited by Guvenc Özel

Aaron Betsky is one of the most famous theorists in the architectural field. And I was surprised when I read that he was born in the United States, in Montana. I met him years ago in Los Angeles. He moved to the Netherlands when he was young and attended grammar and high school there. He moved back to the United States to attend Yale. He is a trained architect and he worked for Frank Gehry. I think he worked there two years. Since then he's been taking revenge on architecture. This is what he told me that he would do today as well.

He wrote many books. I would like to mention three of them tonight. First, "What is Modernism?" is scheduled to be published. Writing on this topic at this time makes him a very courageous guy! He wrote a book in 2000, entitled, "Architecture Must Burn." And this was the first time he stole a title from us. [Aaron Betsky responded from the audience, "It was the second time."] He is a guy who is really talented at camouflaging ideas that surround him. And not so recently, in 1997, he wrote a book, "Queer Space."

He ascended the ladder to international fame while he was the director of the Architecture Institute (NAi), in Rotterdam. He created very famous and fabulous exhibitions. He was also the curator of architecture and design at the San Francisco Museum of Modern Art, which was

built by Mario Botta. He was the artistic director of the International Architectural Biennale in Venice in 2008. He is currently teaching, and has actually taught at every important school in the United States and also many in Europe, including this school some years ago. I would like to welcome Aaron, and I'm looking forward to hearing what you have to say about leaping whales kissing the sky.
— Introduction by Wolf D. Prix

I have made a career out of looking at what other people are making in order to collage it together into ideas and stories about the human-made, designed environment. I have become someone who lectures, writes and organizes in order to keep myself alive. I am not sure that what I will talk about today is a revenge on architecture as much as it is a justification for what it is that I do, which is not making architecture, or at least not making buildings. In the last 10 to 15 years, I have consistently made the argument that we need not make buildings to make great architecture. And I will continue with that argument today as I prove to you why Coop Himmelb(l)au is a great firm that should go back to burning flags.

So the leaping whale is how you have to start the story. When Wolf D. Prix first came to Los Angeles to lecture, there was the leaping whale. For him it represented the magic of an incredibly heavy object levitating in the air and its ability to withstand the laws of gravity, proving that it was in fact possible to move beyond the known into the unknown. Tonight, I am going to talk about the way in which architecture and art try to represent the unknown.

We have to figure out where we are. And in its simplest form, that means knowing where we are in an environment that can be anywhere. Most of us at this point live our social life and obtain our knowledge through the Internet, or through other digital platforms. Strangely, these digital platforms are highly corrosive. I discovered this when I asked my students to design a digital equivalent of the Cincinnati Art Museum. It could have been Internet based, a game, a "Second Life" type of platform, any type of digital virtual equivalent of an art museum. We spent a month on this and finally realized that it was a failure because digital platforms in the end are about speed, transparency and indexicality. They seek to organize in a flexible and fluid manner as much data as possible. They seek to make their organizations visible at such a speed that you do not notice any barriers. It is great in many cases; however, an art museum is built around a strange conceit, which is that it has originals of great paintings, great sculptures, and great sofas that cannot be reproduced, that are material and that you must see to contemplate. The entire building of an art museum is built on that experience and I would argue that it is an extreme version of the problem that architecture faces: namely that if it focuses on making buildings it would be condemned to being useless in a global network that is increasingly based on speed, indexicality, transparency and the availability of information. There will be no need for buildings. I take that back. There will be a

1 W Hotel Room, Midtown Atlanta

2 W Hotel Lobby, Midtown Atlanta

4 Alice Tully Hall, Diller Scofidio + Renfro, 2009, New York

3 Alice Tully Hall, Diller Scofidio + Renfro, 2009, New York

need for buildings as warehouses—warehouses for people to work in, to sleep in, to store goods that are ordered from the Internet, as warehouses for spectacles in which Justin Bieber can perform. We are left without space, and making architecture digital will just speed up the process because all of the fanciful imagination will be leached out by speed, transparency and indexicality.

All around the world cities are sprawling and turning into a concatenation of human dwellings. No place is spared. The center of the city is left only as a kind of museum piece, as it is here in Vienna, where the big corporations, fancy lawyers and politicians have their headquarters. The work goes on in back offices elsewhere. The cultural palaces define images together with the advertising agencies, and the police and judges keep it all together. What controls the sprawl is not necessarily the police and judges who sit downtown, but invisible embedded systems of control. What disappears in sprawl is visible form.

The issue is deeper than what we see, however. Sprawl is only a symptom, though for architecture it is the most important symptom because it is a physical one. It is a symptom, as Karl Marx and Friedrich Engels promised in 1848 "that all that is solid will melt into air." Today, the family is falling apart and the corporation is disintegrating into weaker business units. The state is falling apart as we can witness all over the world, either grouping itself into loose configurations, such as Schengen, or breaking into smaller regions. Everything around us sprawls. Even our bodies sprawl and fall apart, infected by technology from drugs to glasses and artificial lenses to implants that keep us alive.

The rest of the world has as its center, not the dark star of the Angewandte but rather the white star of the Museum of Modern Art (MoMA) in New York. There is no other institution in the world that sets the tone for art, architecture and design more than MoMA. Its stated mission is to not only expose you to modern art but to define Modernism. It is quite a statement to make: "We know the correct way to translate modernity into form, image and space." The

5 Toy Furniture, Greg Lynn, 2008, Venice Biennale

6 Blob Wall Pavilion, Greg Lynn, 2008, SCI-Arc Gallery

architecture of the building in which they do this is reductive and bland, a perfectly composed temple for elitist and isolated forms of abstraction. A few years ago they decided to expand and hired a modernist architect, Yoshio Taniguchi, to design a new temple. Taniguchi said to them, "Thank you very much, now if you give me enough money I will make you a nice building. If you give me more money I will make you a beautiful building. And if you give me enough money I will make the building go away." They reportedly gave Taniguchi close to a billion dollars and he made a building that almost disappears, in a way that leaves the last vestiges of polite modernism hovering around the great masterworks that reside within the temple.

I have a name for this kind of modernism: W-modernism. I named it after the chain of hotels that are currently spreading throughout the world. (fig.1, 2) Hotels are a particularly symptomatic building type. Hotels are the places where the effective elite stay when they are doing their business. For years, including in Vienna, the Hilton Hotel was the place where the elite would gather. It was an emblem of modern, global, and international culture. The W is designed for people like me who do not want to stay in a place making a half-baked attempt to recall past modernisms. We are middle-aged men and women and want to stay in something that approaches modernism, but doesn't hurt and is not too painful. The W knows how to create a minimum level of modernism that is theatrical. It stages the idea that we could all live with—lighting effects, in formal compositions and in the sequences that 150 years of modernism have taught us. We can temporarily reside in good design with everything from Danish chairs to fake fur throws and experience a kind of cocooning of the body that is so much at the heart of the metrosexual culture that now dominates the effective elite.

We live in a global culture where architects are creating fragments of an international culture run by the effective elite. Architecture is, always has been and always will be a built affirmation of the social, political and economic status quo. Good architects, young architects and architects who do not build very much are trying to push that particular language, to reassemble those forms. In the simplest manner, they are trying to make forms that are so minimalist that they question the building itself. Alternatively, they are trying to activate minimalism. It is in fact possible to turn a house or a parking garage into a piece of theater and to make people notice that there is something there called architecture. It is possible to react by going back to the basics. And at the fringes of architecture, we see a number of architects who are trying to push architecture beyond the built affirmation of the status quo.

I also think that a lot can be achieved at the fringes of architecture, not by building but by unbuilding. An example is the Lincoln Center project in New York City, which started out as another billion dollar project commissioned to a famous architect until they realized that they could no longer afford to continue. They then hired Diller Scofidio + Renfro to peel away, redo, re-inhabit and reinvigorate the entire cultural mecca, piece by piece. (fig.3, 4)

I have a small prediction to make: postmodernism is coming back. I assert this now because even the folks who are stretching form through the use of computers are reverting to the fascination of how we can use types and prototypes and how we can use the rendering process itself to build memory, place, recognition, stories and perhaps even jokes into our built environment. Postmodernism will come back. It is even showing up in some of the colors and forms of one of the studio professors here in the sacred environment of the Angewandte. I have argued this point with Professor Greg Lynn, as I think there is quite a lot of postmodernism in his work (fig.5, 6)

In addition, I would argue that there is a tradition that will help us build for this world of sprawl. It is a tradition in architecture that

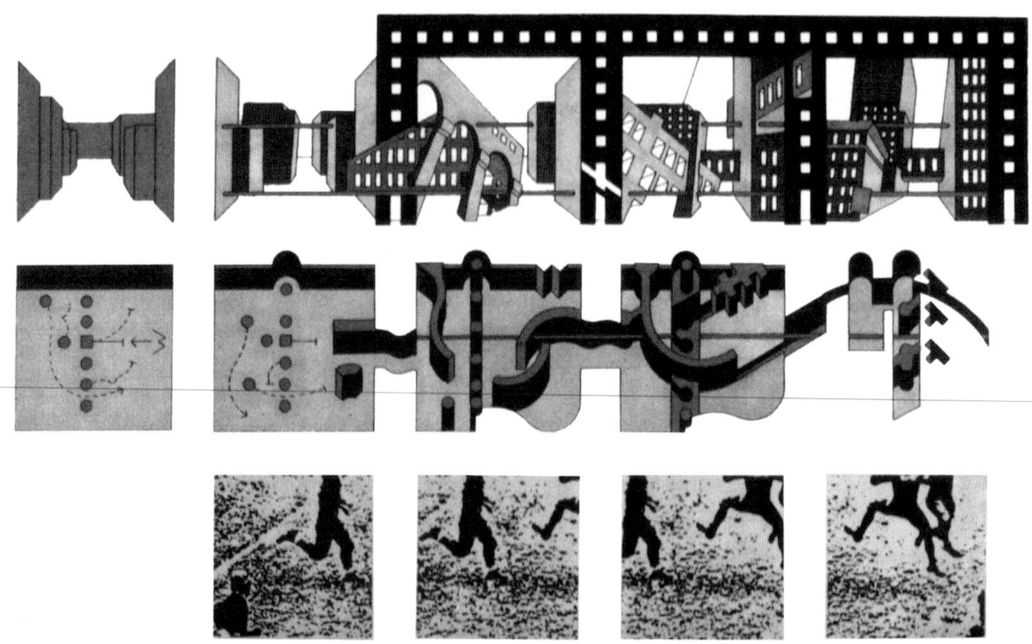

7 *The Manhattan Transcripts*, Bernard Tschumi, 1976–1981

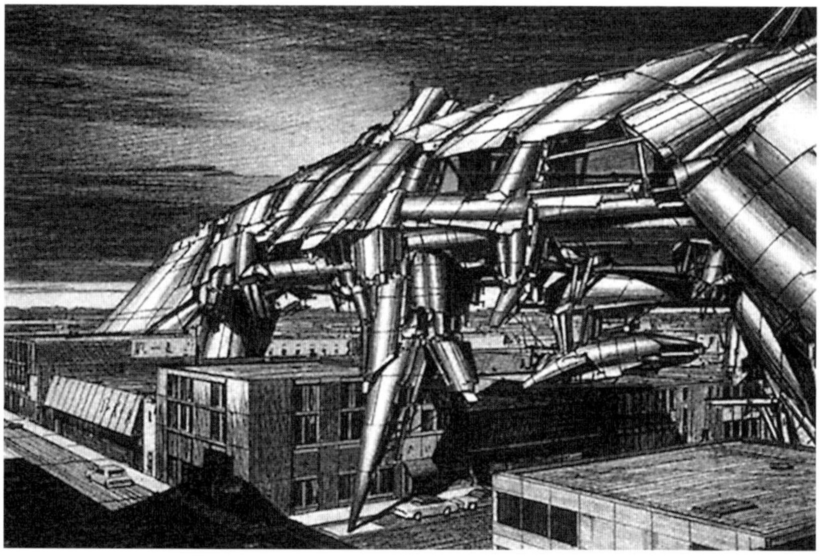

8 *Icebergs*, Lebbeus Woods, 1991

9 *Underground Berlin*, Lebbeus Woods

goes back to the late 1960s and early 1970s. It tries to unearth those aspects of Modernism that we once hoped would create a truly democratic, open and perhaps even spiritual environment. What was essential about the kind of architecture that emerged from New York's Institute of Architecture and Urban Studies, London's AA and strange outposts like Vienna, was that this was not a utopian architecture that proposed perfect static environments; instead it was a rather messy affair. It was what I call experimental architecture. An architecture that was trying to tell stories and believed, as Bernard Tschumi noted in his Manhattan Transcripts, "that you might even have to commit a murder to create great architecture." (fig.7) It was an architecture that tried not to make stable form, but rather unmake stable form as it found an architecture of digging, mapping, unearthing and contradicting that refused to accept reality. At the same time, it refused to propose an alternative, realizing, however unconsciously, that you cannot propose a set form. You have to think about architecture instead as a continual un-

10 *Die Freiheit wird jetzt einfach gesponsert, aus der Portokasse (Freedom is Now Simply Going to Be Sponsored – Out of Petty Cash)*, 1990

folding of the world around us, into a neverending and never beginning landscape and a mirroring of that same reality around us. It is a tradition that looks at unbuilding, at opening up, moving through the buildings of Vienna and Bratislava, for example. It imagines, as Lebbeus Woods puts it, an "anarchitecture." An architecture that rejects order, a structure that may already exist somewhere underground in Berlin, someday emerging and shooting out, destroying the world around us, moving like a leaping whale. (fig.8, 9) Architecture must gather together fragments that already exist to stand witness and to give memory to a world that wants us not to know.

Architecture is a reenactment, a theatrical attempt to restage the world in such a manner that we can all be actors in the world that we would like to make our stage. We must stand witness, as John Hejduk said, to the very destruction of humanity. That should be the task of architects.

Hans Haacke put it best when he adorned a fragment of a building, which was to be torn down to make place for the atrocity that is now Potsdamer Platz, with a work of art that said, "Art remains Art." (fig.10) Can Architecture remain Architecture? Can buildings still be architecture? I hope they can, but I think there is the danger that architecture will always somehow, when it turns to buildings, become appropriated and perhaps even misinterpreted. There is a territory between art, architecture and performance that is undecided, and that undecided characteristic allows us to question how we inhabit our world. If that is the case, perhaps all we need to do is see what we already have rather than to build more.

In fact it should be possible to create something that is not only the blue of sky, but that is the brown of earth, that is as open, as optimistic, as beautiful as a whale leaping to the sky and kissing a guy, but also as real, as contingent, as fragmentary, as messy and as humble as the reality that we all live within every day. I hope that architecture will continue to experiment and someday we might have a true architecture of the open eye, the open heart and the open mind. And I wish you all much luck with that.

Patrik Schumacher

The Societal Function of Architecture

Edited by Robert Neumayr

This week is the English week, the "fish and chips" week. The first lecture this week is Patrik Schumacher. I think it is not necessary to introduce Patrik. Everyone knows him as a patient teacher and a brilliant, intellectual critic.

He was actually the first who introduced a special review system to this school. He invited people from the AA [Architectural Association] and had them talk about computer programs, indicating to the students which programs they should use in order to get certain results. I was thinking they should have rather pushed the other button, the one which would erase the whole program. Twenty years ago architecture was a promise, now it is rather a marketing tool to sell fancy objects. Into this role of superficiality and simplifying thinking patterns, Patrik's book breaks a hole, disturbing the thinking that architecture cannot be focused on a concept.

I think we all know that in our complex society only complex solutions are possible, not simple ones. Simple solutions are old. Complex solutions—and Patrik is proposing complex solutions on many levels—are not optimal but they are new.

Patrik told me that he will not show you any images, only read from his book. Please welcome Patrik Schumacher!
—Introduction by Wolf D. Prix

The title of my lecture is "The Societal Function of Architecture." It is the first time I am speaking about this particular aspect of architectural theory. I've only done a few lectures on my book so far, always supported by slides. So this is a new experience, and that is why I feel more comfortable turning it into a seminar when I am about halfway through. I hope there will be some discussion and questions.

The question "What is the social function of architecture?" is, I think, a legitimate question. It is perhaps a necessary and important question. Important for the self-regulation and self-determination of the discipline, which is the key aspect of the theory of Architectural Autopoiesis—that architecture is a self-regulating discourse with no authority governing it, neither politicians nor clients being able to construct what architecture is and how it responds to contemporary challenges.

Well, what are we doing as architects? We produce buildings. What do buildings do? I mean, you could cite a shelter that provides protection to keep us dry and warm. But is that what requires an academic discipline? Do we need Wolf D. Prix, Zaha Hadid or Greg Lynn to do that? I doubt it. So, what do buildings do? Are we perhaps creating beautiful buildings? So is that what it is? Are we artists, therefore? Or are we creating particularly well-functioning buildings? Does that mean that we are engineers? Or are we just creating original buildings? Does that mean that architecture is a kind of end in itself, a kind of play, like Eisenman and Kipnis sometimes assume?

I want to introduce an important distinction here, which is the distinction between architecture and mere building. Architecture being based on an academic theory-based engagement and on innovative practice being driven forward. Building is just keeping the tradition alive and reproducing what has survived the test of time. And that has been the way the built environment has been reproduced for thousands of years until the big bang of architecture in the Renaissance where we have a kind of theory-based practice, moving into the domain of the paper. For the first time we have fully designed architectures circulating just as speculative constructs on paper.

But what architecture delivers through paper and theoretical discourse is still tied up with what the built environment does for society, and that has been a kind of primordial contribution throughout history. So the societal function of the built environment first of all needs to be questioned, and I would argue that this is a very deep contribution. It is a crucial factor, I would say, in the *Menschwerdung*, in the emergence and becoming of mankind, and ultimately in the construction of society.

I want to elaborate on this by reading a small excerpt from volume 2 of my book, *The Autopoieses of Architecture*, which has just been submitted to the publisher. The chapter I want to read is "The Built Environment as Indispensable Substrate of Societal Evolution:" *"So society can only evolve as a simultaneous ordering and articulation of space. The elaboration of the built environment, however haphazard, precarious and based on accident, rather than purpose and intention originally, seems to be a necessary condition for the build-up of any stable social order. The gradual build-up of a social system must go hand in hand with the gradual build-up of an artificial spatial order. Social order, therefore requires, spatial order. The social process needs the built environment as a plane of inscription, where it can leave traces that then serve to build up and stabilize social structures that then in turn allow a further elaboration of more complex social processes."*

"So, the evolution of society goes hand in hand with the evolution of its habitat, understood as ordering frame."—and that's a very important category I'm introducing. *"The spatial order of the human habitat is both an immediate physical ordering apparatus, that separates and connects social actors and their activities, and"*—which is the second important dimension—*"a mnemotecnic substrate for the inscriptions of social memory. This inscription might at first be an unintended side effect of the various activities, which unfold and produce these environments. Then given spatial arrangements are functionally adapted and elaborated further, then they are further marked and underlined by ornaments, which makes them more conspicuous."* And that is also important. It becomes a kind of quasimemory, as I would call it. *"The result is a gradual build-up of a spacio-morphological system of signification. Thus emerges a semantically charged built environment that provides a differentiated system of settings that help social actors to orient themselves with respect to the different communicative situations that constitutes the social-life poesies of the community."*

So the system of social settings, as a system of distinctions and relations, uses both, the positional identification of places, that means spatial position, and a morphological identification of places (ornamental marking) as props for the social communication process. Indications of this performative nexus between social and spatial structure are bound within social anthropology. They testify to the crucial importance of stable spacio-morphological settings for the initial emergence and stabilization of all societies. In the analysis of the social structure of primitive societies, the drawing of a village plan, for instance, often serves as the most succinct summary. So appropriately designed places regulate social communication by helping to define the situation, reminding actors about who they are and ordering the actors into the appropriate relative positions.

The semiological dimension of the built environment already comes to bear here, as the built environment develops from the state of vernacular tradition to the state where it is advanced by the outburst of architecture and the task of conscious semiological articulation arises.

The importance of the spacio-morphological setting as a defining frame for social communication is also recognized in sociology and social psychology. Erving Goffman, for instance, was very much aware of the need for frames and assemblages of sign equipment, as he calls it, that structure social communication. I'll quote Goffman here. "First there is a setting, involving furniture, deco, physical layout and other deco items which supply the scenery and stage props for the space of human actors, played out before, within or upon it. A setting tends to stay put, geographically speaking, so that those, who would use a particular setting as part of their performance, cannot begin the act until they have brought themselves to the appropriate place and must terminate the performance when they leave it."

That goes for every single communicative interaction. And my whole theory is based on communication theory. And architecture makes a universal claim for structuring frames for communicative interaction, which is the kind of communication operating between people present for each other. And this kind of interaction is always structured by a system of places or spatial frames, as well as clothing, fashion systems, artifacts or props. There is an enormous amount of embedded, accumulated intelligence and information processes within these systems, and we have relatively simple response mechanisms and we retrieve information embedded in these richly layered and sedimented information structures. As Herbert Simon says, "The kind of complexity of the path of the ant is in the environment and not in the ant." We are more complex, of course, but still my argument is that the complexity of social processes is to a large extent in the built environment.

"So the built environment remains a powerful tool of organization, sorting and ordering people and their activities. The ordering capacity of spatial arrangements and the specific order provided is not an independent objective property of the respective built spatial arrangements, but crystallized only in the pattern of the utilizations that it catalyzes."

The complexity is always in the interaction and that is also how you can re-utilize and re-inscribe meaning into all these sedimented structures. But this is always a relatively slow process. There is a lot of redundancy and some degree of mutation and selection for further reproduction and innovation.

"The built environment and the more mobile artifacts like furnishings, tools, clothes, etc., together engage in an inextricable metabolism of ecology, which is—according to the theory of architectural autopoiesis—best described as a system of communication. As the built environment develops from the state of vernacular tradition"—that brings back the distinction between architecture and building—*"to the state of architecture, the task of conscious semiological articulation arises. Architectural settings are to be designed as framing communication, as permanent broadcasts that function as constraining and enabling premises for all further communication, that is to be expected within the respect of spaces and settings. Architectural settings are a form of communication that helps to define the structure of social institutions."*

At this point ... I'm not finished yet ... but are there any questions at this stage? Queries, challenges?

Q&A

Q [Audience]: Why do you think that architecture is an autopoietic system? In a way any discourse could be approached in a relativistic way, claiming it was autopoietic. So why does architecture have a privileged status of being autopoietic?

You are right. Every social system is a kind of emerging autopoietic phenomenon. I'm not privileging architecture. It is one of various types of social systems. But there is one very important category of social communication systems. Niklas Luhmann calls it "the great function systems of society." Societies where you find these great function systems are so-called function-differentiated societies. And you could say that architecture is one of those systems, like the political system, like the legal system, like the economic system, like the mass media system. These are special types of function systems, which have a few hundred years of history and have developed a specific discourse, categories, values and methods.

And that's what the book is about. It looks at the autopoiesis of architecture, as this 500-year-old elaborate intelligent structure, which at the same time needs to be continuously updated. And architecture is one of the great function systems of society. And with respect to function systems, you can ask: what is the societal function? What is the societal function of the political system? What is the societal function of the legal system? And as far as Luhmann is concerned, each of these has a unique societal function, addressing a unique problem or exigency, which all societies have to face. So all social systems represent autopoietic systems. They form very powerful important sub systems of contemporary or modern societies, they are great function systems.

Q [Audience]: Can you be more specific about the evolution of the systems you're referring to?

The distinction between architecture and building is important here. Before architecture arrived, the villagers built their structures themselves as they had always, basically trying to repeat what had been done, maybe integrating small improvements. And you see certain structures emerging, like in self-organizing morphogenetic processes. Some of these structures emerge following local rules and develop global orders. They generate a certain rationality through an evolutionary process of trial and error. All of this is totally unconscious and is reproduced by myopic repetition as it has always been done. And that's what I call building.

And at a certain point in history, there was this big bang, which is the advent of architecture, where all of a sudden—and that is of importance here—architecture was drawn and immediately became a point of discourse, criticism and innovation. The ideal city of the Renaissance was just a rationalization and geometrization of what had evolved as the medieval city. Its innovation was not that large, but once it had been drawn and became part of the paper domain of speculation and one started to write about it, talk about it, ask questions about it, there was innovation. To propose innovations, one has to have a kind of discourse. And then there is a huge acceleration of evolution, and that is the ultimate result of each of these specialized intellectual enterprises, which architecture has become.

But to stick to the political system: initially you have spontaneous political orders, when small clans gather into tribes and discover ways of operating together. And as they evolve, at a certain stage—again at the same time, the Renaissance—you suddenly have political criticism, political theory, ideas that become a project of political construction. These are the moments when function systems are born, with discourses, with theory, with speculation, with self-conscious and the self-referential closure, as discourses. They all then become sub-systems of a larger society, which suddenly has this enormous accelerator. This acceleration and the build-up of complexity are possible through what then becomes a functional differentiation.

Before that everything was much more fused. But these things splinter—it is an evolutionary process—into domains of specially separated, self-referentially enclosed social systems, which at the same time have the obligation to continuously observe what's going on around and adapt themselves, to stay relevant. And that's never guaranteed. Architecture has gone through a number of crises where this expert discourse made itself nearly irrelevant and had to be nearly rebuilt from scratch by new-starters (for instance, the pioneers of the modern movement).

I hope that answers your question: how these contemporary sub-systems of society, called the great function systems of society, have evolved out of initially undifferentiated, tradition-bound cultural developments, which were happening without much foresight, without much critique, without much reflection. And what I call the great self-description of these function systems, the necessity to step out and build up layers of reflection, is an important factor in the overall coordination of these disciplines, because they do run into crises and that self-description is a reassessment of the task, a re-adaptation of the pertinent ways forward, and—in my terms—the development of a new style, which programs and reprograms the discipline's forward trajectory.

The competence of architecture is no longer a technical competence of putting together a construction. That is more and more being taken up by engineering specialists. We become these pure designers. And more and more the question becomes: what is our core competence? In my terms, it is the competence of organization and articulation, which is then unfolding an expertise of dealing with how things are perceived and comprehended. And that turns into a phenomenological dimension and a semiological dimension.

I want to read a few remarks at this stage, which help us to demarcate architecture from science on the one hand and from art on the other hand, and lead us to the discussion of aesthetic values and of the constant category of beauty. My argument here is that design is neither art nor science. It is solely a generous competency. As opposed to engineering, architecture and design take the users of architecture into account as socialized, sentient beings. That is the critical point; engineers never do that. It has to be recognized that built environments function via perception and comprehension. This poses a task of articulation. Architectural order emerges from the components of organization and articulation as the two irreducible constituent components of architecture's task. Organization is involved as physical distancing, separation and connection of domains, and there is framing of communication by physically channeling movement and interaction. Articulation is concerned with orientation and frames communication cognitively. Articulation is guiding movement and interaction via conspicuity and atmospheres, via perceptual as well as semiotic clues.

"Organization operates via social communication's dependency on human beings as mobile bodies in space, while articulation operates via social communication's dependency on human beings as perceiving comprehending subjects. The unique expertise or competency of architecture is therefore the establishment of order, of organizing, framing and priming of social communications and interactions. Framing supports the ordering and temporary stabilization of patterns of communication. As society evolves, more and more complex settings—which allow society to become ever more complex, more productive—need to be continuously upgraded."

Bill Hillier offers a "science" of organization. He calls it the science of configuration. My question is then: can there be a science of phenomenological and semiological articulation? That is all about upgrading the discipline and I think that can and should happen on all three dimensions of architecture's task. We need to upgrade our organizational capacities, our phenomenological intelligence and our semiological expertise. There can be and must be a science-informed normative view of these dimensions, but—and that is important—design is not a science. Organizationally, phenomenologically and semiologically informed design is a different practice from scientific practice. I am not turning architecture into science. It cannot be done.

So that is another theory I bring in: the double code of utility and beauty that governs design is very different from the code of scientific truth and probability. The reason for this difference is that designers need to act and decide quickly in the face of uncertainty and incomplete information. Science in contrast never reaches closure. It has infinite time and patience to follow through the ramifications of hypothetical constructions. We as designers have to react whether we have knowledge expertise or not. There is a kind of necessity to quickly decide in the absence of a fully resolved theory or assessment of the situation. And that is why aesthetic values must come into play. They have to do with this necessity to act intuitively and facilitate quick intuitive decision-making, both for the designer making design decisions and for users making decisions about which space to enter. The recognition of the beautiful is the instant perceptual recognition of the vital, the functional, identified on the basis of its mere appearance, prior to the verification of the entity's functionality.

Therefore, the category of beauty cannot simply be opposed to rationality. Being attracted to beauty is not per se irrational. The discrimination of beauty versus ugly is a culturally defined extension of the fundamental biological mechanism of attraction and repulsion. Organisms are attracted to what serves their survival and reproduction and repulsed by what impairs their survival and reproduction. Aesthetic sensibility is a constant universal feature of all human behavior and action. Some of its aspects I would even argue might be hard-wired by biological evolution. In my belief, the attraction to order and the rejection of chaos might be one of those. Other aspects are culturally evolved and imparted, yet other aspects might be based on individual conditioning. But one thing is important: in an evolving society, which changes its patterns of communication, you continuously have to adapt and develop your aesthetic sensibilities—and also your moral sensibilities. Your sensibilities might be wrong, which prevent you from entering the most vital and actively productive arenas.

This implies that aesthetic appeal can be subjected to rational analysis and criticism. We cannot trust our sensibilities blindly. They need to be subjected to a critique that queries the historical pertinence. For instance, I believe that I can demonstrate that the classical or modernist or minimalist sensibility is impairing the contemporary subject's capacity to fully participate in the most advanced, vital and productive processes of today's life. The question has to be posed, in terms of the state of sensibilities we all rely on: Do we have the right sensibilities? Aesthetic values—and that is the third argument in this paper—encapsulate condensed collective experiences with useful dogmas. Their inherent inertia implies that they progress via revolution rather than evolution. We rely on them and we move with them, until we hit a point of crisis and are forced to change them and relearn them. Sometimes an entire culture is forced to relearn their aesthetic sensibilities, and sometimes a function system, a discourse like architecture, had to be revolutionized. The crisis of Modernism was one of such moments, and in fact people like Wolf D. Prix are the great revolutionaries of aesthetic sensibilities.

Aesthetic values must be revolutionized if societal conditions or technological tools change. Clients vote with their commissions, users vote with their feet. The crisis of Modernism simply meant that the audience was just going elsewhere. The formulae, sensibilities, predilection, methods and categories of discussing art were simply bankrupt at that point. The in-depth rational critique of aesthetic values is a matter of theoretical reflection, often triggered by a crisis—for instance, the crisis of Historicism after World War I, or the crisis of Modernism in the 1970s. Styles become canonized into useful productive dogmas and finally end up as degenerate dogmas. And need to be revolutionized.

Q [Wolf D. Prix]: I love the whole statement, but, you know, I heard a lecture of a young scientist and he argued the same way you do. That they do not know where they are going, that they are operating on a field of uncertainty and they have to decide very quickly in order to get a solution. So why are you separating science from architecture and architecture from art? I understand it as a marketing tool, not in a bad sense, but just to explain the position of an architect, because we're going under…
We all know that our profession is not going to survive the next 50 years.

The distinction between art and architecture is an empirical reality. And I will try to explain what I mean. I'm looking at discourses, systems of communication, and I just notice that the art world and the art system are different groups of people with different languages, different categories, different values. And I don't think that contemporary pieces of art share the same discourse, agenda and criteria of success with the best of contemporary architectural projects. That is not just a description, that is a fact. And it was not like this in the Renaissance or even the Baroque. Michelangelo was the sculptor, the architect, the painter. The cathedral was a synthesis of these. But art has become something very different. And I think the bifurcation happened in the early twentieth century. You can observe it at the Bauhaus, with the split and separation and elimination of the artist from the institution. And that is simply a fact. But I can rationalize it by saying that the artists have quite a different societal function. And it is a much more open-ended and vague function, but, as far as I am concerned, the art system offers this kind of freewheeling platform of experimental communication for all the other subystems of society. Mass media uses the art system to experiment with new forms of electronic communication, new forms of filming techniques. Designers and architects use the art system as well—and when you go into the art system, the success criteria is quite different. You actually have to avoid making any performative claims. You cannot say this is something pragmatic and useful. You just go in there and use resources to experiment with material techniques, with morphologies and so on. That is how we use the art system, and we use it more in revolutionary and transitional periods and less in periods of higher self-certainty of where we are going. That is why in the transitional phase of the 1970s and 1980s, the assimilation of architecture and art was happening for a while, with figures like Tschumi, but I feel it happening less and less now.

> *Q [Greg Lynn]: But I would say, critically, what you're excluding from your discourse is building. What you're including is anything that is architecture. But I honestly believe that your argument would exclude certain architects from the autopoietic project. I mean, is there anyone you would exclude? Like I would think you would exclude Rem [Koolhaas]?*

No, no, absolutely not. Because there are key texts he's been delivering, he has been a central node in the discourse. He has been coming to the AA every two years. He's been teaching there …

> *Q [Greg Lynn]: But by his force of will, or by his residence in culture?*

By what he lives, what he seeks, what he thinks his audience is, by what he wants to contribute to. He has been teaching the discipline about [John] Portman. I think he is very central. I would not exclude him. And I cannot exclude mainstream either. The vernacular, the traditional building is outside. But any architecture, in its commercial form, is at the back of an evolved discipline. Maybe not at its latest stages, but they are participating and they are delivering something, which the discourse has worked up, and to a certain extent they are also picking up continuously from the avant-garde. Look at what KPF is doing, what SOM is doing—how versatile their repertoires have become, using more complex geometries to adapt to more complex sites. I'm not against that. You can criticize it, because it is not driven by the theoretical agendas we would promote, but they are still participating. So I would exclude all vernacular, but all professional architects are included somehow.

> *Q [Greg Lynn]: Included as long as they have a discourse? Or even Michael Graves, John Hejduk?*

Yes, they are for sure included. I am saying it is a contested field, what architecture is. It is not a settled issue. I see a convergence and I want more force to be brought behind this movement because I think we are still far away from transforming what happens out there, because what happens out there is still largely Modernist, Neoclassicist, postmodernist or minimalist. And very little parametricist. So there is really a danger, that this project gets stunted. The institutional support has been withering away, with Columbia going elsewhere, with even the AA to a certain extent. So I do feel like there is a need to foster, promote and inject new energy into this movement. But the autopoiesis of architecture is always the totality of the discourse, which also includes the Postmodernists, includes even Roger Scruton, or anybody who is entering the debate, who has a voice, who puts up a show at the RIBA. And I'm in debate with all these characters, and the students are exposed to that. And that is all part of the autopoiesis of architecture.

> *Q [Audience]: How would you integrate or exclude the capitalist project in the theory of autopoiesis and your Marxist reading of architecture? Because the capitalist project is intuitively forming the structures of society on many levels, not only economically but also psychologically, semiotically and so on.*

That is a very good question. My theory is not based on Marxism, but it's based on social system theory, which comes out of the tradition of complexity theory brought into sociology. But it has many similarities to the Marxist approach, in terms of its deep comprehensive historical approach. But the point is this: the difference here is that in Marxism the economy dominates society, and in the social system theory the economy is just one of the co-evolving subsystems. And yes, contemporary economy is a capitalist economy, it is a market-based economy. That is actually a moment when the autopoiesis of the economy is the emergence of the market economy.

Q [Audience]: You don't consider capitalism a despotic system?

No, no, no, not at all. If I would think that we are living in a despotic system, where we would require a revolution to overthrow the system, then I wouldn't be an architect. I realize that I have made the decision to work within a contemporary advanced society. I do not think it needs radical overthrow. I think you can make architecture in contemporary society. And one of the tasks of architecture is to observe and evolve and deliver to a society, which has an evolving economic system. And one of the great transformations from the Fordist economic reproduction model to a Post-Fordist economic reproduction model is something where the architectural discipline has to adapt itself to society and also to economy. So I have made peace with the market economy. The political system emerges as a self-referentially closed subsystem, through ultimately a democratic system. Democracy is the contemporary state-of-the-art form; the Post-Fordist form of capitalism is the state-of-the-art form, so I am fully buying into this. I am not an anti-capitalist.

Q [Audience]: What about Foucault's concept of—when you talk about discourses—and Foucault showed very well how power and power relations are very well assimilated within discourses. So you simply bracket out all these teachers in your theory?

Well, I believe to a certain extent in the rational side of the real. The collapse of communism, globalization, all these processes, which we have been observing for the last 30 years, coincide. There is an enormous increase in the level of productivity, technological innovations and new levels of freedom and communications, the Internet. They exist within a market economy, within the capitalist environment. I reject this kind of abstract utopian stance of radical critique. I am not blaming Foucault for it because in the 1960s things were less clear. There seemed to be the potential for global world revolution and the establishment of a different order and so on. But, you know, history has gone elsewhere. But that would be volume 2 of my book, *Architecture and Politics*. I made my position clear there.

Q [Audience]: It is a little bit surprising that you say that at the moment things seem to be very clear, when the whole of North Africa is in a state of turmoil, where nobody knows what the course of society is. And the other thing is even if productivity is at levels it has never been before, it might also be so efficient that we kill the planet. If you only argue on this technological level, I think you are bound in a kind of tool discussion, but you don't really discuss the answer.

If I look at, what is called the Arab Revolution, I don't see radically different models appearing. I see just a kind of catching up of parts of the developing world with the most advanced global models.

If they will manage to achieve it, whether they have an understanding of all the necessary conditions like sophisticated rules of law, a multi-party democracy with institutional guarantees and processes, that I do not know. But the model they are looking for is just a catching up, overcoming anachronistic regimes. There is no different political system in view and there is no different economic system in view. But I think each of these systems evolves a kind of global best practice. We are in an era where there are only systems of world systems: world science, world architectural design, world economy, world politics, more and more. There are, I would argue, global best practices, of how to set up a well-functioning financial system. How to configure the ingredients of a proper political system, the ingredients of a proper economic system, a proper state-of-the-art science with an apt methodology and epistemology. And Parametricism, in a sense, I would argue, could be that state-of-the-art best practice in architecture, which would be the equivalent of a sophisticated, multi-party democracy.

> *Q [Audience]: So it is basically a scale-less operation, which would mean that it can be used for designing a building, a city or a political system?*

Well, the autopoietical political system is for politicians, in its own autopoietically enclosed discourse. We can only observe and adapt our own terms to that.

But yes, across scales, I would argue that in interiors, buildings, urban quarters, whole cities, even in all design elements, you can see the same principles, the same rejection of simple geometric primitives, like circles, squares, triangles. They have disappeared out of the design world; they have disappeared out of architecture, out of urbanism. I think that these principles are universal, but at the same time they are very open. They offer degrees of freedom unheard of, with their internal richness and multi-trajectories. But in a specific direction. Yes, I think to this extent it is scale-less.

> *Q [Audience]: So how can it be specific?*

Oh, one of its premises is: be specific. Be contextually sensitive. Be sensitive with respect to internal operations. You cannot just start with a brief with a list of five stereotypical types of spaces. You need to unravel programs in terms of parametrically differentiated event scenarios, with multiple audiences, with multiple event parameters, in a dynamical system, with crowd simulations. That's the way you work on program. So that's why I'm saying there is a particular way how our style is picking up, interpreting and handling briefs, which is different from the Modernists, which were different from the Classicists. These principles in a sense are very abstract. This is kind of the most sophisticated *best practice*, which this discourse has evolved, and that's the kind of struggle of debates, struggle of ideas we're engaging.

So we leave it like this? Okay, thanks!

Zaha Hadid

Edited by Robert Neumayr

I recently saw two very impressive buildings at Zaha's office. The one is the MAXXI, the Museum of Modern Art, in Rome, and the other one is the Guangzhou Opera House (Building), in China. I think that the MAXXI is not a museum for modern art, it's rather a kind of museum for liquid space. And the auditorium in the Guangzhou Opera Building is a space where, I think, all of us would be able to hear the color of architecture. Not only the sound of the music, but also the color of architecture. These two buildings are intelligent pools in the desert of simplicity in our world. And I think they are opponents of superficial thinking. In the last 20 years, I think architecture was a promise. And I have to thank Zaha for keeping this promise up with all of her buildings. So thank you very much!
— Introduction by Wolf D. Prix

Thank you very much. It is a bit strange, that I have been teaching at the Angewandte for 10 years and this is my first lecture here. I want to thank Wolf [Prix], not only for his introduction but for convincing me many years ago to come here, and Gerald Bast for making it happen. Thank you, really.

I have a long history here in Vienna from the age of, I don't know, seven maybe. I didn't like it when I was young. I came here when I was 15 years old to spend the whole summer with my family, and it was deadly. But anyway, I have come here very frequently since I finished at the AA in the mid-1980s because of my connection with Wolf—coming to his reviews and his events—and also because of Peter Noever and the events at the MAK. So I've had a long relationship with Vienna.

Wolf and I met many years before that, when I came to Vienna with my unit trip. I came to Vienna in 1976, many of you were not even born ... Maybe your grandparents were born then [laughter]. I remember sitting under the palm tree in the round room in your [Wolf D. Prix's] old office. Anyway, it was very interesting and I think that back then the work of Hans Hollein had a tremendous impact. There were very few heroes at the time whom one could relate to as a student.

I also have to thank Patrik [Schumacher]. I am sorry I missed his talk yesterday. I heard it was very animated. Anyway, I did not meet Patrik in those years. I met him in 1988 when we did the

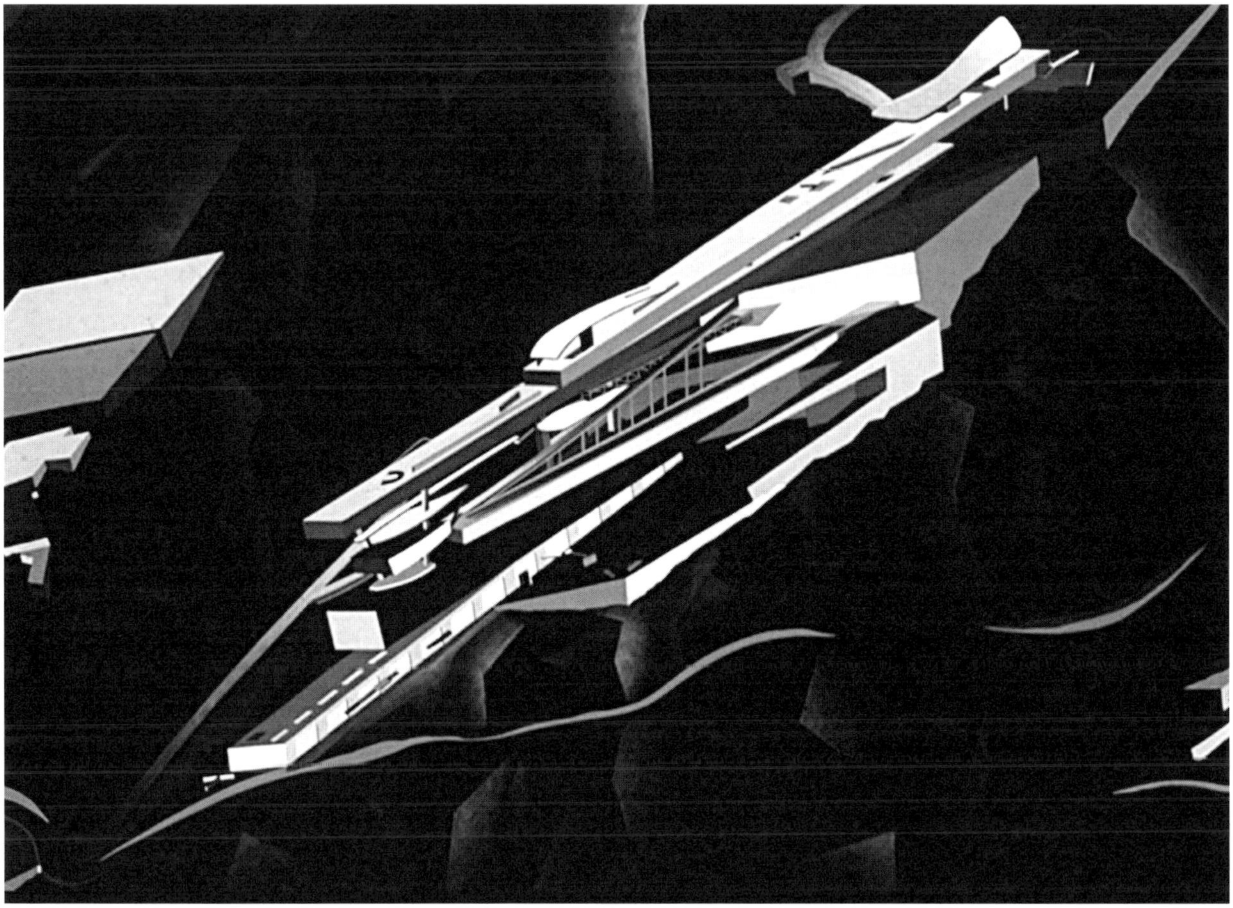

1 *The Peak Leisure Club*, 1982–1983, Hong Kong

Decon [Deconstructivist Architecture] show in New York, which was also a very important moment. He has been a tremendous contributor to the office and a very close friend and ally to me, and I want to thank you, Patrik.

That doesn't say that we don't have our problems and differences [laughter]. Which makes it into what he thinks is an interesting, well, discourse.

THE LONG WAVE THEORY OF INNOVATION—BUILT PROJECTS IN THE LIGHT OF PRIOR DESIGN RESEARCH.

This is a drawing, which I did in 1983, after I won the *Peak* [Peak Leisure Club, Hong Kong], which in a way for me is a very seminal project. (fig.1) A lot of the methods used were graphic methods. And these ideas and methods became the way to develop my projects. And there was—even then—the idea of being interested in topography, landscape and geometry, as an approach.

We had a MAK show, I think eight years ago, which was also a tremendous opportunity, with a major installation called *Ice Storm*. But it also collected all the paintings and drawings so it was more of an archival show with an installation in the main space. It really took tremendous chutzpah on the part of Peter Noever to actually do the show. I also want to thank him. He has been a tremendous friend and support to me. And I will say again that one of the reasons I came to Vienna was because of people like him and Wolf and Hans. They

2 Qatar Museum (model)

kind of urbanized the city, by activity and by work.

This installation also came at the same time as the idea of fabrication and being able to reconstruct a whole domain in one large installation. I got hold of all the things, which I will show today: Rome ... I don't know what the other things are [laughter] ... the Abu Dhabi bridge, Glasgow, Channel, the tower in Marseilles and the opera house.

EXPANDING THE REPERTOIRE: CONCEPTUAL MORPHOLOGIES.

So these are some of the projects, which were about landscape and topography: the Qatar museum, the museum in Graz, Rome, other kinds of installations, the science museum in Wolfsburg. This is a project for the Royal Collection and a diagram for the Quebec library.

And some interesting early diagrams of the Islamic Museum in Qatar. (fig.2) It took maybe a few takes to understand how to translate a field of striations that are clashing into each other into a body with separated volumes, and how that could become gallery spaces. The Citadel: the project for a museum in Qatar, where we started to use gradations, gradating space, from very small spaces to very large spaces. Then the translation of the landscape in terms of the library as a tree of knowledge, and how these valleys that are the reading rooms become the root of enlightenment, in a sense. So the roots of the staircases are between these crevices. And these kinds of ideas really emerge later on in the built work, the crevices between the volumes, or the idea of a very large volume encompassing many different programs, almost a city on its own in one continuous volume.

And the idea of carving also emerged in these projects, not only in the way you carve the earth prepared for a program, but in the way we did all the models, where it was like strata—that it is cut. You know I think that some people in the office had to cut this thick plastic by hand, like for a month.

What I'm saying is that these kinds of graphic explorations became the project. And that is why I think it is exciting for me. They emerge again somewhere and somehow in a built form.

MAXXI: GENESIS OF A PROJECT

Rome. To explain its genesis, I think I will start with the Peak. At the Peak there is this series of beams, resting on each other and leaving in between them a space that is a public domain. And there is the idea of a space of suspension, where the whole program is suspended within, almost like planets on their own. But it is also about the adjacency between the library space and the swimming pool or the motorway, the closeness of different (very different) entities tied together.

Further, there is the Vitra Fire Station, which forms a void carved into the factory's domain. We were looking at these volumes that intersect and intercept each other, bifurcating the space and bringing it back together, achieving lightness through a material like concrete, learning how to achieve transparency within the building.

For the Qatar museum we did many studies about these colliding or striated volumes, but really at that time we did not know how it could be interpreted. The gradation in the museum in Qatar with a superposition of ramps, almost like a field of motorways—it becomes a space to move from one space to the other, up and down through different spaces.

The BMW building in Leipzig and Strasbourg's car park bear similarities to Rome. In Strasbourg the field is slightly tilted out of distortion, and the car spaces follow a geometrical kind of curve.

There is the competition for the IIT [Illinois Institute of Technology] in Chicago, where this idea of intersecting volumes also occurs in one space. Soft volumes versus hard volumes.

Coming back to Rome. The site in Rome was an industrial site, built as a factory in 1904. We had the idea of striated fields and how they stem from one beginning. (fig.3) Looking at the L-shaped site we did many studies where we operated parallel or perpendicular to the street, but then the lines began to emerge as diagonals from the outside, and that really disturbed the early compositions, making it all really confluent. It is interesting how the space in the front is squeezed by the two existing buildings. So we decided to keep one of these buildings to squeeze that site and let the building flood the site, almost like streams. The main galleries are on the major streams and the minor spaces are the bridges. It is almost like a river delta flooding the site.

The areas which are left open are supposedly for the second phase of this project, which I personally think will never happen, but

3 MAXXI National Museum of the 21st Century Arts (spatial diagram), 1998–2009, Rome, Italy

4 MAXXI National Museum of the 21st Century Arts, 1998–2009, Rome, Italy

this is not a complete composition. But there is another thing: in these cases the field provides you with the idea of a composition that can actually be built in stages. So if you have three phases without the fourth one you can still have a complete composition.

The design is going back to the idea of layering which was done in the Peak, but the layering of the beams occurs in a much more compressed way, so there are layers between each other, where you can have cascading or sloping galleries. The way the striation is translated into geometry lets you find your way onto the site, into the galleries, but also allows to hang the drawings or light the building.

Also, the geometry of this composition always addresses an existing geometry on the site. Wherever you are around this building, you have one of these façades or spaces parallel to you. As you enter the space, under one of these minor streams you see the terracing of one of the galleries. You walk through the main space, through this series of staircases, which connects you to the vestibule, where all the beams and all the streams mix and intertwine into this one continuous vertical space that ties it all together. (fig.4)

The louvers allow for natural light so it's a totally day-lit museum, and can also be used for rigging pieces of art. In the original competition the museum was supposed to house a show for Arte Povera. These are very large pieces, which could have been hung from these rigs, but now some of them can also be used to hang walls for paintings, as it is done now.

There are views where you can see two sides of the building or through one floor into the next building. It's the idea that within the space you can see many layers, vertically and also horizontally. The terracing allows you to see objects or exhibits from above, like a terrain. This could be appropriate, for example, to show architectural models or very large objects.

And in a way, if you flip the diagram of the Rome project you get our Montpellier project [the Pierres Vives building], where the streams are on the edge. It is not completed yet, but it's also a kind of a marriage of maybe too many ideas. One of which is the idea of the aggregates, where you have not only big concrete pieces aggregating together, but three programs for that region of France. In this governmental building the archive, the library, and the sports department are clustered together, with the veins of the glazing following the lines of this very large object.

GUANGZHOU OPERA HOUSE

This is the exterior of the opera house. There is this idea of a crevice between two volumes very tight together. These are two volumes which are going back to very early studies of the Cardiff Bay Opera House, to the idea of a public space as a land mass. (fig.5)

For the Cardiff Opera House we had the idea of an "Inverted Necklace," where a band is wrapped around the perimeter of the site, housing all the supporting facilities, and suspended from that are the rehearsal spaces and the main auditorium. The main auditorium has a symmetry, so that sound in the auditorium is energized. And all of this rests on a curve or a bubble as a kind of topography for the public space. So in all these projects there was always the intent to create a public or civic space. I'm not sure how it happened, but in the presentation for the Guangzhou Opera House it was referred to as two pebbles on the Pearl River.

The idea of nesting or sitting over each other or very adjacent to each other, especially in audito-

5 Guangzhou Opera House (exterior rendering), 2003–2010, Guangzhou, China

riums, came earlier in Luxemburg, combined with the idea of topography. (fig.6)

I was really staggered in China when I was there recently because when we won the competition there was literally nothing on the site. None of these towers existed. And I actually never thought they would exist when we opened this building. It's extraordinary.

One thing that is not very obvious in these photographs is that this opera house sits in a park, which stretches throughout a big part of the city. The opera is an extension of the landscape and it is only slightly higher than the ground. And because the park is quite active, it's rather nice to see people using the park all day and throughout the day around the opera house.

What is really exciting about the main auditorium is that it still has symmetry, but it is one continuous surface, incorporating all the lighting and all the acoustic conditioning. Here are studies of other interior spaces of opera houses we designed. So they form a kind of family of opera spaces, of theater spaces or conference halls.

I gave a lecture in the opera. The only thing about operas, if you are not singing—and I am not singing—is that you cannot see the audience. It's a very weird experience.

SHEIKH ZAYED BRIDGE

This bridge in Abu Dhabi has been going on for so long. They have been knitting the steel work for the past 15 years. It is like a dune.

6 Guangzhou Opera House (interior rendering), 2003–2010, Guangzhou, China

And somebody sent me a text message the other day and saying he's been going back and forth on this bridge for the whole afternoon in a car. That is true. It is choreography as a landscape, as a kind of structure. So there are two buttresses and they go up and down till they meet at the end and they become flat as a motorway. The substructure is in concrete and the main structure is in steel. These buttresses are so enormous, they could be occupied. The idea of occupying structure came from there.

HEYDAR ALIYEV CENTRE

The Baku project [Heydar Aliyev Centre in Azerbaijan] combines three programs—a performing space, a library and a museum—in one space. It's almost like an Acropolis. It sits on a higher raised ground which is a park, and then it will float into the landscape. The steel structure is a bit like a rollercoaster. The person there wanted it in blue; there is no other reason for it to be blue. A blue rollercoaster.

CAPITAL HILL RESIDENCE, MOSCOW

Want to jump off [laughter]? It's onsite as well. The client is very fit, so he doesn't mind running from his living room on the ground floor five stories up to his bedroom [laughter]. But actually, what happened is he bought the site, and it is such a great site. It is in the forest, but the trees are high and when he is sitting on the ground all he can see are the tree trunks. So we thought it would be kind of "El Lissitzky" to put him on a platform above, so he would see the trees from above. The entirety of the ground is a spa. It is really beautifully done actually. These are views of the interiors. We had to do the interiors too. So he is looking out into the trees. They had to have a test for this by security, in case he wants to snipe at Putin who owns the neighboring site. I hope there are no Russians in this room [laughter].

But let me come to the end. That's it! Thank you very much.

Sir Peter Cook

Slithering towards a Non-solid Architecture—a Realization

Edited by Kristy Balliet

Good evening! This is the last lecture in English week. Peter Cook is an old friend, a great teacher, and a very generous mentor of young architects. We all know him as the architect of the blue alien, "The Friendly Alien" in Graz. It is not a museum, it is an exhibition place for space. The real contribution is that he articulated outer space in the context of the old city. It is very provocative, very exciting and very alien.

His history is as important. A long time ago, in the early sixties, there was a magic word. It was floating through architecture schools. The word was "Archigram." No one really knew what Archigram meant. It was a glimpse of upcoming architecture. The Archigram comics were like secret books circulated under drawing tables. On drawing tables all over the world you could see Peter Cook's Plug-In Cities. It was influential and had a strong architectural impact. It brought fashion, lifestyle, leisure time, drugs, music, and architecture together.

I met Peter in the early sixties, in his very small office. He was sitting there with his long hair and long beard, very precisely developing his Walking City. We went back home and said, "Okay, this is the future. Go to London, go to the AA." Peter, thank you for coming.
—Introduction by Wolf D. Prix

This is a watershed point, and I mean this seriously. It is probably 40 years since I first gave a lecture in Vienna. I remember it: there were two guys, probably older than I am, in the small room—two Viennese architects and they went to sleep almost immediately. So I was trying to use my stick to keep them awake. I cannot remember what I was talking about, rather trying to keep them awake, probably the plug-in city. And Vienna was one of only two or three places in the world that has this mythical significance at this time of my life because of the people who are there. The other ones are Tokyo and Los Angeles. Berlin is interesting for other reasons, but never made it.

As a matter of a fact I had met the awesome Austrian mafia the first time in Los Angeles, and then moved backwards to the source point. And now the watershed cast … for what seems to be bizarre and unnecessary reasons, your great neighbor and friend Peter Noever has been kicked out and Wolf has to retire from his class. So one museum director or one professor goes, what the hell does it really matter? Who cares, they come and go? No, guys like them *don't just come and go*.

When you get to my age, I feel architecture schools and museums are so closely linked, both historically and physically through personalities and what they propagate. These are terminally fragile institutions. I rescued two such institutions; they are very fragile. You cannot imagine. You guys are unbelievably lucky, if you know what is going on in this platform of architecture, whether you like it or even if you hate it wonderfully, it is still better then studying somewhere in a shit-ass place, where nothing ever happens. That is in most places actually. Some of you were studying at these shit-ass places before you got here. So this is a watershed moment in Vienna, and your culture, since you are a small country. It is also fragile. It is a statement of fact. Our own country is fragile. Too many people on a small island, damn.

My lecture is a realization rather than a statement of a position … Or getting the sniff, perhaps what I like or what I do leads you to non-solid architecture. I am pissed off with these pompous solid objects. I will slither insidiously towards a position of nonsolidity, and, having reached it, perhaps slither equally insidiously away from it.

THE REALIZATION

I come from the seaside; I lived in a very small and undistinguished town called Felixstowe. I had not realized when I lived there that those objects which were surrounding me are unbelievably interesting. One is a kind of a mega structure. Not a very good one, but wooden. Next to it is a piece of East-Anglican art deco. And underneath is a funny rockery building. Think of it: a green house, a mega structure and a piece of conscious styling. I did not know at the age of 10 … I didn't start to want to be an architect until I was 12. [laughter] But the older I get, the more I am aware of surrounding architecture and the influence of it. If you stand at a bus stop, there is always something: a funny doorway, a bus with a funny back, or a dog with a funny collar or a lampshade or something.

The second seaside town, where I spent much longer in and went into my first architecture school, a much larger town, called Bournemouth. There is a cliff lift, and at that time, you paid a penny to go up the lift. If you had a lot of money, you paid another penny to get down. It is a mechanical thing. I think the notion and observing mechanical had an effect on me. Not that I was saying *that* is mechanical, *that* is a building, or *that* is a tree, but it all slithers one-into-the-other.

We entered a competition for a bridge. They just wanted the footbridge, but I am a great collector of kiosks. I said, "Let's have a kiosk on a bridge in Ljubljana. They can sell ice cream." And then Gavin said, "Hey let's make the kiosk move—it will cheer up the whole bridge." (Cheeringup things is an old Archigram term which we are deliberately reviving.) So we installed a bar/kiosk there. One doesn't just want to sell ice cream, there is a bar for the evening. So the bar is a piece of mechanism. *The cliff lift lives.*

When I was a student and consciously reading architecture, taking every book out of the library, I started to read Le Corbusier. And then I suddenly saw this picture. It was unlike anything I had seen before in England. To me it looked like an aeroplane: it sailed, it was translucent, it was marvelous. It was torn down before I saw it and there were never any color photographs of it, only some paintings. I still find it fascinating, although the more you examine it, you could explain it in a certain way. It was Gunnar Asplund's Paradise Restaurant for the 1930 Stockholm Exhibition. (fig.1)

1 Paradise Restaurant, Gunnar Asplund, 1930

The things we are exposed to leave us with a certain innate approach. But there are differences of approach within one culture. Let's take Norwich, the city I lived in also, a city with a variety of pieces of architecture, including 40 medieval churches. "You've seen one, you've seen them all!" Not quite. What is more interesting is the actual make-up of the city. There is almost as much open space as architecture. There is crapmedieval and real medieval, British provincialism and Neoclassicism. It is a very good city for understanding there is no position in the position—or: it is a bit of this and a bit of that.

Another day I was holed up in Syracuse, upstate New York. I couldn't get out of the building because it was snowing, so I took a photograph out of the window. It told me that the psyche of North American cities is very much a box, a box, and another box, another box. Compare that with Norwich, it is a totally different psychology. I think this also underlines one's attitude.

We have of course a tradition both in the UK and certainly buildings representing certain political position in Germany. Both have traditions of pomposity. We are looking at the 1930s. We can look at Speer, we can look at his French counterpart. Well that is a long time ago, it is all right, it went away. But did it go away?

I don't think it did. The new pomposity has returned.

AND THEN THE TAKEOFF ...

One looks back at one's background, what it subconsciously and half-consciously leads to. You went to listen to Constant, and when you look at his drawings you see how liberal he was, even if the gang he hung out with were narrow-minded. You look at Ladovsky, who was actually a teacher at the time, he made this drawing. So teacher's doing a nutty drawing. *Get it?*

Back to Norwich, to point out the things I am looking at: my god they did stuff fluently in the twelfth century (the flying buttresses of the cathedral), they were amazing. But if they could do it, you can do it. They didn't have computers; they didn't even have reinforcing bars. And so wherever you look, you can find it: an extension of our designship into detail.

So Plug-in City is about *that*, whatever the *that* is so far. It was about putting this and that together. It was a cri de coeur for romanticism, because in our day job we were doing prefabricated housing panels. We knew that they didn't have to be so boring. We are suspicious of pompous guys.

And if you have an instant city, you could have an instant village and an instant house. You name it.

THE TOWER AS A PERCOLATION OF SPACE

If one can percolate culture, could one percolate the space? The old 1963 Montreal Tower, the precursor of the Plug-in City. And then we designed a succession of towers investigating different things, all site-specific.

One puts half a building in the water so it is not really there. One brings the English vertical vegetable garden up to the building. These towers ought to be seen as architecture pieces, but also responses by myself, to what I read as being the psychology of these particular places. An early urge way back in 1986 in Brisbane was to design two extremes of a tower. One, long before the Gherkin, presupposes the air conditioned office building, a completed sheath, with a naughty handkerchief on top.

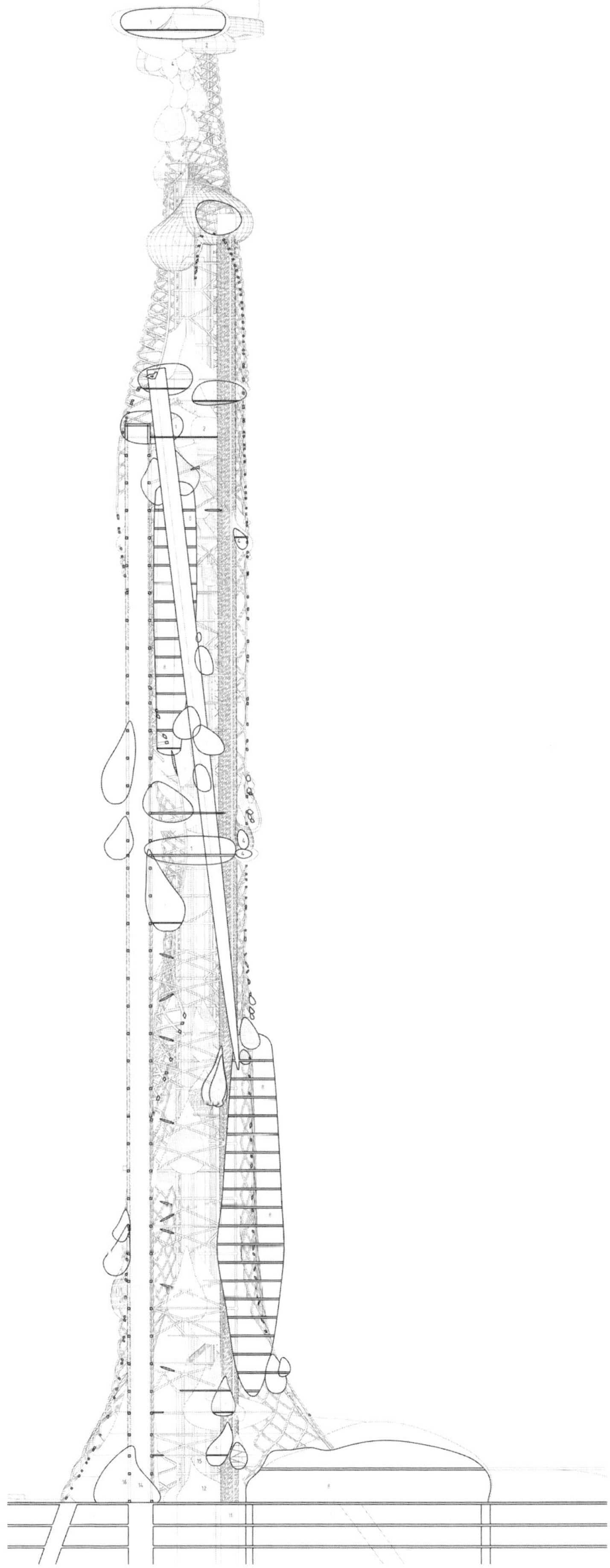

2 Taiwan Tower (section)

The other looked at Brisbane itself. For months I had seen bungalows, houses up on stilts, that allow the air to flow through even in that climate. I asked, why can't we make a tower that is effectively these bungalows one on top of another? I was also fascinated by this freeway. There is something funny, something about its legs, slightly more filigree than many. I integrated it into the project.

I like Oslo, a town I know very well. It has a certain kind of light and it gets to you, especially if you think about what they did 100 years ago. They used big lanterns that suddenly make the place cheerful. I borrowed that and I made towers that would use the same lanterns. I borrowed from what I observed in local culture.

PYLON AND DROPLETS

Very recently we made a project in Taiwan. It also uses the light, and the air passes through most of the structure. It has similarities to the Montreal Tower. It consists of giant testicles hanging up on the building. (fig.2) These are carrying growing pools and they are organized so the public can move up and down. It is actually growing algae. The architectural proposition is not of the tower but this aerated percolating pylon, where things can hang off it. It is really the principle of the coat hanger—the air percolating through the pieces of building, as in a forest. Can we ever produce a city as good as that?

The Japanese have a great tradition of contriving to incorporate the found, the growing, and the positioning. I don't disregard the value of precise positioning. But also, the position of things can be melted or have the effect of time. A number of projects I have done over the years have incorporated the idea of metamorphosis, the first stage slithering into the second and becoming the third. In the Vegetated House, the vegetation creeps forward and forward and becomes completely out of control, at which point I pull the plug on the project.

Now in the context of my title of the lecture, the question is whether the Kunsthaus should be in the lecture at all? Because in many ways it is very solid. It is ambiguously solid, because in a sense the solid parts give way at night; it becomes just lights. It almost disappears into something else. Solidity has to be dealt with in a sort of way. There were disassociations of parts. That is another area I am intrigued by. When you look at the building, you are constantly seeing bits of derelict parts within it. I am honest enough to tell you that the most inspiring drawings I ever looked at were in a Chernikhov book. Upstairs at the AA, the librarian was standing there with the key, in case we nicked it. Only three of us knew about the book. I carried consciously for many years memories of what was in there. In was only in 1970 when I got to Berlin and saw the pink pipe water tank building and thought, "Oh my god, Yakov Chernikhov lives." There is something about the needle part of Graz that excites me more than any other part of the building. This needle is what I am carrying in the back of my pocket from my student days.

Some conditions of the skin, the blisters, we were allowed to do only two, but they are conceptually

3 *Hidden City* (drawing), 2009

important. It says the skin is only a film; there is no presence of a window. I have always thought the tradition of the window is a kind of tyranny. I think there are two tyrannies that we inherit as architects. One is the obsession of ground plane—we are held down by it and the other is the window. They are extremely difficult to manipulate and they corner you.

In a drawing two years ago, I was interested in formulation. I started the drawing as a proposition of landscape, but very quickly and of course intentionally incorporated parts of the landscape, where it is debatable as to whether the elements are actually growing or are manmade. I have always been interested in dangling the constructed amongst the as found in a very causal way. The naughty boys on the left, the clown-like, were very consciously toys as buildings. Some of the others are buildings too, the creeping blue part made out of straight components is also architectural. (fig.3)

COLOR IS ANOTHER FREEDOM

Peter Behrens made a wonderful drawing of his Hoechst Administrative Building in Frankfurt, a wonderful drawing, many wonderful color propositions were made as drawings. And then people say it

4 Soak City (rendering)

is very artsy stuff, but they will not actually build it. But he did! Not only is it a spooky old building, but the color brings it to another level … Inspired by such things, or needing to find them.

This relates to our next proposal, a housing project, which was commissioned by the city of Madrid. This is a blue building, in fact my third blue one. Madrid is full of these terracotta color buildings. All the same bloody color wherever you look. I appreciate context and I am fascinated by the people of a place, but sometimes you say, "Fuck off, I am not going to do you another terracotta building, I am going to deliberately fly in the face of the bloody boring insistent repetitive tiresome locality." So you do a blue building.

This is not quite a part of the color sequence, but I wanted to show it. London may or may not flood, but if it did flood, there is a kind of organic response, a kind of a mega structure, made of anything you can find organic. The mega structures pile up like open old tree trunks, like a do-it-yourself architecture. It has a few favorite elements such as growies and hangies and not many gadgets. (fig.4)

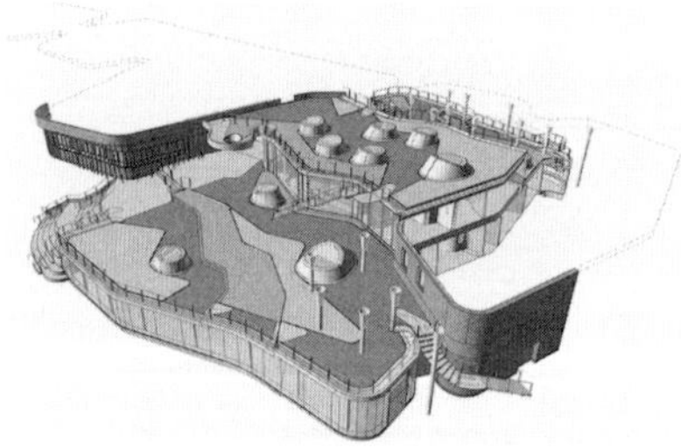

5 Law Library (rendering), University of Economics, Vienna

NOW *ALL* THESE KIDS ARE AT UNIVERSITY SITTING IN RECTANGULAR CONCRETE BOXES

SCI-Arc is one of my favorite schools. It is a fantastic long building, but sometimes you want to get out so they created this tectonic floppy tent. At the École Spéciale d'Architecture in Paris there are rooms to relax. And they have a garden, which is very pleasant. I knock their inability to work hard, but I like that they have a garden. My point being, why should these students be in four-squared pompous boxes?

Well, the Economics University of Vienna is going to do something about it. I presented a cartoon at the competition representing your culture, all the potential, were the authorities open-minded enough to allow you to enjoy it. (fig.5) The notion being that there can be special shared spaces that are not teaching rooms, not just circulation—they are places to deliberately hang out. It doesn't have to be squeaky clean and perfect, the Prater should psychologically be allowed to come in and it should be enjoyed. And the air slithers around it.

The passageways are the most important part of the project,

the places where you simply hang out. You don't have to be in a four-square room. We tried to avoid them. It's a rather exotic library plan; it shows places that could be replaceable and slightly vague, pods as secret gathering places around ambient conditions. There are always percolated conditions moving through, across, and views diagonally.

And finally, another competition win, this time in Australia. It is also for students. It is the architecture school for Bond University in Queensland. In Queensland it is hot and sweaty; there are lots of bugs, lots of jolly people, but potentially bored people if you put them into their square boxes again. We feel the architecture school should have more of a presence, a place that you go to and you can remember what it is like. When you enter, there are double height spaces, studios up and down, places for gathering. (fig.6) In this instance we added scoops. Each scoop is slightly different, acts to pull the air down and support the roof structure.

You have to bear in mind: I first started teaching architecture in 1962. I have observed for more than a couple of years architecture schools. And in this sense the building not only follows principles, it follows anecdotal information. When one walks along the passages, ascends the staircase or looks out into the corridor, one is remembering the anecdotes of the three schools in which I have been most associated: AA, Bartlett and the Städelschule, but also the 20 or 30 other schools that I have spent more than five days in. It is made up of a series of components on the bottom. We see the digging out of the ground for the workshops, above it the deck, because in Australia you are always hanging out on a deck. Then the skins, the scoops, the walkway, the tighter rooms—it is a building with scoops and wraps. It is based on anecdote [showing comical cartoon examples]. (fig.7, 8)

I enjoy students who make things. The models don't quite work and they cause a lot of trouble. But for every school it is important to have a pit/balcony where every visitor can look and say, "What the fuck is that student making?" If my building in Queensland is a success, there will be some crazy loony working away. This will happen if it is a good school, unlike some schools where you are not even allowed to put something on the wall. To me, that is *not* an architecture school.

Tweaking is a very important aspect of any work. You have to have sufficient energy and enthusiasm to cheer it up.

Thank you.

6 Soheil Abedian School of Architecture, Bond University (interior rendering), 2011, Gold Coast Australia

7 Soheil Abedian School of Architecture, Bond University (cartoon), 2011, Gold Coast Australia

8 Soheil Abedian School of Architecture, Bond University (cartoon), 2011, Gold Coast Australia

Peter Noever

Now

Edited by Justin Diles

Peter Noever is a designer, writer, architect, curator, director and artist. He is also a very great, generous friend and a fighter for art with his very powerful voice. I can best describe his attitude with a phrase he printed on a T-shirt long ago: "Don't compromise or you will pay the price." This is a perfect description of his character. Like Raimund Abraham, Peter came to Vienna from Tyrol to prove that the Viennese are the most stupid and stubborn people you can imagine. And this is exactly what Peter has done for the last 50 years—25 as an "Aktionista" and 25 as the director of the MAK. Before heading the MAK, Peter was already very famous for his annual poster appearing in the hotspots of Vienna to announce a motto for the coming year—mottos like "design is thinking," "buried vision" and "go ahead my friends." He was also well-known for his political cultural magazine UMRISS. My best translation for the title is "How to Kill Mediocrity." The magazine was a real pain in the ass of the bureaucrats in Vienna. They became very pale when Peter's name was mentioned because he took a stand for art. I'm very glad to have Peter Noever here, and I always say this when introducing him: "No ever. No ever glad, so he is not sick. No ever rest, like the mountain. Peter Noever forever."
— Introduction by Wolf D. Prix

Site is always the main interest to me: the site of art, the site of an artist and also the site as time. I have always tried to be very curious and to react in the moment. Curiosity drives me—curiosity about what is going on now. One doesn't have to know what is going on; it is always very complicated. But certain questions can drive us forward. Where is art coming from? Where are artists now? And who are the artists of today? To find answers you don't need to go to a museum. I know a little bit about the institution called *museum*, and this is not the place where you will figure anything out. I don't want to condemn institutions—though I have a lot of criticism for many specific institutions—but as I try to answer these questions for myself, it is always the site that is critical.

A dedication to new art comes from curiosity about what is going on in contemporary art. But my specific interest is always the site of art as a manifestation of *the here* and *the now*. I'm fascinated with art that can create a context and influence social consciousness. The most interesting thing for me when working with an artist is the creation of a space that did not exist before. When an artist can generate his or her artwork for a specific site and control the overall circumstances, it becomes the site of an artist. This is something more than an exhibition, a reception or media coverage. It is the opposite of a splendorous yet meaningless museum. An irremovable site created by the artist is the real manifestation of art. When this happens successfully, it completely transcends what can typically be done in an institutional setting. The site of an artist is an excursion to the unpredictable. There is a lot to learn as a curator, and it is also new for the artist. It doesn't work every time and it is always an experiment. But I think art without experimentation would not work, and an art institution without experiments is not an art institution anymore.

If you run an institution, you have to run it outside. You have to go from inside to outside. If you are in a community like Vienna you must also pursue and advance your own interests. Of course these interests are personal, not democratic. But nowadays you cannot just show something. Instead as a first step you are expected to bring people together for discussions about what to do, and these conversations lead nowhere. So I think it is critically important for individuals to retain the right to promote their interests, bring new things forward and create the discussion.

Site-specific art imagines the world of the future. I want to show an example, *Solar Tree* (fig.1), by the designer Ross Lovegrove. This was created for the Museum Angewandte Kunst (MAK) during the 2008 European Football Championship. City officials wanted to dress up Vienna to host the championships and had cast-iron streetlamps, replicas of a nineteenth century design, installed on the Ringstrasse, including in front

1 *Solar Tree*, Ross Lovegrove, MAK, 2007

of the Angewandte and the MAK. I was very upset about this, so I quickly worked with Ross and an Italian industrial producer. In two months we created the *Solar Tree*. It was just a rendering but it was important to show that not everybody sees the idea of creating streetlamps the same way. The Ringstrasse has various styles; there should not be a single solution for it.

2 MAK Plattform, Peter Noever and Michael Embacher, 2009

3 MAK Terminal Ausschnitt + MAK Terminal, Peter Noever and Michael Embacher, 2009

A second project, done with the artist Chris Burden, started from an idea to enlarge the storage of the MAK library (fig.2). The new Wien Mitte commercial complex is under construction across the street from the museum, and our strategy was to use the library expansion as an opportunity to bring something into this project for the public. We proposed to enlarge the bridge over the Vienna River adjacent to the MAK and hang the storage depot underneath. On top, 180 special lamps from California would create two axes, an urban structure, linking two districts of Vienna that are not really in love, the 1st and the 3rd. The head of the city didn't like it.

I have spent a great part of my life on this specific site, the MAK. I could not have done this without the support of the University of Applied Arts. It is very healthy to have these two institutions in dialogue. Through this close relationship we collaborated on a project for a new institution: a research center responsible for discourse at the interface of art, design, architecture and society. We wanted to make a unique site for facilitating cross-border projects and addressing the crucial issues of our time. Raising the right question is all you can do. It's very hard to give answers, but every exhibition in an art institution should raise new questions in many directions. The MAK-Terminal (fig.3)—a Schaulager or Exhibition Depot—was a building proposal related to this initiative. We imagined a highly visible head office sitting on top of a large crane that would be used to reconfigure the work. We wanted an institution that would literally move itself and be constantly renewed.

To create a site you have to put in energy, not just take it. You have to act. I want to show you an example of an artist who is divisive, both for his strength and for his absolute language: Donald Judd. However you see him, he was a great artist. First of all, he didn't want to work with me in the MAK. He claimed that any museum kills the work of art and didn't want to be encaged. But we managed to convince him and held the exhibition *Donald Judd Architecture* in 1991. The sculpture he developed for the show, *Stage Set* (fig.4), was the biggest he ever produced. Afterward we worked to get permission to install it in a public space in Stadtpark, the city park near the museum. This took us five to six years. It was a conflict to put it there, but we managed it.

To put something in a public space, to erect it, is a confrontation. If society is consuming art and you say, "You have a Donald Judd sculpture in your park. You may not like it but you can find more information on the Internet."

4 *Judd Stage Set #22*, Vienna

5 *The City Inside Us*, Vito Acconci, 1993

This is not going to work with everybody. Judd found an alternative to this problem. He bought land in Marfa, Texas—34 or so military barracks and even a part of the city, which was bankrupt at the time. He slightly modified the existing buildings and inserted 65 sculptures. There is absolutely no museum director who could or would do something like this. A director would be fired before it was even finished! But this project relates to the question of the art site. What is its meaning? For me this question is of constant interest.

Here is an exhibition that explains what I think it means to really make a show. Of course this is site specific it couldn't be more site specific. The artist is Vito Acconci, the year was 1993 and the show was called *City Inside Us*. (fig.5) After it was finished we were standing in Stadtpark and he had tears in his eyes. He had never before done a show that took all his energy. What he conceived was very simple. (I remember that architects hated that!) He simply repeated an existing space, the central exhibition hall of the MAK, one to one. But if you repeat it, you have to shift it, to fit it in. With this shift he also wanted to create the sensation of walking on the ceiling of the museum, and a glass ceiling at that. So we did it!

It is my strategy to build up new spaces; for me that's what it's all about. After the MAK building underwent a very painstaking two-year restoration, I was a bit scared. Scared that it would become a new building, very different from the ugly, beautiful space that it had been before. After the renovation I felt it was very important to make a clear statement of now and the contemporary. We brought in the Czech artist Magdalena Jetelová, who installed *Domestication of a Pyramid*. (fig.6) Immediately after the restoration workers left, she moved in. It was not a permanent installation in the building, but it was permanent for the memory. It was definitely important for the

6 *Domestication of a Pyramid*, Magdalena Jetelová

7 *Shooting into the Corner*, Anish Kapoor, 2009

building, for the curators, and it was very important for the artist. Recently we commissioned a related piece from Anish Kapoor called *Shooting into the Corner*. (fig.7) It is now in the Contemporary Art Tower (CAT) in Arenbergpark. Kapoor donated this piece to the museum and it has a value—everybody now talks about the "value" of art—of something like 20 million euros. He's an artist whose work now commands great sums of money.

It is very hard to do projects like these. The Republic of Austria is always running out of money, especially for art, and it is difficult to fund this kind of work. Further complicating the matter is that the orientation of an art institution cannot be the public. Society is not the orientation, it is the artist. An institution, the curator, has to serve the artist—has to connect with the artist and bring out the work. Then perhaps you can sell the idea to a wider public, but one should never ask the public what they want to see because they only want to see what they know. As a result you have museum programs all over the world that are completely senseless and have nothing to do with art.

8 *Open University of Diversity*, Koen Vanmechelen

At this point I want to give you an idea of what I am doing now. I am collaborating with the former director of the Guggenheim, Thomas Krens, on a project for the Forbidden City in Beijing. I am also currently making two shows for the upcoming 2011 Venice Art Biennale. One is with the exceptional Belgian artist Koen Vanmechelen. We have rented the Palazzo Loredan dell'Ambasciatore for six months, the entire duration of the Biennale, to make the *Nato a Venezia*, the *Open University of Diversity*. (fig.8) My interest with this show is how science and art meet. During the show, Vanmechelen will crossbreed two varieties of chicken and produce a new animal. A new chicken will be born during the Biennale! Many sculptures from Michelangelo and the busts of numerous Renaissance celebrities are housed in this palazzo: Palladio and

Dante Alighieri. All of these figures, so important for Italy, will now appear together with a newborn animal.

My second exhibition consists of interventions for the city of Venice outside the Biennale campus. Perhaps people who are not interested in art will also have the opportunity to see the work. Everything is still in process and under construction—many problems with permits and permission. Some of the work is in a show called *Glasstress.* Partially supported by Venetian glass companies, the work will be exhibited in another palazzo, Palazzo Cavalli-Franchetti, next to the Accademia Bridge. One artist from this group who I appreciate very much is Kendell Geers. He is creating a large heart—over 2.5 meters wide—from LA police batons made in glass. There are also pieces by Zaha Hadid. Some of them have very complicated surfaces and the glassmakers are being challenged. Venetian glass companies are not able to do what they could 200 years ago. So it makes sense to give them a provocation.

Then there is an interesting project with Erwin Wurm, an Austrian gift for Venice. This sculpture is in dialogue with the palazzo. (fig.9) The palazzo, you can rent it out—anyone could have it. So it is an empty case. Erwin Wurm's *Narrow House* contrasts with this. It is a replica of the house that he grew up in but it is squeezed into just 1.6 meters. The art society will like it.

The final piece I will discuss is *(Des)Orientation* by Magdalena Jetelová. (fig.10) It is difficult to explain. She will put a moving mirror in a space in the palazzo, and everything will shift. The whole environment will shift in another direction and dimension. I want to finish my lecture with the statement that will be printed on the mirror: "Everything moves but not the right thing moves."

To that I will add that the greatest risk is the avoidance of risk.
Good night.

9 *Narrow House*, Erwin Wurm, Venice

10 *(Des)Orientation*, Magdalena Jetelová

Hitoshi Abe
Scuse Me While I Kiss the Sky

Edited by Guvenc Özel

I would like to welcome my friend Hitoshi Abe. Hitoshi is the director of UCLA and is close to the peak of the Japanese architectural world. But the funny thing is, and we had a discussion this afternoon, that his buildings all look very different. He differentiates every building, and I think this is why we should discuss what develops from wandering between worlds. Born in Japan, he studied architecture in the United States. I knew him as a student at SCI-Arc. We should take a closer look at his approach to every task and how he is integrating these two cultures. I'm wondering, and this is a little bit against my theory, is every architect tied unconsciously to the roots of their landscape, of their hometown? For instance, the Viennese architects, whether they want it or not, are tied to their baroque way of thinking, meaning that the secrets of spaces are very interesting. In opposition to the Dutch architects—and we will see it when Winy Maas will come here and lecture—that the Dutch guys are going to follow the diagram of architecture. So, I'm wondering how Hitoshi will explain his two worlds. We should welcome Hitoshi Abe. Thank you for coming here.
— Introduction by Wolf D. Prix

Architecture is motivated by the subject's desire for his environment. Just as a kiss only exists in that moment when the lips touch, architecture arises only in that moment the subject encounters his environment. Architecture cannot independently exist before or after that moment. We, for that moment alone, become connected to the world and continue to wander in search of the next connection.

Wolf [D. Prix] always calls me "the wanderer." Even though I really do not know whether he means "somebody who is still in search of a place to settle" or "somebody too free to settle" or even "somebody who is just too immature to settle." The name points out some truth in my mentality, which constitutes an important part of my work. "A wanderer" is forever in search of some place to which he can attach himself because he does not belong anywhere and never will.

This strong desire for movement defines the essence of "the wanderer" and is also the main motivation that drives my practice.

A series of experiments conducted 25 years ago, such as a cocoon made of a membrane of air that surrounds the body and a spherical black helmet to cover the head, constitute a group of works that signify the recognition of the dissociation of the self from the environment. The act of eliminating that disconnect reveals a strong desire for architecture to become the medium that anchors the self to the world. For me, architecture is the link where "the self as designer" and "the various events that make up the unique environment of each project" merge—the contact surface of their moment of meeting.

The environment that confronts the subject cannot always be perceived by its surface. It always manifests itself as a contact surface. Through this contact surface, the subject comprehends the environment, creates a connection. Form is a part of the environment signified by the continuity of this contact surface. Therefore, form demonstrates the relationship between a coherent environment, its related subjects and the medium. Architecture, through the action of the designer, goes beyond the mere understanding of events into a more aggressive act of redefinition: the history of relating self and environment recorded and expressed through form.

The form as a medium is outlined by the following four principles.

FOUR PRINCIPLES OF "FORM"

1. Form is a medium, hence form in itself has no inherent meaning.
2. Form is the boundary between interior and exterior (adjacent environments) and their contiguity.
3. Form is a medium that requires a body.
4. The strength of form is dependent on the degree of precision used in the process of creating a continuity of interior and exterior.

FIRST PRINCIPLE:
FORM IS A MEDIUM, HENCE FORM ITSELF HAS NO INHERENT MEANING

If architecture is the medium that connects project-specific events, architecture is generated in those moments of connection; it is something reborn with each new project. The attitude that considers this kind of design as generative stands counter to the stylistic school that treats architecture as something that inherently exists 'n' the absolute as a derivative variation within individual expression. Form is only the result of a generative process, not something with a priori meaning.

When explaining this distinction, I often use two American actors as examples. Regardless of the situation he encounters, the face of comedic actor Buster Keaton remains impassive. He suppresses his facial expression but produces comedy by calling attention to the absurdity of an escalating situation by running in different directions on the screen. The antithesis to the way Keaton functions as a medium is how John Wayne, who possesses

1 Shirasagi Bridge, 1993–1994, Shiroishi, Miyagi

strength of character, redefines the situation on screen whenever he appears.

In the design of Shirasagi Bridge instead of borrowing a regional icon to ensure monumentality the form is generated by manifesting the invisible rules that constitute the site conditions—achieving symbolism without resorting to the use of icons, as it would happen in Keaton's comedies. (fig.1) Seventy-four regularly spaced steel right triangles envelop the existing bridge and act as the medium through which weight limits, bridge lamp positions, water levels, the minimum clearance level and height requirements of the handrail are visualized. Abiding by a given set of transformation rules—rotation, scaling, translation, truncation—like a runner clearing each hurdle, the trajectory of these elements jumps over and under each parameter, becoming the shape of the bridge.

SECOND PRINCIPLE: *FORM IS THE BOUNDARY BETWEEN INTERIOR AND EXTERIOR (ADJACENT ENVIRONMENTS) AND THEIR CONTIGUITY*

Architectural form fundamentally exemplifies the boundary of internal and external space. It not only demarcates the separation of the internal and the external, it defines and visualizes their relationship. It might be something like a soap bubble. Bubbles are defined by their inside and outside, while at the same time their shapes are dependent on the balance of the internal and external environments. Bubbles as boundaries are very weak and soft, hence their shapes reflect the wavering relationship between inside and outside. Similarly, architecture as a boundary must be weak and soft to accommodate fluid and diverse contemporary events. In doing so, architecture is not only a barrier that distinguishes adjacent events, it is the medium connecting them and functioning as an interface.

Form derived from tracing the contact surface of adjacent environments is observed in many of my projects, such as the Setsugetsuka Restaurant and the Media Guest House. (fig.2, 3) In these works, the contact surfaces are fundamentally one or two surfaces that separate the inside and outside, but the O2 building for Vienna University, which is currently undergoing construction, tests the multiple lamination of these boundary surfaces configured across all regions. Work is moving forward, slated for completion in 2013, on five buildings for a new campus on a site facing a park near the Danube River that runs along the northeast side of central Vienna. Zaha Hadid, Carme Pinos, CRAB Studio/Peter Cook, NO.MAD, and our firm were selected through an international competition.

Our scope entails 21,000 square meters of floor area with offices for five departments, various seminar rooms, a small library, brasserie, gym, supermarket and other such facilities for student living combined with features such as a kindergarten. The building is a mille-feuille of linear contact surfaces between alternately layered, elongated atria and office spaces arranged in parallel. These contact surfaces undulate along the rules set by the site context, program relations, structure and daylight conditions to create a unique space.

THIRD PRINCIPLE: *FORM IS A MEDIUM THAT REQUIRES A BODY*

While form is something that ties together various events, it ultimately requires the transformation to matter. Architecture is that which is produced by the physical contact surface between environment and subject; however, the unifying event is not always limited to a simple boundary. New architectural opportunities lie where ties beyond mere physical connections are attempted by simple matter.

The design of the French restaurant Aoba-tei facing Jozenji Street in Sendai relates to the town's symbolic zelkova-lined streets. (fig.4) A soft boundary between the internal space and its exterior context is established through the insertion of an interior wall made of a thin metal plate spatially mediating between the first and second floors of the existing building. The inner wall made of 2.3 mm steel plate is perforated with thousands of holes across its surface. These holes, spaced at computer-controlled 15 mm intervals, are 4 mm, 6 mm and 9 mm wide opened by an NC turret board based on data from the deconstructed image of zelkova trees. Behind the inner wall are lighting elements that recreate the light and shadow patterns of the exterior context. These holes that we have named the "graphic hole" when seen through low-resolution cameras emerge as a realistic depiction of the actual trees. If you think about it, reproducing an image as a set of points of light is a primitive imaging technology. If that is the case, the inner wall that constitutes the boundary of the physically separated interior space of the restaurant and the tree-lined exterior street space is the material manifestation of the recorded image.

2 Setsugetsuka Restaurant, 1997–1999, Sendai, Miyagi

3 Yomiuri Guest House, 1995–1997, Zaou, Miyagi

4 Aoba-tei, 2004, Sendai, Miyagi

5 Reihoku Town Hall, 2000–2002

FOURTH PRINCIPLE: *THE STRENGTH OF FORM IS DEPENDENT ON THE PRECISION OF THE PROCESS OF CREATING A CONTINUITY OF INTERIOR AND EXTERIOR*

As mentioned before, if form is the medium that connects elements in its environs, whether one shape is superior to another depends on its performance as a medium. In other words, it depends on the accuracy of the information conveyed of the environments it separates/connects. For me, increasing the accuracy of form, seeking out the principle that makes this possible is of utmost importance. For example, in Reihoku Town Hall, the form of the building essentially consists of a singular principle of the fluctuations of a line organized as "tomographic sections." (fig.5) The fluctuation allocates space with a large amplitude, controlling the auditorium surface to create a wall that moderately diffuses sound, thus changing the frequency depending on the requirements of the location. The frequency of this fluctuation is integrated with the configuration of the small wooden elements that produce the expression of the façade surface. The amplitude of deformation on the surface determines the width of the cedar boards and machining dimensions of sane-wood, the size of the glass and provisions for the estimated dimensions of the frame, all together determining the pattern of the outer wall. By reducing the glass plate into small pieces, angling the window frame within the range of the frame dimension and maligning each one a little at a time, the elements correspond to the twisting of the walls. The glass pieces become smaller in areas of large deformations.

For the Kanno Museum, the complex principles governing the form of soap bubbles are used—spatial composition, structural principles—all of which are integrated for a precise finish. (fig.6) In the design of a private museum for the permanent display of eight sculptures, situated over the hills overlooking the Pacific Ocean in a small town, we carefully considered the condition of the town, the program of the building and the spatial requirements of the museum. I thought it was necessary for the museum design to have enough strength to stimulate the local art scene. Hence, rather than a white cube that accommodates any exhibition, I aimed for a design that produces a unique landscape.

For the overall massing, we devised a shape derived from blowing up eight soap bubble-like elements, each corresponding to a specific sculpture, into the predetermined 10 × 12 × 10 m volumes. This form results from the equilibrium between the internal pressure of each individual cell that makes up a small space and the overall envelope of the building. Visitors experience eight sculptures while meandering through these continuous cells that are linked across the various elevations of the site. Each cell that configures a room is constructed of 3.2 mm thick steel plates embossed 25 instances per square meter. By welding together the groups of embossed bumps of adjacent cells back to back, honeycomb panels are formed—a unique structure recalling a collection of soap bubbles. While the embossing that appears inside and outside the building was determined by strength and workability requirements deemed structurally necessary, the Corten steel produces beautiful simultaneous effects of light and shadow that result in a tasteful play of textures.

Finally, I will discuss the plans to build "Where to Kiss the Sky," a project currently in development in Los Angeles. Lenticularis is a grand roof that will cover the square by Isamu Noguchi in Little Tokyo, Los Angeles. The grand roof will span the space without touching the historic square designed in the image of the Japanese garden. Lenticularis by definition is a cloud of unique form created by circumstances particular to a geographical location like terrain, air flow and humidity.

Just like its inspiration, our Lenticularis is also determined by its context, namely the shape of the plaza and legal requirements. The structural form complements the characteristics of the site so that the singular 60 × 40 m canopy appears to be floating in the air. The double membrane ETFE roof is printed with a unique pattern on the surface in order to achieve the effect of a cloud as the observer moves through the space. The oculus in the middle of the cloud is in dialogue with the projected profile of a disk at the center of the Noguchi-designed plaza. This oculus, a unique form of stainless steel with a mirror finish, is where the intersecting boundary of heaven and earth is projected, and there, people kiss the sky.

On March 11 of this year, a massive earthquake and tsunami devastated northern Japan. Many lives were taken, many towns and villages were totally eradicated. It is almost impossible to continue believing in the tie between "self" and "environment" there, but still I believe that architecture can once again nurture that bond.

6 Kanno Museum, 2003–2005, Shiogama, Miyagi

Nicolai Ouroussoff

Architecture and Ambiguity

Edited by Justin Diles

Good afternoon, good evening! It is a great pleasure and a great honor to welcome Nicolai Ouroussoff to Vienna! Is this your first time in Vienna?

Ouroussoff: The first time in fifteen years!

Prix: So it is your first time in Vienna, because Vienna has changed a lot. Nicolai Ouroussoff is the architectural critic of the New York Times. He was educated as an architect, doing his master studies at Columbia. He was formerly the architectural critic of the LA Times and is now at the New York Times—two major newspapers. He is writing a book about the modern architecture of the last century. This is the last century, so you are a little bit too late; perhaps you should write a book about the next century. This will be the next one. He will talk about that!

Actually his writing about architecture is very explicit and if you do not read between the lines, you could think he is a critic of modern architecture. And I think he is interpreting all the buildings like they were modernist architecture. If you do not read between the lines... When I came to New York, I think twenty years ago, I had an invitation to have lunch with Philip Johnson for preparing the exhibtion "Deconstructive Architecture." People told me, "Watch out, please watch out. There are two people in New York, who can kill you. One is Philip Johnson and the other one is the architectural critic of the New York Times." So please welcome Nicolai Ouroussoff!

— Introduction by Wolf D. Prix

When I was just beginning my life as a critic in the spring of 1992, the world seemed to be emerging from a long period of darkness. The Berlin Wall—and the whole Cold War—was quickly becoming a memory. Across the Atlantic, 12 years of Republican rule was coming to an end and, as many of us hoped, Bill Clinton would soon bring a measure of sanity back to Washington if not usher in a more egalitarian vision of American society. In architecture, Bernard Tschumi's Parc de la Villette, Coop Himmelb(l)au's Vienna Law Offices, Peter Eisenman's Wexner Center, Rem Koolhaas's unbuilt Jussieu Library and Zaha Hadid's Vitra Fire

Station—all designed in the late 1980s and early 1990s—not only represented the long overdue recognition of a generation of architects who had cut their teeth in the aftermath of 1968, they seemed to signal the dawning of a new era of creative and intellectual freedom. What I saw, often buried beneath too much theoretical posturing, was the framework for a new, more heterogeneous worldview, one that included an emotional dimension that Modernism seemed to have completely ignored, without reverting to historical parody. The work of these architects seemed to represent a worldview that, whatever its other faults, at least seemed to be more tolerant of difference—more accepting of the "other." As someone who had always identified with outsiders and misfits, and was as interested in exploring the city's subcultures as looking at its architectural landmarks, this seemed like an attractive idea. Maybe even something worth fighting for.

As a critic, one of my roles was to give voice to these ideas—to act as a bridge of sorts, between a still insular profession and a suspicious public. I didn't simply want to educate people—although that was part of it too. I wanted to demonstrate that, if utopia was now a dead subject, if the age of the manifesto was over, then architecture could still be about ideas; it could still provide alternate models for how to live in the world. Part of my task then, as I saw it, was to nurture an architecture that was disobedient, that challenged accepted formulas and broadened the range of creative and social possibilities.

As it turns out, that optimism was premature. The first big architectural event of the twenty-first century—the effort to rebuild Ground Zero in New York—may have been the first sign that something was going terribly wrong. The few architects who participated and took it seriously were used to give cover to what was essentially a parody of an architectural competition. The basest form of kitsch was presented as serious, thoughtful architecture. The program itself, which included a gargantuan underground memorial surrounded by 10,000,000 square feet of commercial space and littered with half a dozen undefined cultural spaces, was grossly overblown in scale and an exercise in political posturing. The proposals that survived were perfect expressions of the political and economic forces that were *really* shaping the site: the flag-waving jingoism, the commercial greed and political hubris. It was a lesson in how architecture, as late as the twenty-first century, still could be a tool for government propaganda.

Things haven't gotten better since. Nowadays even the construction of the Guggenheim Bilbao feels like it was an empty triumph. The creative freedom it seemed to unleash was remarkably limited in terms of social scope—and it has placed architects in a perverse position. The push for privatization that began with Ronald Reagan and Margaret Thatcher and accelerated in the past decade or so has radically shifted the playing field for architects. Large-scale public projects like affordable housing have become increasingly rare. In the United States, civic projects of any kind evaporated. So has the idea of a democratic public realm free of commercial interests. Instead we've reached a point where those at the very top of the profession seem to work almost exclusively for global luxury brands or quasi-authoritarian states that treat architecture as a propaganda tool—a context where they are encouraged to be formally daring as long as they don't probe too deeply into sensitive social or political issues. The formal freedom these architects have won has even become a convenient tool for advancing the cynical agendas of developers, who use the cultural cache that architecture can provide to mask a social vision that is all about conformity, whether we are talking about the gentrification of existing cities or the creation of new self-contained worlds.

A nice example was the Saadiyat Cultural District, which includes Jean Nouvel's Louvre Abu Dhabi and Frank Gehry's newest Guggenheim. Whatever you may think of it as architecture, it was a sincere effort to create a viable cultural forum against ridiculous odds. The site is a spit of land at the edge of a desert wasteland with few cultural references to grab hold of. There's no local population. And the entire project will be embedded in the kind of high-end suburban subdivision that can be found all over the Middle East, but rarely in such isolation and on such an expansive scale.

The situation is just as dire in New York. Many of the most significant buildings to go up in the city over the past few years—Jean Nouvel's 100 11th Avenue, Frank Gehry's 8 Spruce Street, Norman Foster's Sperone Westwater Gallery—are targeted toward Manhattan's super rich, or those who strive to join them. And it has reinforced the public perception that architecture is an art that only serves a small, exclusive elite—and that has no impact on the lives of ordinary people.

Given those realities, it perhaps shouldn't be too surprising that any architect of a certain stature today is routinely dismissed by the mass media as a "starchitect"—a nasty term that is supposed to mean that they are vain, self-indulgent divas, indifferent to the needs of either their clients or the general public. Few critics are willing to take the time to make distinctions between serious efforts to work through what has become an abysmal situation and those who cynically embrace this new world. Less than two decades after the euphoria that surrounded Bilbao Guggenheim, in fact, it feels as though the profession—or at least the part of the profession that thinks—has never been so under attack.

Not surprisingly, many architects I know have begun to see the optimism of the 1960s and 1970s as a kind of heyday—the last time that architects were allowed to contribute to the discussion on major social issues like public housing and large-scale urban renewal. It was also, touchingly enough, the last time that they could dream of having a positive impact on society's future.

Over the past few months I visited a few projects that seem to suggest one way out of this trap. They don't represent a movement. But they capture the mood of our times: the sense of uncertainty over architecture's place in the world, over its own future. One of these is Koolhaas's CCTV. When I first saw the design years ago the monumental scale of the building, and the fact that it was being built for a state-controlled television company, brought to mind early 1930s Soviet architectural designs like those for the Palace of the Soviets. More specifically, it made me think of the agonizing struggles that the great Soviet architects of the period went through to balance their own ideals with the desires of an authoritarian government at the exact moment when the utopian fervor of the 1920s was being drained away. Koolhaas was condemned in the West for taking on the commission, which for some was the ultimate example of architect as propagandist.

But the building is really about instability—its meaning is intentionally slippery. Two giant legs joined by an L-shaped bridge-like structure that cantilevers 50 stories above the ground, it's neither a tower nor an office block. Nor does it have a recognizable scale. The floor slabs are obscured by a matrix of irregular cross bracing, making it hard to decipher where they begin and end. And the forms completely distort your perspective of the building: it seems to flatten out from some angles and bear down on you from others.

The building's form seems to say something about the elasticity of our global culture. But as an image of political authority, it's also strikingly ambiguous. Imposing at one moment, shy and retiring the next, the building's form seems to say as much about collective anxieties about the future as it does about centralized power. It's neither a monument in any traditional sense of the word nor subversive commentary, as some Chinese critics have claimed.

Steven Holl's Vanke Center struck a similar chord. Holl says that it's the length of the Empire State Building, knocked over on its side. But when you first see it it's kind of an anti-monument. It's made up of a series of horizontal bars, joined together end to end in a vaguely zigzag pattern and lifted 60 feet off the ground, so that when you approach it the building virtually disappears. What you see is a series of earth forms, and beyond that, the mountains on one side and this scattered development on the other.

In SANAA's Rolex Learning Center in Lausanne the relationships between inside and out, individual and collective, are even more fluid. There aren't any walls; the interior is contained within a roof and floor made of undulating concrete slabs. Holes are cut into its surfaces to let in light and create collecting points, like eddies in a pool. Raised platforms create periods of calm. Formally, it's a blend of landscape and building.

What all three of these designs suggest, to me at least, is the emergence of a more elastic architectural language, one that is trying to bridge, in a new way, seemingly incompatible conditions: the inner life of a single individual and the scale of global society, the need for privacy and the longing for community. They may not represent a zeitgeist, but they seem to resonate in a world that feels increasingly unstable, in an anxious state of transition where we have no idea where the future is going.

Still, I'm wondering where the optimism is in all of this—or have we reached a point where that kind of thinking has become impossible? Is the role of the architect simply to accept the world as it is? Or is the role of a serious architect to create some kind of resistance to it? And where is the space for that kind of project?

Q&A

Q [Audience]: Architects, for the sake of their own sanity perhaps, tend to stay a bit naïve about how much they can really hypostatize quality and embed it in their work. Can you say something about the basis of architectural quality from your perspective as a critic?

A: I think the real issue is control—control over your tools, control over space, control over structure, control over material, and being able to use those tools to make an argument effectively. And to do that, you have to control those tools very well. Let me take two examples: Hadid's Contemporary Art Center in Cincinnati and Diller Scofidio + Renfro's Institute of Contemporary Art in Boston. The ground floor plans of both buildings have a very similar approach conceptually. You enter from the corner, and then you move diagonally across the lobby and up to the gallery. In the Cincinnati building, those relationships are very fluid and carefully mapped out. The understanding of how a body moves through space, its rhythm, the way your eye reads a space and pulls you through it—this is all mapped out with incredible care. In Boston, the architects seem to be trying to convey a similar experience, but it's handled in such a clumsy way.

So in the end the point of view doesn't matter because of the way you tell your story. It's like controlling language for a writer or knowing how to move paint around a canvas if you're a painter. If you don't know how to move that paint, if you don't understand what paint is then there is no reason to look at it for more than two seconds. In the end it can be both technique and argument. You need the argument too; you need a point of view, and this point of view has to be something that connects to people. Finally, the problem for architects, unlike painters, is they often don't control their tools because contractors control some of the tools, the client controls other tools. It's much more like filmmaking in the sense that it's collaborative. This is what makes it such a difficult art form.

Q [Audience]: You spent a substantial amount of time talking about the problematic term "starchitect." I'm first of all curious how this bears on whom you decide to write about? Second, are you satisfied with the speed at which the architectural community responds to changes in society? Finally, what do you feel is your responsibility as a critic?

A: In terms of whom I cover, before I took this job I told my editor that I would have to be on a plane all the time if I wanted to do it right. So I set out to explore parts of the world that I feel I don't understand fully. The things that I find fascinating about being an architectural critic—more so than, say, an art critic—is that you can use it as a lens for analyzing so many things—political issues, social issues. When I set out to write my series on the Middle East last year I knew I'd be writing about a lot of iconic buildings because those are the major projects there now. But for me it was an opportunity to explore how cities are being built today in that part of the world and to try to understand the forces that are shaping them.

The second part of your question has to do with whether or not architects respond quickly enough to these shifts, and the answer is no. The explosion of development during the last decade meant that architects who had spent 15 to 20 years working out their ideas, often with few opportunities to build, were suddenly allowed to build quite a bit. But the rules changed, I think, under their feet. We have a free market system that has run amok and architects are still struggling to find a way to navigate this new economic and social landscape. I don't think either architects or critics have figured out what this shift really means for architecture.

Finally, regarding my role as a critic, one result of both the Internet and architecture's globalization is that people are only responding to images. They're not responding to buildings; the two are not the same. This is something that has been disastrous for serious architecture. So maybe my most important contribution has been simply to make the effort to actually go and see buildings. I get the chance to see a lot of work, and I try to convey that experience to my readers. On the one hand, I have opinions about buildings, and on the other hand, and maybe more importantly, I've tried to act as a conduit between the ideas that circulate in the world of architecture and a broader public. In a way that's probably the most important function of my work.

This question relates more generally to the role that journalism plays in our culture. Newspapers feel very much under attack today now that their traditional function has been undermined by the Internet. But what a newspaper does is give you reporters on the ground who actually interview people and see events with their own eyes. And these reporters come with certain skills. With reporting, the interest is to gain a deeper truth. This is something that all journalists share and believe is the essence of what they do.

> Q [Audience]: Do you see yourself as reflecting on buildings or do you see yourself as teaching your audience about architecture? If so, what do you assume as the level of entry for the discussion?

A: Well, I start by trying to explain the buildings to myself, and as I'm doing that, I formulate an opinion. And usually I don't form the opinion until I sit down and write. That's a more personal answer, but it's really what it's about. It's about the way you work, really. In terms of the audience, one of the problems I find with what's happening to journalism is that the audience has become so diffused, and I think this is a real problem. You don't really know whom you're talking to anymore. And I find that for me—and this isn't true for all journalists—it's sometimes easier and more effective to write to someone. This is hard to do when the audience is constantly shifting. I find the conversation with the reader becomes less and less personal.

Q [Wolf D. Prix]: Nicolai, what is more important to you: the image or the word? How do you fill the gap in between the power of the image and the power of the word?

A: Well, I used to always help the photo editor pick images, but at a certain point I realized I couldn't control the images enough. At some point, the process became a kind of surrealist game. The headlines I don't write, the captions I don't write, the pictures I don't choose: it's an exquisite corpse. After a while, I decided this was something I just needed to accept. It's just the reality of working at a newspaper and something that is maybe positive in its own way.

Q [Wolf D. Prix]: So, it's the same as in architecture!

A: Yes, exactly. You accept the absurdity of the situation and then you have a drink and then you're much happier. (*laughter*)

Q [Audience]: You described the scenario in the early 1990s. Would you say that architects then had an image or an idea of utopia? Can or should architects have an idea about a personal or collective utopia?

A: Well, I would say that the first reaction against orthodox Modernism was a complete retreat into nostalgia—some people wanted to pretend that the 20th century never happened at all, which was silly. But in the 1990s, this first reaction was followed by a real desire on the part of some architects to re-establish a sense of continuity, to acknowledge that Modernism had happened and that in fact the Modernist project was not finished. But they still contended that Modernism had been a closed system and it somehow had to be broken down and opened up, that it had to be more heterogeneous and needed to make room for outsiders, oddballs, and all kinds of other things. Part of this came out of what people think of as identity politics—the feminist movement, the gay rights movement. It was a kind of liberation. And it was a reaction against the gray uniformity of the period of postwar social democracy.

And there was a moment of euphoria when suddenly, after working on these ideas for decades, these architects were accepted by a general public. And I think people forget just how euphoric it felt that suddenly this work, which was being done in places like the Angewandte—behind closed walls as part of a subculture—was suddenly out in the world, and everyone thought that this was a really cool thing. Why wouldn't it be, right? But it turned, in some ways, into a disaster. It spun completely out of control. So how do you deal with this situation when during the euphoria you suddenly run up against a brick wall, and the situation you expected to find yourself in is something completely different? Is it possible to just keep doing the same work? That question is an important one. It is an open question for me.

Q [Audience]: Do you kill architects, or are you trying to prevent some of them from getting killed?

A: I worry more about preventing them from being killed. I think that especially when I started writing—and this has something to do also with how the climate has changed for me—consciously or unconsciously there was a real sense that a certain kind of work had to be nurtured, because already then you could feel that there was a public that was antagonistic towards it and that if it wasn't nurtured and explained, that it could actually die before it even bloomed. That was what went through my head at the time, but now of course there are completely different sets of issues.

Q [Audience]: Who do you think is killing the architects? Gehry is so successful that he's designing jewelry, interviewed in *Playboy* and building prestigious buildings all over the world. So I'm wondering why you think somebody is killing him and why we need to return to the euphoria of the 1980s and 1990s?

A: The backlash is very real and also cyclical, because it's happened before. At the end of Modernism, the backlash was so intense that the architect was defined as someone out of touch with reality. For decades after, architects were not allowed to address really essential parts of what it is that architects do, like public housing for example. It's a bigger question of where that backlash is coming from and where it places the architect in relationship to the world.

> Q [Audience]: At the beginning of your lecture, you talked about architecture in search of optimism. Do you have an image of what optimistic architecture would be like? Is it a volume, is it a memory, is it a color, is it a flash? What would make architecture optimistic?

A: I'm not sure, and I really feel that it's like a blank, what's coming next. One thing that scares me is the constant pressure to find formulas that level everything. New Urbanism is a good example. Every city in the Middle East and China has a New Urbanist plan with pedestrian paths and trams. The plan for Al Ain, outside Abu Dhabi, is all New Urbanist. It's unbelievable. How does this model translate to a desert environment with 130 degrees Fahrenheit in the summer? It's completely absurd. Some other formula may come along next.
In a healthy culture these formulae are constantly being challenged and rethought. And I feel like that's becoming less possible and that there is a pressure to always establish some kind of a formula that then everyone has to conform to. And I don't know how you break out of that. As you know, that's your job as architects.

Gerhard Matzig

Gerhard Matzig baut ein Haus: Architekturkritik als Ernstfall

Edited by Alexandra Graupner
(This lecture has been translated from German.)

It's great that you can give a presentation in German here in Vienna. Gerhard Matzig has decided to give his talk in German for poetic reasons. I am very pleased today to have the opportunity to introduce to you the critic Gerhard Matzig. I just found out that Gerhard Matzig has studied medicine, philosophy, political science and architecture. I know that there is nothing worse than giving critique as a critic. But I would like to now say a word to German architecture critics, as well as the Austrian ones. [Insertion Matzig: Should I go so far? Prix: No, don't worry about it, on the contrary, exceptions always confirm the rule.] I think the first task of an architecture critic, and we have also sensed this from Ouroussoff, is to deliberately make the unconscious of the architect conscious, put it into words, and, perhaps, also make it understandable. However, you not only need sharp intellect and sensitivity to do this, you also need—and I find this missing in many German-speaking critics—an eye, an eye that can see and allow for reflective interpretations in speech and writing. In this sense, I think that Nicolai Ouroussoff is not the only exception. Gerhard Matzig is one (but not the only) outstanding exception in the German-speaking world. When one reads his reviews, they not only describe architecture, they are also an associative chain of thoughts similar to—and this is a compliment—those of the former critic Herbert Muschamp: an associative chain of a description that describes not only the architecture and the building, but also the background. Today, he will attempt to describe—and I find this fascinating—the disparity

between architecture and building owners. We'll see if he succeeds.
— Introduction by Wolf D. Prix

Grüß Gott. Who understands that? Who doesn't? I could have of course kept parts of my presentation in English, but then they would become a lecture, which would have been a bit exhibition-like: "Next picture, ground floor, aha, next picture. Section. Next picture." I think you know this. My tool is not the floor plan. I build bridges, but in the figurative rather than literal sense.

This is about the relationship between the clients and the public. The public is always a kind of client—private clients, the public sector, the companies: it's about the relationship between the client and the architect. I don't know why I am so fascinated by this. I think it's because I've been writing about architecture for 20 years and I've noticed that it has become less about architectural criticism and more about reporting from the front lines. When building owners and architects meet, there's really a clash of cultures. So my thesis is: they come from different worlds, they don't have much to say to each other, they wage wars against each other and the conditions under which construction and architecture occur are accordingly difficult. How do you think the public sees the architect?

Architecture and the modern architect are often seen in this way: he has a sardonic grin, he is of course dressed in black and, for lack of a better idea, he drives a Saab. He is unsympathetic to the builder, however—and this is where the "starchitect" enters the picture—he is an artist that you would gladly invite to a party, but you wouldn't let him build your house.

I will now read you something from the not-so-horrible newspaper, *Die Zeit*: "I propose making the crime of architecture a punishable offense. The paragraph could read as follows: Those who contribute to the planning, financing and construction of buildings, or to the authorization of buildings—those who, after all things considered, interfere with the aesthetic common good more than necessary or ruin the cityscape or negatively and permanently affect the *joie de vivre* of the citizens of Germany—will be sentenced to at least two years of imprisonment. The attempt is punishable by law." And further on in the text: "An architect who embarrasses his fellow man by exposing his private parts in a parking lot"—we wouldn't write this, we are a family newspaper, but *Die Zeit* would—"will be punished or entered into a clinic. But if the same architect exposes or erects, instead of his private parts, a shopping center in or next to the parking lot that would be just as shocking to sensitive observers, and significantly larger, he gets off with impunity." This was not written by just anyone, it was written by one of the most important columnists in Germany, Harald Martenstein. He's no architecture critic, but this could be read in a very prestigious newspaper for the educated elite. And this judgment on architects, this malice, this thoughtful wit, is very deeply rooted, and not only in Germany. An example from a provincial newspaper: "Architecture is not uncommonly seen as a large-scale test of the people: what can they bear, how much can they endure? There are individual buildings, streets, residential areas and entire cities of undefeatably depressing ugliness and shabbiness: monstrous urban status-seeking and architectural vanity that makes the observer wish for blindness on a daily basis."

This was written by Wiglaf Droste, also a well-known columnist. You have Martenstein, Wiglaf Droste, a major weekly magazine for the elite, and a paper called the Märkische Allgemeine: everywhere, the same findings. To begin with, architecture is contemptuous, and architects are a mixture of vain, stupid and very nice—so long as they are not allowed to build anything. These are, in case any aspiring architects are out there, the professional conditions into which you are entering. In my opinion, you need to know this, but I don't think your professors tell you this.

This is a design by—does anyone know? [image] Call on your building history knowledge. Who could that be? You should recognize it by the pencil lines! Frank Lloyd Wright. He designed this villa for Marilyn Monroe in the 1950s. At the time, Wright, whom I worship, was one of the first starchitects, and predecessors of people like Prix, for example. At that time, he was a world-renowned architect, and the most famous actress of her time, Marilyn Monroe, naturally wanted to have her house built by the most famous architect of her time. At the time, she was married to Arthur Miller. When you read Arthur Miller's biography, you come to a beautiful part of the book that talks about something which you never encounter in architectural history. In his memoir, Miller wrote about how he visited Wright, who lived at that time in his hotel in New York. The house would be in Connecticut, a two-hour drive away, and Miller wanted to drive out there with his architect and show him the property. Miller wrote: "Wright slept the whole ride. When we arrived, he ascended the small hill, turned with his back to the wind, peed and said, with a view of the property: 'Yes, oh yes.' Then I thought it would be time to speak with him about how we wanted the house to be. But Wright made it clear that my opinion did not interest him much. Four weeks later, he sent us a preliminary draft: a small colored pencil drawing." You can see it: he estimated that, even if he had converted his entire inheritance into money, he would have been able to pay for the supporting wall of the pool and that's about it. It was never built.

T.C. Boyle wrote a very nice book about Wright, who was also a very big ladies' man, and one of the pioneers of the so-to-speak popular media-loving starchitect, a role he played very consciously. A client once called him and said, "New house, it's raining straight through the roof right into my soup bowl, how is that?" And Wright said, "Move the bloody soup bowl somewhere else." This is all true, a wonderful nugget from architectural history.

This house is Falling Water, you all know that there are entire book series about how brilliantly and ingeniously this location was implanted by the architect in a huge joint project with the client, a certain Kaufmann, a rich man. The truth is quite different: Wright was practically broke, but he had this school of architecture, kind of like this one, although a bit sect-like. The young student Kaufmann wanted to help and said, "My dad has lots of money, build him a house."

Wright had no desire to at all. But Father Kaufmann said, "Okay, Wright should build a beautiful house for us, here's the property." Wright never went there, only the students were there and measured it. He never made any plans and Father Kaufmann eventually wanted to know, "What about my house, when will it be done?" Wright would always say, "Next month, I'll send you some plans." It never happened. He was always putting him off, until one day, Kaufmann called and said, "Ok, now I want to see the plans, I'll be there in two hours," and hung up. At that point, Wright began to draw. He had never seen the property, but the house was designed.

Architects are not so simple. This should be the first message. Architects are already very difficult contemporaries and were actually always this way. But what about the client? Is the client really the innocent one in this dysfunctional marriage?

If you go on the street in Vienna today with a microphone and take a spontaneous poll asking, "Who is Zaha Hadid?" I suspect that eight out of ten answers would be, "Hadid who?" or "Zaha who?" Architecture is no longer part of the canon, even of the educated. I have 20 years' experience in the newspapers and I know that one can talk with anyone about literature, theater, music or art, but not about architecture. I studied art and my teacher didn't know who Le Corbusier was. This means that there is a huge general ignorance regarding architecture and only this can explain why everything contemporary is always assigned with the same terms—cold, inhuman—and that pervades throughout. You will see later that I am a defender of architects. You must not view me so badly, it will all turn out good. This is a lecture with a happy ending.

Nevertheless, let's stay with the disasters for a moment. This is an excerpt from a photograph by the photographer, Pavlitschko [image]. These are all buildings that, within one year, 2001, were built in Munich as private residences. He took the photograph on a simple 1:1 scale, and when you stand in front of these 500 images, it really becomes clear what is going on in the world. Take a good look at this architectural landscape. That is what people want. I assume it's not what they produce. So somewhere there is a gap between the production, supply and demand. This brings us back to the broken marriage between client and architect. This has something to do with the critique of modernity. The critique of modernity is as old as modernity itself. When Gothic cathedrals were built, they were tremendously innovative. It was a sensation, it was pure utopia, it was modernity and progressive thinking at its purest, which many people were already not liking at the time. But at the time, architecture was only being negotiated among the elite. Now it is being negotiated everywhere beyond the elite. And this is very important—or it should be—to your understanding of how the reception of architecture works.

In 1972, it was a different time. You know the Olympic Stadium, Behnisch. You know the story of how Frei Otto, who was the engineer, did not really know if the roof would work. And then they reconstructed it with stockings. Frei Otto told me that every time he is in Munich, he gets in a taxi, drives out, takes a look at it, and can't believe that it's still standing. At that time, he offered a ten-year warranty and not a day longer. So the city of Munich built something for which they had no idea how long it would hold and everyone knew that the cost analysis of the architects was just a bunch of numbers. No one knew what it would cost. In the end, it had a 1400 percent cost increase, and yet it still has become a symbol of that time. Munich is incredibly proud of the fact that it is the only symbol of modernity in Munich today, although there are in fact a few others. Considering this utopianism, this furor over a time that is lost to us, in this situation you're supposed to be inspired by architecture. A difficult task.

MATZIG BUILDS A HOUSE

This ends the first part of my presentation and now I come to the second, which doesn't lend itself to the most seamless transition.

Now it gets a bit shorter, and now comes the good part: my own house.

Why am I introducing you to this? First of all, it's exciting when someone, after 20 years' experience with architectural criticism—who has seen the most beautiful houses in the world, fantastic villas, and gotten to know great architects—builds himself a house, and realizes that, damn it, he has never asked how much it actually costs. I had the problem of not really wanting to build a house until after ten years of brainwashing by my wife and my three children, and after living in an apartment on the fourth floor with no lift and three children, my wife finally said, "It's a house with a garden or that's it." Yes, I let myself be blackmailed. I had no money and had to search for an unwanted property: something located in the air corridor of the airport or a radioactively contaminated ground. It's still Munich, but I really live in the outskirts. I found a narrow piece of land that was extremely cheap, simply because nobody else wanted it.

This property is 12 meters wide, 50 meters long, and what the building code specifies as the cubature for a house: exactly 4.80 meters wide and 60 meters long. I didn't get too involved with the details, although I should have taken into consideration that, with three children, this could be difficult. I just looked at the price and said okay, this is the only property I can afford in Munich, I'll take it. Then I thought at first, I'll design it myself. I did indeed once study architecture and thought, I could do this better than most. After four weeks of a marriage crisis and many ugly drawings, I went crying to an architect of my choice, Andreas Meck, whose architecture I appreciate. I didn't have the guts to ask Wolf D. Prix, and Zaha Hadid was too busy, so it was Andreas Meck.

It has actually developed into a stunning house that works very well within the means of the architecture, although we only have 130 square meters, some extremely low spaces and some six-meter high spaces. In the next photo above, you see three equally large rooms. Can you see them? These are the children's rooms. I can't shake the feeling that one day, social services will come and take my children away from me, or that my children will become horrible mass murderers, like Erfurt-2 people, and someone will then see these plans and say, "You know, one should have thought of that in advance." Indeed, the children don't only have these six square meters, they each also have this two-story house within the house, so they each have a tiny house, a hut, to themselves. Overall, the architect has—with sliding doors, with the way in which the door jamb is implemented, where that light falls—accomplished a miracle, in my opinion. As a client, it has become clear to me that it doesn't work without architecture. It has become a smart house, a very simple house. Yet another point: I negotiated for two months with the local building commission, which had specified a 4.78 meter width, until they agreed to 4.80 meters. Then they said, "That's it." Then I Googled: what is 4.80 meters? A Porsche Cayenne is exactly 4.80 meters: the width of my house [image].

We opened up our site. We tried to be friendly, we did not close ourselves off. But the neighbors felt that this was elitist. I think that this is a very intelligent response because basically that is what it is. In an environment with all these "beware of the dog" signs and garden gnomes, a certain aggression is hiding behind the good intentions. I'm planting like a madman at the moment because my goal is to block out my surroundings, which coincides well with the interests of my neighbors. The color by the way was the biggest catastrophe for the neighborhood. Everything there is candy yellow and pink. Ours is black—a total disaster. All the old Tyrolean farmhouses are black, because in the old days the wood was flame-treated so that the pores would close up, which made it weather resistant. It's actually an old theme: dark wood is ordinary but aggressive. Something else about the architect: we're getting along again, we're talking to each other again without lawyers, but one thing was really difficult: he has the image copyrights. The house was featured in some living magazines, and I was young and needed the money, so I allowed it to happen. But we couldn't agree with the architect about what images should be shown. This is the most beautiful picture, says the architect—it shows the interior [image]. And that is something which drives a living magazine editor to drink. This is how it basically looks [image]. But the architect says, "That's quite something, but we have completely ruined it all with our furniture." Every time the architect comes over, of course he feels sick. But we live there with children. This is something that architects just can't come to grips with. This is an image that my wife smuggled in because she thought you wouldn't like my presentation and that you would find me arrogant.

If you bring a picture of your nice children and wife, they will like us. And now this is the book that I have written, you will recall—I was young and needed the money, and above all, I built a house and I couldn't pay for it.

Thom Mayne @ *This Moment*

Edited by Guvenc Özel

To introduce Thom Mayne means to bring water to the Danube or wine to our studio. But nevertheless I called the office this morning and said, "Can you send me Thom's biography on my cell phone?" And it was nine o'clock in the morning and it's still running. [laughter] Maybe you don't know a few things from his biography, including that he was cofounder, supporter of creating the famous school SCI-Arc. It's very important because the influence of this school is worldwide. I wrote a piece for him a long time ago and there is a quote I wanted to repeat because it describes not only our friendship but also my respect for his creative process, for his drawings—he is the master of drawing, actually—and respect for what he is doing in the field of architecture. The piece I wrote for him five years ago was titled "Call him Thom Mayne." "Call me Ishmael" begins one of the most beautiful books in the world of literature which across countless pages describes Ahab's battle with the white whale. One of the best descriptions of architecture can be found in this book, namely, "Would now the wind but have a body. But all the things that most exasperate and outrage mortal men, all these things are bodiless. But only bodiless as objects not as agents." Thom Mayne's architecture can be described as the white whale if you will and he is Ahab. Let's welcome Thom Mayne!
— Introduction by Wolf D. Prix

I have been working with a series of predilections that are the discursive part of the work. There is this constant connection between that which is more intuitive and that which is discursive. And for me this has been incredibly important because from the very beginning there was a sense that architecture was collective, there was a modest critique of the autonomy of architecture and the single authorship of architecture which directly came from my time. I have been interested in context, it's kind of odd being an LA boy and maybe it is precisely because I grew up in LA. I was a classic middle-class American Protestant. I was the kid the sixties were invented for. But I think it also has to do with a critique of the context you're in.

And somewhere today when we were together—Wolf and I—it occurred to me that his rooftop law office could only have been produced as a provocation to the history of Vienna. And so I'm in LA with no context, my provocation is to build my context and it started very early with the very first projects. With that there has been a commitment to specificity, the idiosyncratic: the notion of neutral to the differentiated is to separate architects in terms of their output. All of the work from very early on has been interested in the relational, not in the object but in the relationship between things.

One of the things I want to lead to tonight is the notion of resistance, of the critique which is absolutely rooted in my generation of the sixties and was of course connected to the broad political, cultural, social and environmental milieux at that time. It was not solving specific social problems but in fact in itself was pushing architecture in terms of its innovation and its language that was somehow parallel to that notion of challenging the status quo. And again the resistance became a connecting tissue of a huge amount of my generation. And I am at this point questioning whether this project is not exhausted and whether the trajectory of language in particular—the formal aspect of architecture—has reached the place where it is no longer in any way connected to its original association with the social, cultural and political. I see the world as complex, and I'm interested in absorbing versus marring it. I have never been into complexity for its own sake. I see complexity as the reality that our world operates in and an enormous amount of information that finds its way into our work.

Methodology became a critical concern starting in the mid-eighties and it was very much tied to the work in the academy. And what took place was an extension of the simpler, more intuitive notions of developing architecture, which was still linked to a classical plan, section, elevation, to certain approaches of functionality and a more or less orthodox notion of Modernism. What took place was a shift in strategy which had to do with complexity and the ability to deal with information on multiple planes and it shifted towards operational strategies. The operational strategy in my case was parallel to a collective practice. The work was reinventing and reinterpreting the system that develops the work. And the final work is a set of relationships that have to do with the production of complicated buildings which have a necessity for multiple systems.

COOPER UNION

When we won the competition for the Cooper Union, it was a project I knew well. I knew the institution and the type of project that I wanted to see. This is a really typical American project: highly governed by the client and as you may know, in the States clients are kind of meddlers. So the first question is: Where are we? What is the project? As in later projects you can find it in the public space, the undefined space that has to do with the connecting tissue. So the notion is to take something

1 Cooper Union, 2006–2009, New York City

that is absolutely arbitrary and meaningless with any broad cultural term and make it willful and purposeful. This is a project for an architect over 50 and it requires a lot of discipline. Where are you going to put the resources available? It was quite clear to us that we would invest it in the street level. We were interested in giving this building a certain kind of energy and a very un-New York Yorkness. We used every functional element as part of the formal language. We were extremely concerned with its relationship to the existing community. There are two different ways you can look at this: the literal way, which is the way most people look at it—in terms of language, a shiny silver thing next to a 100-year-old building made out of stone or brick; and as another having to do with the connectivity of the street and the general form of the building. (fig.1, 2) The site is the East Side of New York and it's extremely gritty—the real New York—and for me this building is like that and when you see the building you find it in that environment. The skin was operating as both an urban idea and in terms of performance and environment. It's an extremely transparent building where you are not sequestered in an academic environment but you are always a part of the city.

2 Cooper Union (nterior), 2006–2009, New York City

PHARE TOWER

I can remember when we were invited to the competition and showing up to look at the site. You didn't know you were there; there is no there. Site information is crucial to our work. In this case we literally started by constructing the site and not building.

So the building is not one but four buildings making up a constellation, a grouping, an urban cluster, which allows you to perceive the building in very different ways depending on your approach—it constantly changes its relationship to the skyline. (fig.3) We were very interested in attacking the simplicity of the tower today, which has become similar to perfume bottles. And again we're trying to locate the project within architecture—where it exists and where it has some depth and some comprehensible capabilities. You move around this thing and

3 Phare Tower (rendering), 2006 (ongoing), Paris

each time it keeps shifting in terms of its reading. We are studying the nature of the public space as it has layers of skins that are both part of the environmental program and part of the layers of structure, internal skin, etc. All of our work has elements which are evolving, which allude to the future, which allude to its incompleteness and alludes to its relationship to its basic biological evolution—ideas that are always in an incomplete state. Of course today we have mechanisms to rationalize this and we can do it with the layers, whether it's structure or skins. We can put them in families and we can take something that has the size of 11,000 parts in its structure and 5,000 in its skin and we can put them in families. In the last four years we've started scripting. (fig.4) You write a program which gives you the output of the pieces. If you can read each one of those little pieces, every strain has data on it that tells us the use of this strain in relationship to functionalities.

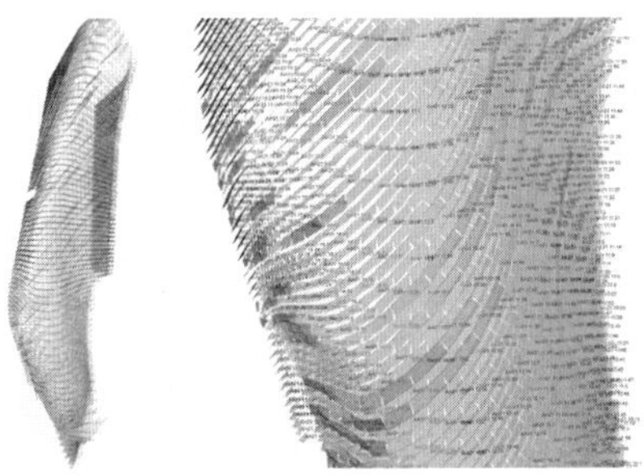

4 Phare Tower (optimized skin rendering), 2006 (ongoing), Paris

Today one of the things I find the most interesting in the digital environment is that you work across scales. We were trained in schematic design, loose drawings, design development, construction drawings, etc. And it was somewhat limited in terms of the synaptic activity. Currently everyone is working on multiple scales from the beginning and I find this extremely useful. It has to do with the direction you take in a project. So some projects like Cooper were dealing with a highly pragmatic material from the get-go. Halfway through schematic design we had to prove to the client we could actually build it within the budget. Because of that we were building instead of drawing. Strangely enough it took me back to the beginning of my career as we did little projects. We were building. Up to the fifth house we were constructing them—really building them. I mean going out and really figuring things out. And it's actually taking us back to that. We're actually making things and it's really an interesting process. When you produce something it is reality, it is not something representative. It is a thing which is a hugely different environment.

With highly differentiated architects today we look into computation creating huge diversity out of a single system versus architects looking at multiple systems and the collaboration of systems solving complex problems. What I am interested in is the ability to make infinitely complex, incredibly flexible organizations. Of course now the relationships are through association; they no longer have specific mathematical rigors that came out of the classical program.

OLYMPIC VILLAGE

So a couple of years later we won the competition for the Olympic Village. (fig.5) And what I'm interested in now is strategy. And we decided early on that given the site—the spectacular site along the East River looking at Manhattan—that open space was a key element. We produced a scheme that produced 70 percent open space. I asked the jury if anybody was on the same track and they said no. And I went back and said, "It's ours, we've got it!" It's nothing about architecture, it's about the strategy. When we presented it to Mayor Bloomberg we were whispering the talking points into his ear. As he presented it to the press, the first words were, "This is a legacy and the city is going to

5 Olympic Village, 2012, New York

give Queens its largest park within four miles." The legacy is we will be giving a 41-acre park to a city which was 70 percent of the land. And we increased the growth by ten percent. It's a win-win. We are again looking at the programmatic elements because we are dealing with the continual flexible notion of what those elements are. The park itself is a complex project in terms of paralleling Central Park or Hyde Park as you really study those as social and environmental resources. It is then architecturalized to some degree. It shows up as sectional. It shows up as spatial and we can look at the implications of our interest. We gave an illusion of an idea of architecture. And it's not about the architecture. The architecture is only a single reading as it follows certain conceptual interests.

Now at last I want to take you to the exact opposite. You will all find the same thing. You will find different outlets for your interests, both intellectual and emotional. So for years I have done stuff. I don't think ... This is the time that I do trust my instincts and I more or less work intuitively. For years I have been working on quasi-conceptual models. They use materiality in a certain way and they are definitely works of an architect. Recently I have started another project. What I am doing is producing a series of three-dimensional paintings. They operate on a five-foot by five-foot by five-inch frame and all of them have the same four components. There is an x-y line which is thin, medium and fat and there is a z line which is thin, medium and fat, and the fat one has a space in it. There is a surface—the same surface—and one object, and the object can only change in its thickness. All of these pieces are made through collaboration between these four elements. And they have to define the site with five edged [surfaces]. I am looking for mechanisms of differentiation and for the characteristics in terms of solving complicated problems with an extremely disciplined framework. What I am looking for is a range of differentiation that I can find with these simple four elements within the space of the thick canvas. All of them are identical in their make-up. (fig.6, 7) I have a series of things that I am pursuing: I am interested in the notion of beauty, if it is relevant as what it is, my sense is connected to some type of coherency and that's probably more biological than it is cultural. I am definitely more interested in the biological than the cultural and the nature of predictable behavior that produces this because I am again interested in the way we organize things.

You are constantly searching for a direction or redirection to challenge. I have realized that we have reached some sort of boundary and I am trying to challenge that boundary. Self-similarity: I am not interested in that, but if you produce it then you have to face your own critique, and I'm looking for my way out of that.

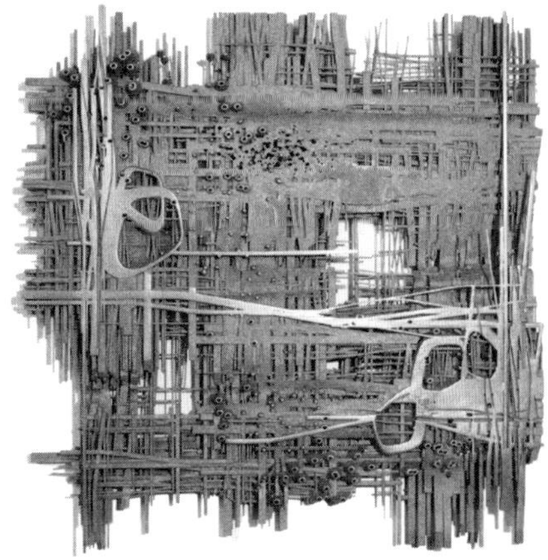

6 *YONKXI.*

7 *YONKXI.* (detail)

Eric Owen Moss

Build Your Cities on the Slopes of Vesuvius

Edited by Justin Diles

How should I introduce Eric Owen Moss? He was the curator of the Austrian Pavilion at the Venice Biennale last year and there was a lot of controversy. How can I describe him as a person besides that he is the Director of SCI-Arc and that he is a great architect? If Thom Mayne is the master of drawing, Eric is the master of the world. He is not only an architect; he is also a philosopher, a poet and a catalyst. Sometimes we communicate, Eric and me, only by quoting Bob Dylan songs. But perhaps the best way to describe him is by revealing the secrets found in his latest book. It's very heavy, about three kilograms, but in it you can find everything that he has been thinking about architecture: details, plans, sections, drawings. But I must warn you. If you try to copy these details in a building, you will be fired immediately from your commission, because he does things that are not so easy to do. To describe him in a short sentence I would say that $Em = c^2$. It means that Eric Moss is faster than light.
— Introduction by Wolf D. Prix

This talk is a little bit different than any talk I have attempted to give before. Probably because it's in this place, which is a distinctive place, and I have to say largely attributable to Wolf D. Prix and to Peter Noever, who made—in a pedagogical way and a design way—this stop an essential one on the tour through the discourse of international architecture. And the person who pioneered this parade is of course Prof. Hans Hollein, who sits here with his arms folded, ready to render serious judgment. This lecture is in a way for everyone and for no one. In a sense it's very ordinary. The way we really should do it is have each one of you in turn do what I have done, and put together a collection of images of various kinds. Serious, profound, hilarious.

1 *Medusa*

What I'll show tonight forms part of a collection of images that I've made over a number of years, just piling up things that I see from different places in the world, and somehow using them. What I'm going to discuss are the issues that for me really sit underneath the architecture and provoke the architecture and stimulate the architecture, or to which the architecture responds. One listens to lecture after lecture, looks at images from very unusual and talented architects, and one of the things we're all axiomatically told to follow belongs to a quote from a famous German thinker. (Well, he used to be a German thinker but he has trans-mutated now as an American thinker.) His initials are F.N. and he tells us: "Build your cities on the slopes of Vesuvius." This means obviously: "Go take a risk!" Everybody should take risks and everybody agrees with that. So now everybody is taking risks. In American advertising it's called, "Being outside the box." But the problem now of course is that everybody is outside the box. So the real meaning of risk is a question for all of us. It's certainly a question for me.

What is the meaning of risk? If you look at things which at one point were very difficult to do and were unlikely to be done, they were rare. Risk had something to do with being isolated, being unique, being separate. So what I'm saying is that real risk has something to do with separating yourself. Be careful of the image, the form language, of risk. If everyone is taking the same risk—if there is similarity in the images—it ain't very risky ...

I like this image very much. It comes from an underground Roman cistern across from Hagia Sophia in Istanbul. (fig.1) The image is of Medusa's head, and what is important to me in this image is that it suggests a way that

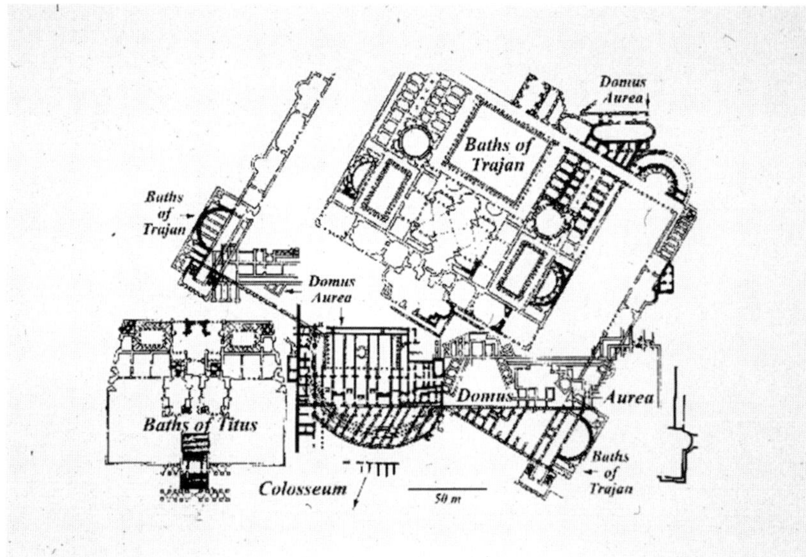

2 Trajan over Nero

architecture moves. All of you want to move architecture—discover, change, alter and see it differently. How does that happen? In America in many cases there is the congenial notion that it moves incrementally, step by step. Some acknowledgment of yesterday integrated with today, looking for tomorrow and so on. This image suggests a very different proposition for the way things change. The following interpretation belongs to me, I have to say. The Romans ripped down the Greek temple, tore it apart, took the columns and used the columns to support the cistern. They turn the columns upside down. They took the Greek story, flipped it upside down and stuck the column heads in the water. Another example along this line comes from Rome near the Coliseum before there was a Coliseum. The emperor Nero builds his well-known Domus Aurea. Emperor Trajan comes along not so long after. (fig.2) What does he do? He dumps his baths on top of the Domus Aurea. He stuffs the two together as a kind of intersection of one over the other, one force meeting another force. Now you go into the Domus Aurea and you can see the consequence of what Trajan did. Like in the cistern, you can't destroy history, but you can bend it around substantially. These are examples of how ideas go forward in architecture. It's aggressive.

A critical question for me and maybe for some of you: What constitutes a building? How do you know? There are very conventional dictionary elements and components: this is a wall, this is a window, this is a door, this is a floor. But once you decide that the definitions that you find all around you aren't adequate to say what you need to say, then it opens up an infinite number of possibilities. So "What's a building?" becomes a perpetual question. Related to this question is a hypothetical discussion I picked up between Marco Polo, who traveled from Venice, and Kublai Khan, for whom he spent 20 years or so working:

Kublai: Marco, when you return to the West, will you repeat to your

3 Angkor Wat

people the same tales you tell to me? Marco: I speak and speak, but the listener retains only the words he is expecting.

This discussion—which takes place when Marco Polo is about to return home—touches a very important point pertaining to our lives. Kublai says: "Hey Marco, what're you gonna talk about?" and Marco replies, "I'm gonna tell them what happened, but they are not gonna listen. What they're gonna hear is what they already know." What they hear is what they already know. This is what he anticipated would be the result of telling someone something he or she hasn't heard. The question is, working in architecture, can you listen for something you haven't heard? Or can you imagine something you don't see? Can you do that? Or do you just hear yourself talking to yourself? If that's the case, it stays the same. Can you listen for what you can't hear?

This is Angkor Wat in Cambodia. (fig.3) A lot of discussions in architecture are about the durability of architecture, how it lasts, how it endures and so on. Durability is completely true and completely false. In one sense—I know this from some of our own work—architecture is extremely fragile. If you touch it or you bump it, it becomes in an important way something very different. On the other hand, because of how it's made and the way it's made and out of what it's made, it has the capacity to endure. Not only to endure but to also outlive the cultural content, to outlive the cultural arguments that were part of its initiation. And therefore at a certain point we don't know what it is or why it is but we can guess. This for me has to do with the meaning of building. Very, very durable, enduring, and very fragile, very ephemeral. Both, simultaneously.

A number of years ago, we made a book called *Gnostic Architecture*. And the tool for making it was a sculpture called *The Helmet* by Henry Moore. (fig.4) The size of the sculpture is literally the size of a helmet. But it's not the helmet of Achilles, which is congruent over the

4 *The Helmet*, Henry Moore, 1939–1940, Scottish National Gallery of Modern Art

head for obvious reasons of protection. Moore's helmet is done in a different way. There is a shelter, an enclosure, but it's not total. And then there is something else, which doesn't fit. This "something else" is an element inside, which is nominally the head protected by the outside. And when putting together our book we made an argument that this sculpture serves as a conceptual model for making architecture. Here is the way it works: the outside of the helmet is the outside of the outside. Inside that, there is the inside of the outside. Then there is a space and an element in the middle—the space we call the glue. Ultimately we found five regions in this sculpture: outside of the outside; inside of the outside; the glue; outside of the inside; inside of the inside. Different aspects attuned to different qualitative issues in a project with tensions created between the different regions and elements.

5 *The Desperate Man*, Gustave Courbet, 1843–1845

Speaking of tension, I always liked this painting *Le désespéré* by Courbet. It's the eyes that really get you, you know. (fig.5) I used to use it to open lectures with the declaration, "Architecture has to be the act of a desperate man." And everybody would laugh. They didn't believe it. A few people believed it. But there are actually a lot of translations of the title of this painting. Misfit is another translation. And I think the idea of misfit goes along with the other points I've been making. Misfit is precisely where you wanna be in order to be outside the kind of formulated conception of the way you ought to think, the way you ought to learn, the way you ought to understand and the way you ought to build. So outside of the outside means misfit, means risk, means a path you're taking that you might not have taken before ...

Now we come to a very different topic but one of great interest all over the world: the question of race. A few years ago I got stuck in a parade in downtown Los Angeles. It was a parade of roughly 350,000 Hispanics complaining about various things. Many of the complaints were extremely valid. But what struck me was that, for all the current globalization, ecumenicalism and egalitarianism, there were only Hispanics protesting. So you can see that there are still very important differentiations, separations, social differences and political differences. It's a mistake to ignore these, and this project from our office relates to these differences. A few years ago the Foreign Affairs section of the *New York Times* asked us, along with other architects, to design the border between Mexico and the United States. What I like about the assignment is that, again, it took architecture out of the normal discourse, and it put it in a very different realm of public policy and political priorities. At the time there were a lot of complaints about tunnels under the border. So we made a project that actually suggested a whole series of what I would call "public policy positions" as they affect the attitudes of countries to one another and to social and cultural exchange. (fig.6) This is a role for architecture for sure, and it's an important subject for me particularly with respect to the public side or the collective side, vis-à-vis the private side and individual use.

There are two projects that, for me, really touch on these issues. One is the Carpenter Center at Harvard University by Le Corbusier. The other one is the Staatsgalerie, James Stirling's museum in Stuttgart. At the Carpenter Center, just outside Harvard Yard between Prescott Street and Quincy Street, Le Corbusier made a public ramp. If you're a student who is running late, and you are literally running from English to Physics, instead of going on the normal street you will run through the arts building. You run through the arts building! It's pragmatic and it's practical. It's not in order to see sculpture and graphic design and art and so on. But what it does is connect a private realm to a public one. Most people going between English and Physics probably don't give much of a damn about what's going on in the arts building. But Le Corbusier's ramp works as an important way—a public and urbanistic way—of not differentiating between private use and private purpose and public use and public purpose. He puts the two together, operating in a single building, and makes it easy, useful and practical. He's not insisting that you have to go look at a Van Gogh. But he puts it on the way, and by doing that he points that part of the culture, just as Stirling did in his Staatsgalerie, into the life of the public realm. They are both very interesting precedents.

Maybe this is obvious and self-explanatory in terms of the priorities in the world, but it is fascinating when you look at the arguments we hear so frequently about making it green and making it sustainable—all of the saintly,

6 *US-Mexican Border, 2006*

virtuous associations with architecture and engineering. If we triple-glazed every new building for the next 10 years, it's not gonna make any difference if someone puts a missile on the refineries in Riyadh. Oil policy is an international topic. Alternative fuels are an international topic. This is not to say that unusual works of architecture can't illustrate, as exceptions to the rule, how energy might be more intelligently managed. But the subject is not architecture's subject. It's not engineering's subject. It's a different subject in a different realm. It belongs to a different group of people to manage it and they're not doing a very good job.

Now for an extremely optimistic forecast of what architecture and engineering can do in the broadest sense—in a social sense, in a political sense, in an environmental sense and in an economic sense. Enormous projects are not fantasies. Colossal projects for your generation are plausible, doable, should be argued for and should be pursued. They are more complicated because they

7 *Make It New*

require a discourse with very different people. An interesting example that appeared not so long ago in the *New York Times* concerns how the entire Mississippi Delta could be rebuilt intelligently. I mean, it's audacious, there's no argument about that. It's audacious, aggressive and every environmentalist on the planet would say don't touch it. Yet there are very intelligent, plausible arguments for rebuilding the Mississippi Delta.

Another example I picked up a couple years ago was an article on an election in South Korea. The candidate who ultimately won made a fascinating proposal concerning two rivers in Korea: the Hwang and the Nakdong. They're huge rivers up in the mountains that run into the sea in different directions and don't connect. So the politician proposes that for 30 billion US dollars, you go up into the mountains and connect the rivers. And then you can sail from Japan through Korea to China. It's a fantastic idea. Though they haven't yet done it, that a proposal like this is countenanced on a political stage is indicative to me that this isn't just the realm of fantasy. This is our subject now and we can talk about it.

The Gotthard Tunnel is not so far from here and it's colossal, the longest in the world. The final breakthrough just finished recently and it's about 57 kilometers long. They did it. After I don't know how many thousand years of falling down the mountains, they made the tunnel.

The final example is the Yellow River in northern China, which is sometimes called the river of sorrows because it floods, turns to mud and has been for centuries a problem. Now China is moving the river. They're actually moving the river—with a lot of arguments and so on—but it created so many sorrows that part of the argument is that it won't get worse and theoretically they can make it much better.

We can debate the efficacy of all of these things but for you people I think it's important to recognize that these kinds of projects are being discussed. If these projects are being discussed in America, Korea, Switzerland and China, all over the place, they're gonna happen. And the discussion of projects at this scale for architects is very critical.

***QUOD ANTEA FUIT IMPETUS, NUNC RATIO EST*: WHAT WAS BEFORE IMPULSE, IS NOW METHOD.**

The last image is Chinese and is made from three images pushed together. (fig.7) It's translated: "Make it new." Of course it turns out that "make it new" is not very new. Make it new is old, in fact. This comes from the washbasin of an emperor named Cheng Tang from thousands of years back. Emperor Cheng was, I guess, a famous guy and on his washbasin, when he got up in the morning, he had this image to remind him. Whether he lived up to it or not I can't confirm, but it was on his washbasin. So this is a suggestion to all of you, when you go home tonight, of what to put on your washbasin. To me it's at least an interesting idea, because there are people who are saying that make it new is getting old, that resistance is getting old, that it's all old. And it is, in a way, unless it's not the words "make it new" that make it new. It's instead the thinking that dissatisfied people and disappointed people want to see the world other than it is and understand that the world can be other than it is and needs to be that way. And architecture can take it there. That's how we continue to make it new.

Thank you very much.

Marie-Therese Harnoncourt

Tactile Scenarios

Edited by Robert Neumayr

I would like to welcome Marie-Therese Harnoncourt, co-founder and —together with partner Ernst Fuchs— member of the nextENTERprise.

I remember very well coming to this school 20 years ago, smiling but with my fist in the air. And if I had to describe Marie-Therese and Ernst Fuchs, I would give them the name "smiling but fist in the air." That means: very good networkers, very clever designers, and if they come to the point where they have to decide, "Should I build it?", "Can I build it?", "Will I build it?", they are always going the right way.

Marie-Therese and Ernst Fuchs, former students, now friends, have a biography I really like to read as a former teacher. I know, it is very hard to hear that. When I was a student and a teacher of mine was standing in front of me saying "This is my former student!" I hated it.

So I am sorry that I mentioned that, because they are standing on their own feet, and very strongly.

They are not only building and doing architecture, they are rethinking architecture by doing other things more connected with art. When you think on different levels it again influences architecture. I am very excited that tonight I might get some insight into the design process of Marie-Therese and Ernst. Please welcome Marie-Therese Harnoncourt.
—Introduction by Wolf D. Prix

The roots of our work can be traced to this place and certainly to the period when we were studying in your class. When you started teaching here, it was like an explosion. Not just for the school—confronted with a studio that was suddenly shifting and moving all the time, appropriating found material from the basement to build models (I am thinking of the Raumabdruck exhibition here)—but especially for our minds. We were confronted with new programs and topics, and with a review system that gave place to our ideas within an academic discussion and with your openness and curiosity for ideas even if they might have seemed far-fetched. In the end, what counted were results in terms of spatial visions.

In this lecture entitled "Tactile Scenarios" I want to show a cross section of our work like an associative reading, from telling architecture through drawings and models to building as a materialized experiment. The purpose of a space can only be found by using it. For us, ideal architecture does not exist. We talk about spatial qualities and their potential of activating space. Architecture to us means imagining future scenarios. The planning process is an iterative approximation of a future reality. We believe that the purpose of a space can only be found by using it. We create spaces that ask to be conquered. This approach opens a discourse that values events that cannot be planned or predefined. We have no preference for a particular material. The choice of material evolves from the spatial concept and intensifies it.

The Zirl House is an architectural manifesto for a single-family house. (fig.1) It is an open, flowing spatial continuum with distinct spatial qualities zoned by the differences in height. The inhabitants are explorers that take over a climate-controlled volume they have discovered. At the core of this inner topography is the kitchen with its views and vistas. On top, the cantilevered roof volume extends to the maximum allowed by the building code. The footprint below is reduced to a minimum and reaches into the ground where an atrium collects air and light for the lower floor. The south side has a large glass front with different degrees of transparency reaching down to the atrium. The shadows that are cast onto the south façade by the neighboring buildings are part of the overall sun-screening concept.

The house was generated from a three-dimensional conglomerate made from scraps of architectural models, fragments of ideas about space, shape, structure and program that were placed onsite. With this approach we wanted to kick-start a process that would allow for the unexpected and accidental, would undermine any preconceptions we might have about a house and would bring in alternative, informal, atmospheric and personal notions into the production of space. Space is carved out of this block of data in iterative, almost archaeological steps defined by a subjectively chosen set of rules such as building code, technical guidelines and personal interpretations, like the vision that a house on this site already exists by the three-dimensional shade of the surrounding buildings. The shade space of the neighboring houses, superimposed on the data block and carved out of it, had a strong impact on

1 Zirl House, Zirl, Austria, 1997

defining spatial qualities and opportunities for use, both within the house and in the space between the house and its neighbors.

This found space was transferred from model to two-dimensional copies and drawings. Our equivalent to the mill was a photocopying machine, and this process formed the basis for the programming and description of spatial qualities. The data field can be used to store ideas, graphical descriptions, textures, and to engage and interpret everybody involved in the design process. A feedback system becomes a transforming agent in the project's evolution. Drawings, texts, shapes and conceptual terms—a process of associative reading—were interpreted as three-dimensional models and vice-versa. Our thoughts were the first inhabitants of this structure. The building has changed over time: living and sleeping quarters have switched positions, a separate room for the children was created, the wood has aged, the eastern terrace has become an enclosed space and the covered entrance area has mutated into a garden room.

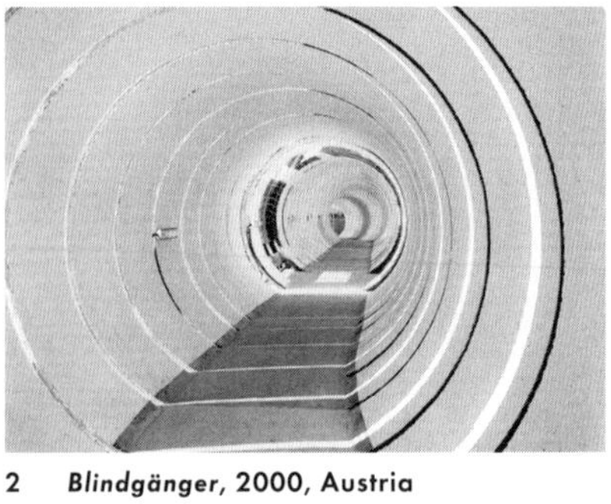

2 *Blindgänger*, 2000, Austria

3 Lido Bath (collage), Caldaro/Kaltern, Austria, 2006

We have continued to explore the concept of spaces that leave room for self-organization and appropriation. We call it alternative movements. They have the ability to adapt to the changing needs of users. This is an important issue within our work in urban planning and housing concepts. For example, for the social housing project at Auer-Welsbach-Strasse, a six-studio team conceived of the development as one continuous building with six distinct parts. A flâneur's walk connects the shared infrastructure and outdoor spaces. The community space in our building is situated under the fun rock, which is part of the attached outdoor playground. The so-called far room is a separate small unit that can be rented as an addition to the apartment or separate from it as a playroom, an office or a guest room. The apartments above are lit from three sides and incorporate switch-rooms that by their position next to the entrance and services can take on a semi-private or semi-detached character, for example by becoming an office or an almost autonomous room for teenaged children. There are two things we love about making architecture: the endless ways to imagine space and putting space into a social discourse.

Blindgänger was built on the former site of a factory that manufactured prefabricated concrete elements in Lower Austria and was reused as a cultural center and waste collection station. (fig.2) The project evolved from a competition we won. The brief asked for a fence that would separate the cultural center from the waste collection station and would work as an icon, a signature for the Kulturwerkstatt.

We designed a "space containing" fence that separates the different areas and at the same time is a space accessible and conquerable 24 hours. We see culture as part of everyday life, as something that should not be locked away. We imagined an accessible public space that would also reference the former use of the area, could act as a separator but should also be permeable to light. From this we proposed an enclosure made from well rings, a standard prefabricated product as standing hoops. On the inside the sunlight creates a changing pattern of luminous stripes. At night the fluorescent strip lights on the inside, which are hooked to the town's public lighting grid, transform the *Blindgänger* into a 130-meter-long light object.

The Lido in Kaltern focuses the concept of purpose finding and space appropriation through spatial and atmospheric variety and density. (fig.3) Space affects the body. The site for the new Lido is on the northern shore of the lake, a lush manmade landscape with its vineyards in the Kalterer See natural reserve. It's one of the few places where the lake is accessible to the public.

Inspired and fascinated by the natural lake and its atmospheric moods we developed the strategy of "cutting out a piece of lake" and exposing it to view by "pasting it" on shore. This led to the spatial concept of a water-filled platform, suspended above the site. This organizing principle resulted in the addition of two new spatial qualities to the existing Lido: the suspended platform called the Sun Deck and the hollow space below called the Aquarium. A spatial typology for an outdoor pool, organized on two levels. The Sun Deck is joined to the landscape at the highest elevation of the site and extends it like a horizontal plaza towards the shore. It is an elevated platform with panoramic views of the lake, a meeting place for bathers and flâneurs. The Aquarium below is a fluid spatial continuum, a continuation of the existing sunbathing lawn. On hot days it's a cool and shady outdoor space, on rainy days a shelter with a whirlpool, the rain room, the whispering rock.

4 Lido Bath, Aquarium, Caldaro/Kaltern, Austria, 2006

5 Lido Bath, Caldaro/Kaltern, Austria, 2006

Conceptually we proposed a suspended, monolithic deck with integrated pools, continuous surfaces fused into a monolithic body. (fig.4) The greatest technical challenge was the cantilever of the Sun Deck and to avoid corrosion caused by the chlorinated water of the pool. These guidelines resulted in the design of a seamless reinforced concrete structure with the concrete cast. From an architectural point of view casting is what makes concrete interesting and while working on the project we tried to exploit this potential in geometry and surface treatment of the concrete.

The 1400 square meter seamless concrete structure is supported by individual structural cores with piles used for the foundations. A total of six cores support the cantilevered Sun Deck. (fig.5) The aquarium can only be experienced by moving through it and discovering the shifting spatial sequences and views. They are framed by the volume of the whirlpool, rain room, whispering rock and glow room with their enclosed hidden spatial pockets. The different ways in which natural light, is used reinforces the identity of the spatial zones.

Atmospheric fiction or atmosphere intensifies space. Staging a room for a brief moment, appealing to all senses with sound, smell, taste, and light is another experimental ground we use. This is exemplified in *Ice Canal Number 1*, a project for the opening event of our studio on Schottenfeldgasse. *Let it Storm* was another intervention within the Zaha Hadid show at the MAK. (fig.6) For that evening we wanted the installation to float in an imaginary landscape for exactly as long as the budget converted into dry ice and rented fog machines would last. Christoph Cargnelli provided the soundtrack.

6 *Ice Storm*, 2003, MAK

7 Warmbad, 2006, Villach, Austria

The potential of staging space was a driving factor in the project *Warmbad Villach*, a family resort with a gym and spa area in Villach. (fig.7) The dense environment gave us the idea to imply an internal landscape. Excavations were difficult due to two thermal springs. Most of the program and infrastructure were densely stacked on the north and east perimeter of the site with views into the vertical bathing scape. An interior cavity branches into areas with very diverse spatial qualities. Carefully placed openings frame views both to and from the outside. The roof, two stories in the areas housing the spa, has light funnels that cut up to 40 meters through the main volume, connecting the roof to the ground floor. Conceptually the ground level is a piece of scraped and carved bedrock with water collecting in its grooves and drains. We used images of Lotusland, an artificial interpretation of a landscape as inspiration for the choice of material and color: moss patches, the stainless steel pools as gleaming, bright water surfaces, the dark bedrock, crystal walls and caves. A sequence of water slides, similar to a slide park, cuts diagonally across the landscape. Users can traverse the whole building in them slipping from a tube slide into a wide bed slide and on into the wild water course. Colored light transforms the track into a stylized lava stream. We like this idea of sliding through space.

A subterranean pool imagined as a remote living room, as an escape from everyday life: We were asked to submit a proposal for an indoor swimming pool on the ground floor of a turn-of-the-century villa. The building code forbids building in the garden but not underneath it. A walkway leads from the entrance of the villa into the depth. In the foreground

8 Cloud Tower, Grafenegg, Austria

light reflected by the pool; in the back the strip window and skylight was built as a stand-in for the pavilion allowed by the building code. To the right, the sauna with the dipping pool. The sand-colored floor coating and the mahogany wood are used to suggest the atmosphere of a living room. To avoid the chlorinated smell we used a reduced chlorine water purifying technology. The pool is separated by a glass front from the living room. Developing space by studying the spatial sequences was essential for this project to handle this very specific light and very compact spatial situation.

The *Cloud Tower* in Grafenegg was built within an open air situation, evolving as well from sightlines and patterns of movement. (fig.8) According to the competition brief the pavilion was to be used for about 15 concerts a year. The rest of the time the pavilion should serve as a destination for the visitors of the park, which is one part of the 31-hectare English landscape garden. We proposed a figure, an object that changes appearance by moving through the park area. The principle of the English landscape garden is the sequencing of sceneries, like in a movie. In this context, the spatial expression of the stage is like an additional scene.

In the competition brief there was no site. We proposed to define a relational field of topographical features and historical

9 Archaeological Center Mainz (model)

buildings—a hillock, depression and castle—and to insert the stage into this field, into the existing topographical depression. Characteristic landscape features such as the trench, the slope, the hill and the trees were drawn on for the spatial configuration of the building. The existing depression was excavated and the soil used to raise the hillocks in the auditorium area. This shifting of masses emphasizes the topographical character of the landscape garden and creates an excellent starting point for the acoustics of the venue. Performances rely entirely on acoustics without electroacoustic amplification. Therefore, parameters like the maximum distance of 45 meters from stage to auditorium were essential. Access to the auditorium for the audience is through the trench, which in the southern part also serves as access for musicians. The auditorium can seat about 1,700 people and is organized into three tiers and lawn seats. The backstage area has a rehearsal room for the musicians, wardrobes and sanitary facilities. The funnel-shaped stage opens towards the audience in order to bundle a maximum of sound energy. The elevation of the stage area was fundamental for directing the sound energy, as were the reflectors suspended from the stage roof. Ten more tons of stage equipment can be suspended from the stage roof.

10 Archaeological Center Mainz (rendering)

Finding the right materials was influenced by the wish to bring out the outdoor character of the stage as part of the landscape garden. This we associated with a mineral material, waterproof and insulated and without the need for a façade layer. In order to build and direct maximum sound energy sound-reflecting materials were required. The earthbound elements are built in fair-faced concrete. The roof is made of steel plates, welded to steel ribs. The formwork was made from laminated wood sheets because we were interested in achieving a textured, wood-grained surface as a reference to the outdoors and the park. Also this technique was most suitable for the monolithic effect we were after.

Finally, a competition we won recently: the Archaeological Center in Mainz. The center is placed in a very heterogeneous urban context. It is dedicated to Roman-German antiquity with public areas for display and areas for scientific research. (fig.9,10) The site for the new **AZM** (Archaeological Center Mainz) is prominently placed at the southern end of Mainz's historical center, between the main north-south road and the train tracks. It appears suburban and is exposed to heavy noise. On an urban planning scale the task was to create a new, attractive entrance situation to the Old Town. From the study of the heterogeneous surrounding and the given program we proposed a building complex that would contextualize the different characteristics of the surroundings. We add a topographic plateau to the site, which we call the Neutor-Plateau: a base serving and connecting the other two elements. The plateau merges the park on the other side of the railway with the townscape and opens visual links between the Archaeological Center, Old Town and the Mainz Cathedral.

We distributed the requested 15,000 square meters of space programmatically between the Scientific Services Building, the Museum Building and the plateau; the buildings' differentiated appearance evolved from their very different functional and spatial characteristics. The iconic volume of the new Museum Building is the focus of the ensemble, the eye catcher. By contrast the Scientific Services Building is designed as a block growing from the base of the plateau and organized around a central courtyard. The museum's split-level exhibition spaces are organized around a vertical atrium lit from above. The atrium is placed at the end of Neutorgasse at the highest point of the plateau and provides orientation, information and quick connection to the cantilevered exhibition spaces. The exhibition spaces are also linked by the flâneur's walk in the interstitial space between exhibition areas and building skin that offers views onto the exhibition and glimpses of the city and its archaeological sites at the same time. The Neutor-Plateau acts as a topographical plaza, to be a pleasant place full of people but also an intimate, private space. As we do not know how the place will develop we tried to densify the spatial potential for the unforeseen to happen.

Thank you!

Greg Lynn

Massive Composites

Edited by Kristy Balliet

It is a pleasure for me to be here as part of this lecture series extravaganza, which is really something special. Preparing this intro speech I found out that Greg Lynn is very well known here, it is not so easy. Most of you know maybe more about him than me, so I thought it is better to skip this intro, Ja. And before you talk about chemical compounds and your approach to mass, I think I just have a question for you.

The question is: Greg, you have so many projects, you are doing these projects in Korea, Italy, Singapore, Spain, Abu Dhabi, Germany, competitions; your exhibitions are in art museums, universities; you have exhibitions on Blobwalls, Design and the Elastic Mind, archi-sculptures, Swarovski exhibitions, Biennale, Triennales; lectures, you have such an amount of lectures, it is amazing. And all the titles, brilliant titles. You are a curator and you have all these research projects. And you make books, there are books on your work, and you are a member of juries, conference member, you received awards, Venice and so on and in the United States. And you have hundreds of articles that are written about you. Beginning with Animate Form, Curve your Enthusiasm, Closing the Gap and PIN-UP 9, and the list goes on and on, hundreds of them. Time magazine named you one of these big heads of the century, one of 100 of the most innovative people in 2001 … Also recognized by Forbes magazine. You know how to use the computer. [laughter] You design architecture and design objects. You are a skipper. You are interested in advanced technologies. And you are a professor here in Vienna, UCLA and Yale University.

But at the same time, and this is the question—no it is not the question, you even know great places for food, like Cha Cha Chicken in LA. But at the same time when we both play this billiards game at bar Shabu, how come we as a team always lose against these beautiful women who are laughing at us? This is not rocket science. [laughter] Maybe you should spend some time for proper training. But let's talk about that after the lecture … Ladies and gentleman, please welcome Greg Lynn.

— Introduction by Gregor Eichinger

Well I am feeling good. I am lucky, that could have been so much worse. [laughter] I am glad you stopped when you did!

This is a very abbreviated and focused talk. Over the last few years in the studio here, we have been talking a lot about composites: not really materials, but an approach to design and a way to think about architectural surfaces and surface modeling. There is confusion when I use a term like mass. Wolf [Prix] will always say, "Mass, mass is about gravity, these are lightweight materials and you keep using this term mass, and how do you use a term like mass when talking about surfaces that are plastic or lightweight?"

What I thought I would do in tribute to the Friends and Enemies lecture series is to put these two things together. I will talk about how I started using surfaces and how surfaces seemed, well, first virtual and immaterial, and later not as things that produced volume and mass, and then move towards a logic of massive surfaces. First to start, there is a very big shift that is happening right now and it is a shift from the way we think about details and the way we think about construction. I will lay this out in terms of composites. When I think about the term tectonics, I think about the layering of systems. A primary structural layer with a secondary structural layer with cladding applied, and with an interior surface applied, but it is always a series of discrete elements that are coordinated at their connections. Typically these connections are mechanical and because of these details take on a very special quality. Details are always at the transition of elements. The detail is either how you attach the layers or the detail is at the transition of the floor to the wall or the wall to the ceiling. Typically that is where we think about the detail, it is where two disparate things connect. The way this all gets managed is with geometry. It is the geometry which allows these alignments and allows us to think about the detail—we are all fascinated with geometry. I think this is the reason that when you start using surfaces it very quickly turns into structural expressionism, where the lines of the surface, the geometry, turn into lines of structure or panels, and this move of thinking about geometry is primary. I have terrible news for my students, which is: in the last few months I have realized in composites that there is no geometry. I could show you some examples, but geometry is absolutely irrelevant when you think about composites. For the next seven or eight years, we will be throwing away all of our geometry.

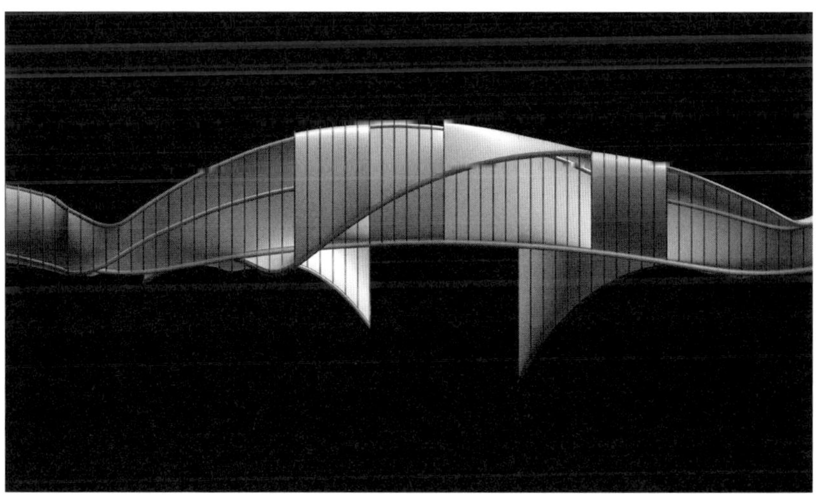

1 Port Authority (rendering), 1995, New York

A trip down memory lane, which I think is in the spirit of the Friends and Enemies lecture series: The very first project where I ever used animation to generate surfaces was the Port Authority Gateway Project, which was for a competition. (fig.1) What was generated was discrete layers, tectonic systems, moving paths of bouncing points in space. I modeled all these values like I was a scientist. They became structural tubes, curved tubes, and then covering those curved tubes I lofted a series of surfaces and I had to slice them up so that it was constructible. You could always get one surface around tubes without intersecting them. All of the principles of this hung around for ten or fifteen years, this idea of a tectonic approach to surfaces.

2 Korean Presbyterian Church, 1999, New York

3 Korean Presbyterian Church, 1999, New York

4 7th Venice Architecture Biennale, 2000

1995: SURFACES AS INTRICATE TECTONIC SERIES

In the Korean Presbyterian Church, (fig.2) surfaces were translated into structural frames and then clad with panels. The intricacy of components, where every component was a little different as it flowed along the surface, was translating surface into tectonic elements and expressing the frame and cladding and the interior surfaces as layers. (fig.3)

2000: SURFACE ORNAMENTATION: SELF-CONSCIOUS USE OF PLASTICS

That move towards layers was countered by thinking about the quality of surfaces and its ornamentation and translation into lightweight plastic materials. This is where I started to discover that this stuff had a baroque quality of mass and volume. Our installation at the Venice Biennale had a massive effect in the room, it was commanding in its gravity. (fig.4) It really looked heavy; it translated what was a thin surface into this super thick thing.

MASSIVE, OOPS?: FOAM WEIGHED MORE THAN ONE TON

The response project was with Fabian Marcaccio, we made a big three-dimensional painting at the Wexner Center called the Predator. (fig.5) This was the late 1990s. We vacuum formed clear panels and put relief on them, digitally printed them and built this hollow plastic shell. Even though it was lightweight, it looked heavy. I realized that these plastic

5 The Predator, 2001, Wexner Center Columbus Ohio.

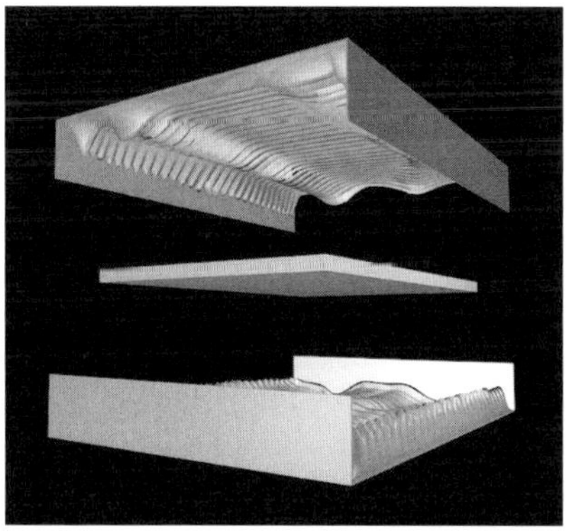

6 Visionaire, 2001

7 Vitra Ravioli Chair, 2003–2006

surfaces, even though they were the closest thing to an infinitely thin shell, actually had the quality of producing Baroque volumetric mass.

At the same time I was moving away from this idea of tectonics, mostly through the design of consumer objects and furniture. I had this idea that you could eliminate parts as a more innovative strategy than adding parts. The promise of parametric modeling is the ability to control vast numbers of different unique elements in a single system. This sounds great, but if you listen to yourself when you go into a room with a furniture design company and you say, "Look, I have this idea for a chair, but we are going to build it out of 150,000 unique parts and it is the most innovative thing," they will look at you like you are insane. They will reply, "So innovation is taking a thing made out of 12 parts and making it out of 150,000?" I realized that this actually did not seem right. Innovation should be reducing the number of components and reducing the steps in the process rather than dealing with greater and greater complexity. I believe it is the same thing with architecture. Being innovative does not mean complicated! Being innovative is reducing elements and having elements do more work than they previously had done before. With these design objects I have tried to take multiple elements and synthesize them into fewer parts, or integrate elements which were previously layered into a single surface. I did not realize it, but all these principles are the same principles that are applied by people that build things in composites: production of components, multiple orientations of surfaces, synthesis of elements and multi-use of a surface to produce the qualities of a structure. This is really what composites are all about.

The first design that represented that was the Visionaire Case, a case that has no hinges or clasps, no mechanical attachments visible. (fig.6) I designed this textured surface that the magazine floated on. On the edges there are a series of teeth in both directions and these teeth bite together. When you close the case on itself you can only reopen it if you lift it in one direction. If you turn it and slide it, it bites together and holds it in place. We got rid of the hinges and the clasps by using a surface and by making that surface nest in itself.

This also led to the Ravioli Chair for Vitra. (fig.7) I came up

8 Sciarra Lantern, 2008

9 Sciarra Lantern, 2008

with this idea of a soft top where the back, the seat, the arms, all the previous elements of a chair would be integrated into one soft shell and then the legs and the support frame, which would normally be made as components, would get integrated into a hard shell, a hard surface and a soft surface that clamped together. In the actual construction there is more going on inside the sandwich, but essentially it is two surfaces that do all the work.

RE: MONOCOQUE CAN STILL BE TECTONIC

Looking at other industries, which I have done quite a bit for material research, I found out that some of these other industries made exactly the same shift. What we like to think of as high-tech, a monocoque frame is actually a very old idea and it is a very architectural idea. It was a tectonic system, so this monocoque shell was really a tectonic language of construction. It is the same thing even with contemporary automobiles, which are also built with primary and secondary structures stiffened by a skin. I looked at what the high end of those industries were doing and the paradigm there was not structural frame with a stiffening skin but a series of fibers, panels and even sometimes hardware all put into a matrix.

COMPOSITE PARADIGM: SURFACE IN A BAG NOT A SURFACE ON A FRAME

The matrix is usually a resin, but it could be concrete or any number of things. The matrix is there to hold the fibers in their orientation, does otherwise no structural work at all, and these things are put into a bag and they are cooked together. The details of this is that you can fuse disparate materials together, they are usually layered without any distinction. The logic is not regulated by the geometry of a surface whatsoever; it is regulated by the stresses that are on that surface, the thickness of that surface. The geometry here is really about defining a fuselage or a surface, and the layering of construction is usually a link to that. The fiber path orientation usually has no privileged relationship to the geometry.

An example is a different kind of a boat. What is important about it is that all of the hardware and components, what would have been big timbers of wood or big aluminum posts, are all put into a single mold and cooked together. They are bonded and glued all in one shot, as a composite sandwich. I started to play around with fiber-reinforced plastics, vacuum forming things and cutting forms. We started working with fiber-reinforced resins, plasters. What you have to do is find a way to think about the economies of molding, which usually means that you are building two things. You build two buildings, one mold and one actual building. It is always better if you can use things multiple times. We started off with luminous fiberglass lamps, originally in the Intricacy Exhibition. Later we did the Sciarra Lamp with two different materials and it is done in parts, (fig.8, 9) one fiber-reinforced plastic part and a series of fiber-reinforced concrete parts. The principle here is that you need to build the mold to then build the parts and you can lay different materials into this same mold, it is not a mechanically attached or mechanically fastened system, it is all glued.

From playing with those materials and talking to people that design airplanes, high and low performance boats, you become interested in the way they think about things. What is funny is that in this world a composite is usually thought of as a fuselage. I think a fuselage has a few qualities. The first thing is that it is a projectile, it is meant to move through fluid. They are usually defined with fluid dynamic software. The other thing about a fuselage is its relationship to the ground is usually dynamic in the sense that it is meant to move.

I started to work for plane and boat companies to start thinking about these design issues of a fuselage. The way you think about being in them is really very different than how you think about architecture because you are more like an insect, in that you are on surfaces; they don't need floors, they need surfaces. (fig.10)

I started a boat company. The first boat we are designing, a trimaran, I am happy to say will be mine. It is not only designed with this projectile idea of motion, it is also all modeled in terms of movement. A lot of the surfaces are modeled in terms of reinventing the terms and language in a very backwards industry. What is amazing is that in the world of boats, unlike cars, they really think of everything above the water like a cabin and they build a lot of stuff in wood and brass, while the rest of it is very high performance. Our design tries to take the language of surfaces into the languages of the entire boat. (fig.11)

10 56' Suncat (rendering)

Everything is like a bowl, there is no ground in it; it is all walkable curved surfaces and sleeping curved surfaces.

COMPOSITE ERGONOMICS: ABSORBING EQUIPMENT INTO SURFACES

The best architectural example I have of integrating equipment into surfaces and thinking about construction in terms of plastics surface is the Bloom House. (fig.12) A lot of the design for the Bloom House came from a visit that I made 20 years ago to Woodland Cemetery where I went into a chapel by Asplund and saw the way he took the bent plywood and used it as a wall material and folded it down into a bench.

SURFACE PLAN & FREE MASS: STEPS, FOLDS, SHREDS & POCKETS

In this house there is a free plan, a one-room living space. But unlike a loft, the rooms are made out of steps and folds in a surface. In that surface we integrated a lot of the equipment. You can see it is the same language as the boat. While fireplaces and shelves get sucked into a wall and absorbed into a curved surface the

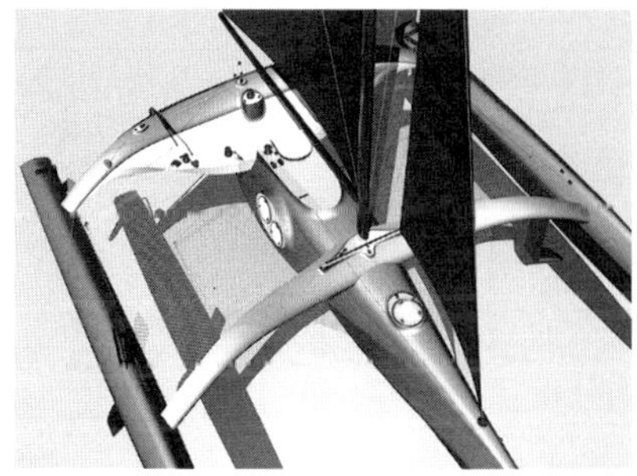

11 Trimaran (rendering)

12 Bloom House, 2010, Los Angeles

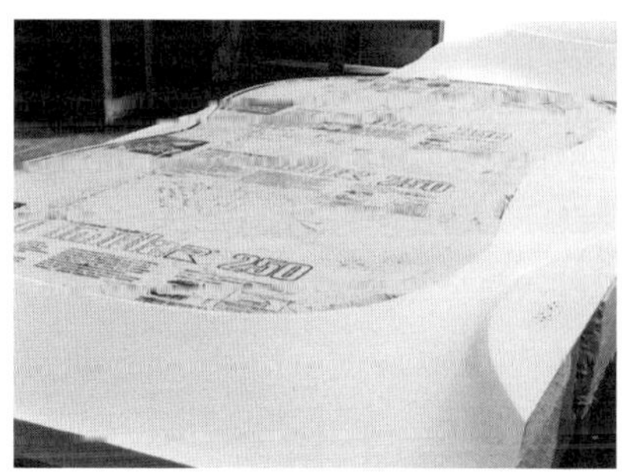

13 Bloom House, 2010, Los Angeles

14 *Triton Fountain*, Gianlorenzo Bernini, Rome

ceiling folds down and makes a large luminous lantern. In all of the wet rooms, like the kitchen and bathroom, we took the equipment and surfaced it into cabinetry and glued everything together using Corian. DuPont worked with us to get a very thin Corian layer. We started with something that is less than a centimeter before it was formed and draped it with balloons, driving it into foam molds. We reused some of the molds for serial elements and wall surfaces. (fig.13) All of those elements get bonded and glued together into a single surface and then the cabinetry and everything is behind. Everything is a monolithic plastic surface. The sinks and toilets are all absorbed into those surfaces. What you get in the end is a fairly *gemütlichkeit* or cozy place that has the qualities of an open loft. You define the rooms by folding the walls and swallowing all that stuff into them so you get one big loft modulated by curves.

INTRICATE PLASTICS:
A NEW HOLLOW BRICK

The last thing I will show has nothing to do with anything except that I just did it and I thought Kristy, Justin and everybody would want to see it. I have been doing these Blobwalls where we build bricks and cut them with a robot arm and then we did the toy furniture, which was here in this space last year. My wife Sylvia kept saying, "The furniture is kind of wrong, it is the wrong scale," she said. "This should really be a fountain. You know Bernini did these fountains that have rustication and these really want to be a fountain."

I started to look at the fountain and I realized something that I think is curious about architecture's relationship to art, and that is sculpture. If we look at Bernini and look at what he did as a sculptor, his sculptures were usually one figure, sometimes one figure on a base. His architecture was obviously made up of tens of thousands of parts. So if the sculpture is one part, the architecture was 10,000 parts and I looked at his fountains and they were around 12 or so parts piled up in a very funny way. If you take *Triton Fountain* as an example, there are four dolphins, two shields, tails of the dolphins around these clubs, keys, four clamshells, and then there is Triton and he is drinking out of another clamshell. It is this hilarious pile of figures. [laughter] (fig.14) I thought Sylvia was actually onto something. I went and looked at these toys and did this fountain at the Hammer Museum in Los Angeles, where we took around 40 whales, we had 22 ducks and the ducks each were spitting, or rather sharks were spitting the water. (fig.15) And that is it. Thank you!

We can talk about Wolf now. Thanks Gregor for the intro!

15 *Fountain*, 2010, Hammer Museum Los Angeles

Brennan Buck

Eine heiße Viertelstunde

Edited by Kristy Balliet

It is significant that Brennan is here tonight as part of this series for several reasons. First, as I look out into the audience I see many alumni and colleagues who had the opportunity to work with him while he taught here from 2004–2008 in Greg Lynn's Studio. Second, he was a co-creator of the IOA Sliver series responsible for the platform that has grown into what it is now. Finally, and most importantly, he represents the youngest generation of architects in this series dominated by established figures in our field.

The work itself exploits contemporary fabrication techniques, employing special effect strategies producing a result that is smart, refined and often eloquently colored. If you have not heard of him yet, I can assure you that you soon will!
—Introduction by Kristy Balliet

It's great to be part of this lecture series, but particularly this year as I understand there were about 20 lectures and I think I'm sandwiched between Greg Lynn and Winy Maas. You guys are the hardcore; I appreciate you showing up to this one as well. I call this talk "Eine heiße Viertelstunde," which, besides showing off my German skills, has two specific meanings. One, it was the name of a theory reader that we put together for the Lynn class five years ago about revolutionary moments in architecture in the 1960s. It is also suggestive of my time here. It will be evident that a lot of the work I'll show has a kernel from here. The title, I think, is evocative of the Angewandte in general. Here time is valued over place. There is an absorption in rapidly evolving images and ideas that are more "of the moment" than specific to a locale. This allows an energy and intensity that you don't find in timelessness or through focusing on locale.

There is an origin to a lot of our work that's here. I want to talk about it in relationship to Greg Lynn, and that's convenient because he was here two nights ago and you just heard him lay out this argument about tectonics in the context of composite materials. I'm going to agree with maybe 90 or 95 percent of what he said, but come out

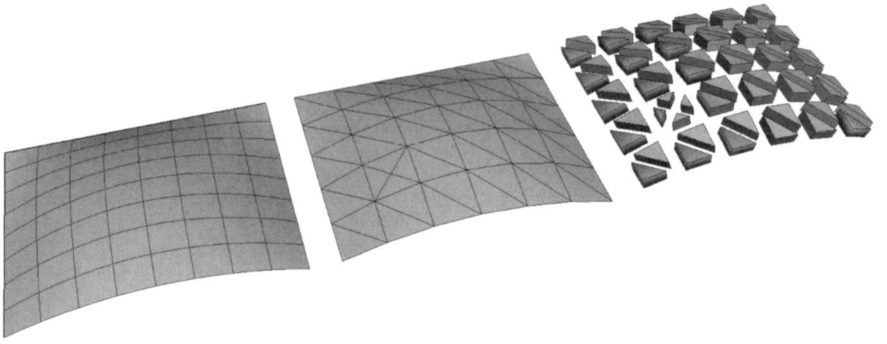

1 Three Geometries

with the opposite conclusion, that there is some fertile ground in the expression of many parts as opposed to few.

In the Semper sketch that Frampton used to define tectonics as a set of essential distinctions between building and ground, between beam and column, the joint is where those distinctions are marked out and recognized, where the two adjacent types are symbolized. In a topological surface or composite surface on the other hand those kinds of differences are absorbed into the surface. This is possible because it's described through calculus, which is the study of differentials, rates of change. There is an infinite number of points in any surface and those points are all described in relationship to their neighbors, not according to any absolute coordinates. In our work computation works the same way: it's a way of managing a large number of parts as a relational system. Rather than expressing it as monolithic continuity, we are interested in the multiplicitous continuity of pattern.

A simple example: a NURBS surface, which is made up of any number of points on the surface. The surface is expressed as a whole. In a polygonal surface, each of those planar triangular faces is expressed through their edges, and yet they are linked together in the same way. Each face is described in relationship to its neighbors and any change to any one of them affects the ones around it. In the same way, what I would call the patterned assembly on the right is still a set of objects expressed distinctly as individual components, but they maintain that same set of relationships from one to the next such that any change of one affects its neighbors. (fig.1) My argument is that these are all cohesive assemblies; only the scale of articulation differs. Composite surfaces have fibers that are woven and glued together with resin, just as pattern does with parts. I think that computation potentially redefines tectonic expression, not as a way to distinguish between essential types but as a way to incorporate complexity and synthesize it.

We are interested in the right end of this spectrum. Buildings are made of parts, and there is potential in using the inherent logic of assembly and construction to produce different kinds of expressive, spatial and atmospheric effects. I'll describe the potentials of these kinds of synthetic but

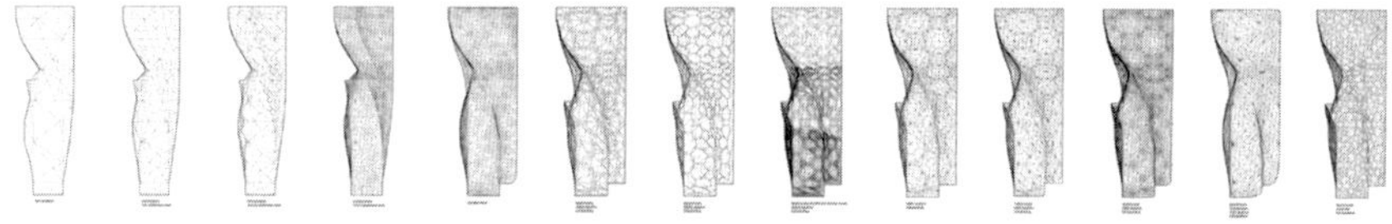

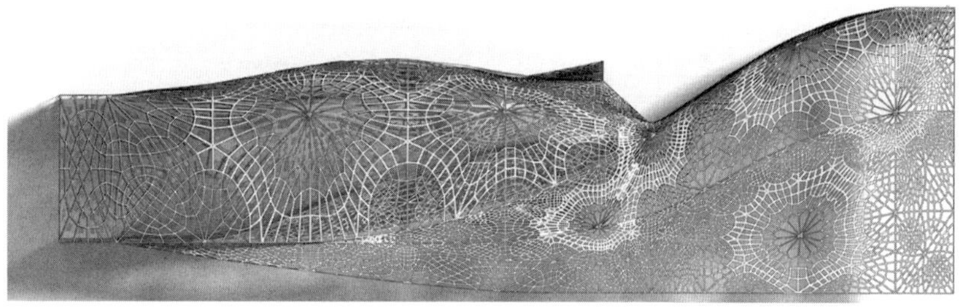

2 *Technicolor Bloom* (drawing), 2008

3 *Technicolor Bloom*, 2008, Vienna

4 *Technicolor Bloom*, 2008, Vienna

atomized patterns at three different scales throughout our work.
The first scale is fabrication and assembly: trying to take advantage of the way things come together to produce different kinds of effects. The second scale is the scale of spaces and rooms. Not all buildings are single-room grand open halls. Often they need to be broken down into individual rooms. Pattern allows us to think about these distinct rooms cohesively. We think about the relationship of one room to the next. The last scale is the scale of the city, where urban infrastructure and organization are generally atomized and segmented or cellular, but they can be thought about cohesively.

The first project, *Technicolor Bloom*, was an installation project here in the Sliver Gallery. We were trying to do two things. One was to build a set of doubly curved surfaces with sheet construction, the most low-tech way possible that we could conceive. The other idea was to try to blur the differences between the facets, between the individual panels, by hyperarticulating them—by subdividing them even further into smaller and smaller visual units, which would cross over each individual panel. The project comprises many triangular panels, each one further broken down into 12 four-sided figures. The pattern helped blur the distinction between one facet and the next.

Formally it was a set of surfaces that produced a kind of tunnel through the middle of the space to interrupt and re-channel the flow of people through the courtyard. We modeled this form (three different surfaces) and then looked at different ways that we could describe them through geometry and pattern. We thought about these as generic, the most uniform and even way to break down those surfaces. Given these generically patterned surfaces, we then introduced a whole series of creases and concentric points of convergence as a way to produce different types of illusions in the surface. (fig.2, 3) The creases were intended to produce the effect of folds. Sometimes there are actual folds in the surface and sometimes there aren't. Sometimes the pattern reinforced the actual form and sometimes it undermined it. We were interested in the experimentation and the relationship between the form and the pattern that produced it.

When the surfaces are unfolded you can see the degrees to which we manipulated the pattern to produce all kinds of small micro-symmetries and objects in the field. There were two other techniques that we were designing with, color and porosity. (fig.4) These were very thin triangular panels cut from plywood and painted on one side. There were a lot of them connected together as sandwich panels. We painted the inside surface of one of the sandwiched sides. By painting one of the interior surfaces you always see color through the screen of the white lattice in front of it. The triangular panels were cable-bound together to produce larger blocks.

The rest of these projects were collaborations with David Freeland, my business partner. There was a series of projects, which we were calling surface poché projects, that produced a porous mass from the layering up of many surfaces. Rather than trying to produce continuity along a surface, we produced continuity through the depth, through extrusion, which I will try to explain. I was also interested in how patterns may be broadly evocative of very generic general categories. In a couple other projects I'll show an interest in the boundary between representation and abstraction. (fig.5) We never want to produce images that have a direct, obvious one-to-one meaning, but I think we are interested in evoking as broad a set of associations as possible. We experimented with general categories, including structure and natural or organic growth, as well as one I call "bank." This last category is inspired by Louis Sullivan's bank buildings in the Midwest, and has the same hierarchy and concentric organization. Each was extruded through a simple cube to produce a space—a generic orthogonal space, but one with a really dynamic orientation and set of views. The structural mesh is extruded through the cube at an oblique angle, resulting in a clear view from some angles and a totally opaque surface from others. Of the four elevations of the cube some are very porous while some are not.

To realize this idea, we entered a competition in the UK to design a pavilion for an art gallery called the Lightbox Gallery. They wanted a pavilion in the forecourt of the building to hold small parties, lectures, and exhibitions. In terms of massing it was a very simple exercise

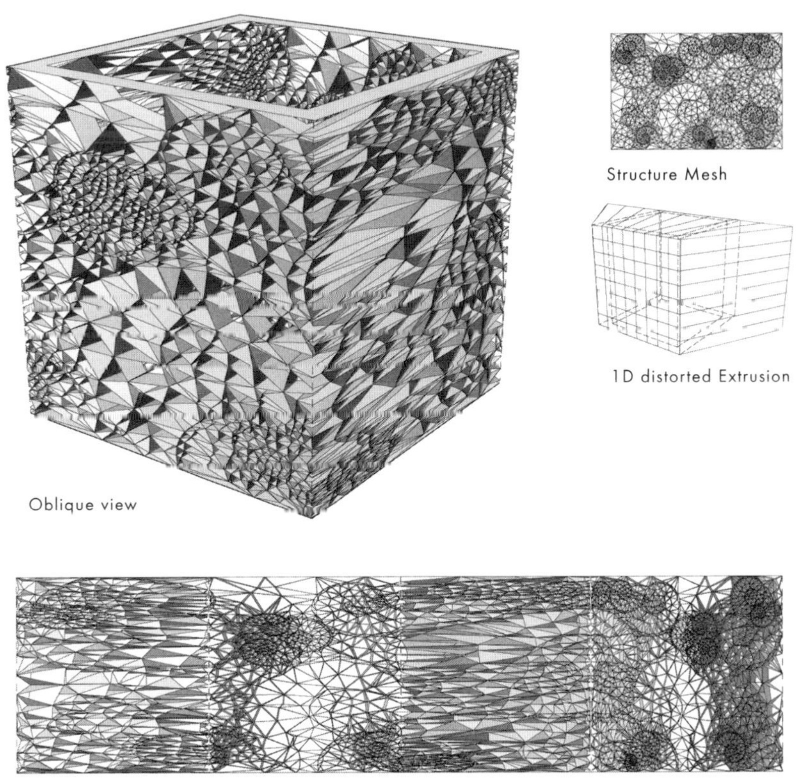

5 *Surface Poché* (diagrams)

6 Exhibition mockups, 2011, WUHO Gallery

of conforming to the site and then making a room, but also making a passageway through the pavilion in addition to that room, which we were calling the canyon.

The competition was sponsored by a company called Facet, which uses a CNC mill to produce modular plywood structural cassettes that are brought to the site by hand and assembled as walls and floors. It seemed obvious to us that part of the brief was to take a non-modular approach to the same idea, that not all of these cassettes had to be the same. We came up with a triangular version that could vary in shape and scale. Each cassette is made up of five surfaces, which are notched together and dry-stacked. They are extruded about a foot for the walls and extruded much deeper to produce the floors and ceilings.

The continuity that I am alluding to is through extrusion rather than along a surface. We started with a generic triangulated set of gradients from small and dense to sparse and large. As the pattern was extruded through, it had to accommodate different things, snap to different geometries. What we got was an adapted tessellation, something that was much more complex and interesting as a result of having to connect these different surfaces together. Through this continuity of extrusion you feel like you are in a continuous semi-solid zone between these walls, like a continuous kind of matrix. (fig.6) Trimming the edge of the doubly curved surfaces opened up a different way of production for us. The implied surface of all these cut cassettes could be wherever we wanted it to be. On the other side of that wall in the lecture and gallery space, the triangular cassettes are expressed differently. Instead of a continuous surface each one is cut vertically and stacked.

That was the small scale, the fabrication and construction scale. This is the room and spaces scale.

Next is a house in Maine, a very rural forested site. We were really interested in the kinds of space that the forest produced, which is a fairly dense alternation of solid and void. In Maine hunting is a common sport. It is often

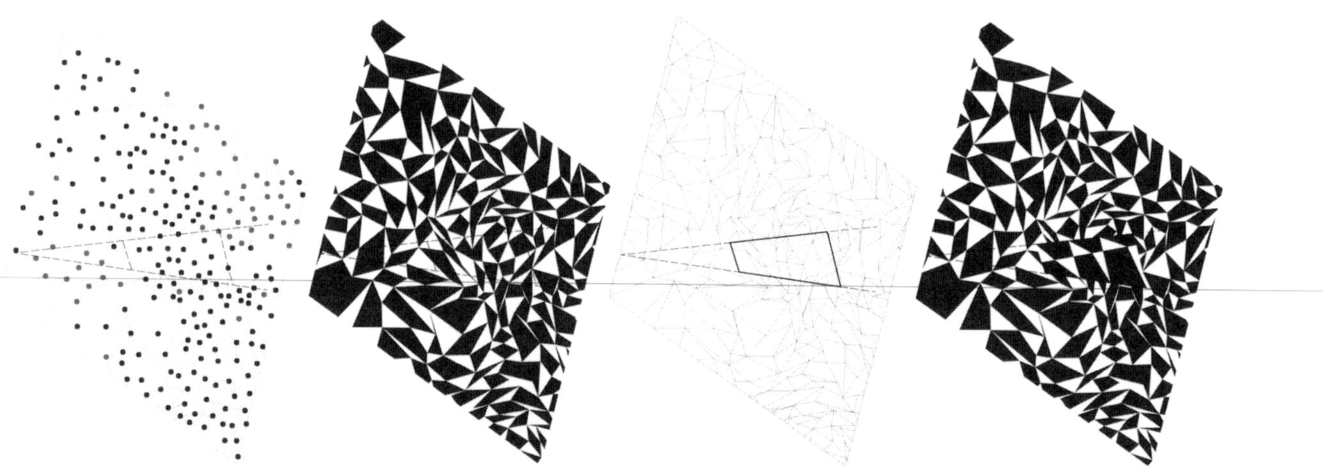

7 Woodlot House Diagram, 2010, Portland Maine

done through the use of deer stands, a platform in the tree that you sit in for a more expansive view over the forest. We mapped the forest itself and then imagined a kind of bizarre repetition of these deer stand platforms between every four trees. (fig.7) What you get is a very even alternation of platform and void. Then, given our massing, which was kind of a wedge, we tried to incorporate a series of solids and voids into that continuous, imagined matrix. The other idea was that we didn't want to interrupt that continuous alternation of the forest with the house. The house is about a mile from the ocean on a hillside. We used the footprint itself as our tree clearing strategy. The wedge of the house would be embedded in the hillside and we would approach it from above, so that the house itself would be a fore-ground for a view out over the trees to the ocean beyond. We designed the massing as a set of rooms and courtyards, which twist in three dimensions. Our ambition was that the figure of the courtyards and the figure of rooms would alternate, never privileging one over the other. (fig.8, 9) You can move through these diamond-shaped openings from one room to the next. There is a lot of looking through an outdoor space into another interior space, and the idea was that by weaving the exterior through the interior of the house, you could get the different colors of light and changing qualities of seasons to invade the house. We were interested in how the figure of the courtyards and the rooms would shift along with the changing tree canopy.

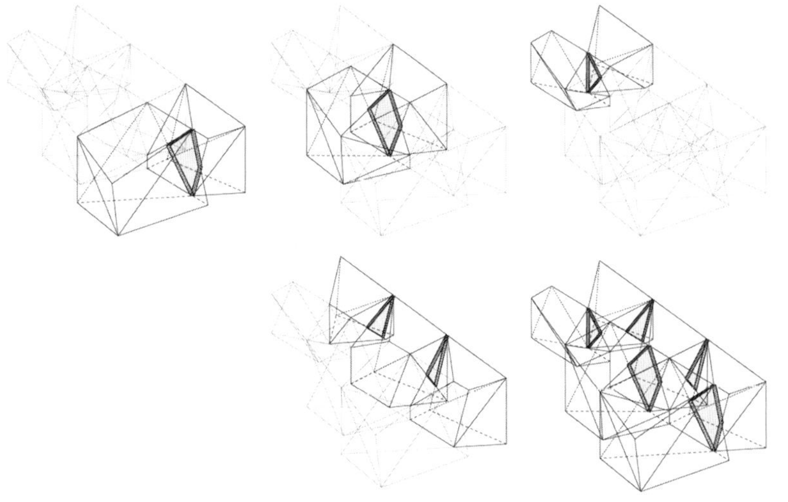

8 Woodlot House (massing), 2010, Portland, Maine

The last project that I'll show is at the scale of the city. We were interested in how pattern could not only be geometric and organizational but responsive over time. This project is in Detroit, famous for being the most dramatically shrinking city in the world. (fig.10, 11) As jobs disappeared, people were moving out of the city over the last 30 or 40 years, and there was no one moving back in to buy the vacant houses. The city started to demolish them, but had a difficult time trying to keep up. We were looking at the pattern of vacancy: the majority of the vacant lots form a ring around the core of the city. What we anticipated, both in terms of the numbers and geography, is inextricable decrease in population. The remaining houses are surrounded by vacant lots of unoccupied land. Many blocks where there were 20, 30 or 40 houses now have two or three. There is too much infrastructure: the street grid is needlessly dense given the number of houses that remain. There is also an additional layer of informal circulation routes, which don't conform to the diagonal grid of the streets.

9 Woodlot House (rendering) 2010, Portland, Maine

10 Detroit Super Division, 2009, Detroit

11 Detroit Super Division, 2009, Detroit

Some of the most obvious solutions were totally impractical here. You can't add infill because no one is interested in buying it. You can't add infrastructure because it is already wildly disproportionate to the population density. We were interested in trying to ease the transition from urban to rural in a way that didn't require those strategies. As a result, we thought about the Jeffersonian grid, which was the way the US government divided up the American West for purchasing and settling. It was divided into an orthogonal grid of townships and then properties, each of which—once subdivided—could be bought and sold and built on. Our ambition was to deploy an inverse strategy: rather than subdividing these vacant empty lands, we were going to try to super-divide the vacant land in Detroit, adding new boundaries that would help scale-up the perceived size of individual lots and properties. We wanted to do that through a technique of rural land division, which is the hedgerow or lines of trees. When a given house was demolished, a series of hedgerows could be planted between it and the neighboring houses on that vacant public land, continuing until reaching some kind of private property. It would re-divide the vacant territory. What you have now are tiny lots that are occupied and surrounded by vacant territory. What we would get instead is a larger scale set of precincts that are newly defined by these hedgerows—a larger expanse of ground that is woven together by this network of forest, agricultural land and community gardens.

This algorithm wasn't just geometric; it was also responsive. Every year the city could map out houses that had been demolished that year and also map out the interests of different communities in this program. The owner of nearby houses could be surveyed and asked: "Do you want to be included in this hedgerow program?" Based on those two maps, a series of hedgerows would be chartered and planted. Demographic changes and level of interest in the program would be incorporated into the algorithm and adapted year to year.

The spatial idea is that you have a series of houses in an undifferentiated, abandoned area. Through the re-division of that land you start to get more clearly defined precincts, a forested zone. There would be no legal wrangling necessary. Legal boundaries wouldn't change, but through the planting of these trees we think that the perceived boundaries of the city would change and would scale up to a rural scale as opposed to an urban one. In the long term this strategy would be aimed not just at the transition to a more rural landscape but also toward stabilizing the remaining houses, and even the communities, as an archipelago of smaller villages, surrounded and woven together by this network of hedgerows and agricultural fields.

And that's it. Thanks!

Winy Maas

What's Next?

Edited by Kristy Balliet

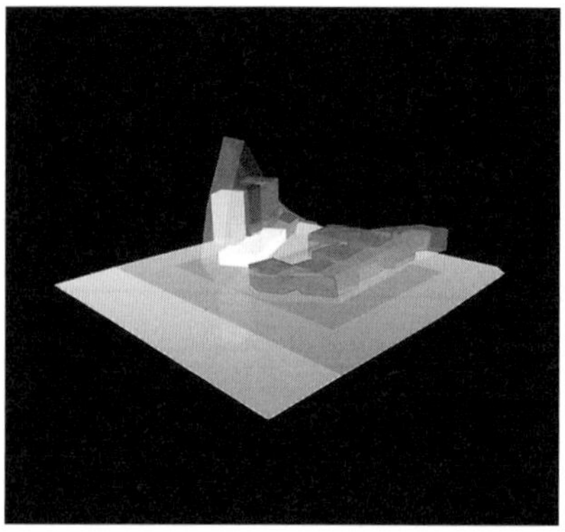

1 Busan Cinema Complex (diagram), 2005, Busan, South Korea

Good evening! I would like to introduce my friend Winy Maas. Winy Maas is one of the co-founders of MVRDV and currently teaching at Delft University of Technology. If someone asks me to describe Winy three things would come to mind. The first is that his name and the name of MVRDV are connected to this pavilion he built years ago. We used to call it the Dutch Hamburger—the super hamburger. The second one is that I remember when we were students there were two groups on the forefront of the architectural discussion, namely the Italian groups Archizoom and Superstudio, both having very critical, utopian visions of the future city. And I think Winy is the reincarnation of these two groups because he is developing some very critical utopian visions of what's next. And the third one is how can we be differentiated? We meaning the Viennese school of architecture and the Dutch architects. Or a better question might be, would it have been possible for Rietveld to build in Vienna? Or, is it possible to imagine Kiesler completing a project in Holland? I don't think so, because of the major differences in background. On the surface I would say it's because of the Calvinistic mindset and the Catholic attitude. Or more precisely, the Viennese would never have invented the diagram. The diagrams of the Dutch are very famous and they follow the diagram in all their projects. Or to put it a more humorous way: the Viennese follow the space sequences and the Dutch architects follow the Gulden, meaning they know what they are doing and they know what's next. Please welcome Winy Maas!
— Introduction by Wolf D. Prix

Enemy or friend? That is what you asked with this beautiful lecture series. And how to answer? This is of course one of the answers that I should share. In an email from Hani Rashid, regarding a gathering that we had a while ago here in Vienna, where humor was invented, our names were nicknamed in reference to our own enterprise. So if you are the big bad Wolf and I am considered a Walt Disney figure, then I'm going to talk today about that Disney-ism, the edge of what we propose, of what we can do.

I learned a lot with you, Wolf. I remember this moment in Busan a while ago. We were asked to compete. We have only competed twice in our lives up to now. In this case, I was intimidated. How would I respond to the possible winner that will build a film festival palace on this very spot? So we did our first "curvy" project. Our office said, "This is what Wolf is going to do, he will make a box and then he's going to push it." Our answer was to push it differently. We tried to compete on a diagrammatical level. We proposed a little box with all the cinemas inside, including all the logistics. All of the seats have been placed on the slopes and we could walk around. This is where Wolf and I differ. Wolf put his open space under the building and we put it on top and made a new chair. We invented a mattress in order to make the bending action possible, collecting the various cinemas inside in order to create a chaise lounge for festivals. (fig.1) We lost of course. I think we didn't control our budget as well as you did, Wolf.

So what's next after this? That's the question of tonight's lecture: what's next for you and what's next in this series of lectures? It is a simple question. In every lecture that I give, I always get this stupid question, "What's next?"

People are so intrigued by youngness, newness and nextness that they kill the baby before it's even born. You in this audience, as a younger generation, how are you going to respond to this incredible eagerness of the former generation that wants to eat you before you have come out of your eggs? So what do we do with that?

The project for Busan was a technique, it was a verb. And like architecture, it was an action. We bent a building—we bent it in order to create more density: a plaza underneath, a red carpet and a super seat on top to watch and witness the incredible growth of Busan City. (fig.2) It's part of a sequence of experiments. The book *KM3* was of course about the space gap, about the awareness that the Club of Rome had given to me and my generation. That was, that we consume a lot even when space is slightly limited. Even if we have the Alps and the Russian Tundra, still at certain points we miss density and we would like to encourage that through our book.

At the same time, the Venice Biennale curated by Richard Burdett was dealing with similar topics. How to address the scale of sprawl? How can architecture comment on what we were suggesting? We tried to summarize this

2 Busan Cinema Complex (rendering), 2005, Busan, South Korea

by saying, "We want more but we have less." It can be described in many notions. One of them was a diagram of our ecological footprint. In other words, how can we compensate for our behavior at the moment? I know there is a lot of discussion about bringing architecture back to the autonomous, only inside itself, only about light and space, about material, about professionalization. And I hate that discussion. I think it is so normal to do that. I expect from you that you are all super professional and that you take that for granted. The issue is how to deal with the profession in a wider sense. Can we talk with artists? Can we communicate, use our politicians to make things better? And how do we do that? I think architecture can be very clear. It must be so clear that people start to understand it—and that's of course what Wolf started to say—the diagram can be a one-liner. The diagram can be so small that it doesn't cover everything, or such that you don't want to come back because you have seen it all at first glance. So how to combine the zone of "mixity"—say, Austria—with the zone of clarity—say, the Netherlands—and to make that combination fertile?

So architecture as a device, as a tool to enhance, that is where the verb, the action, the painting, came from. Of course we did many verbs ...

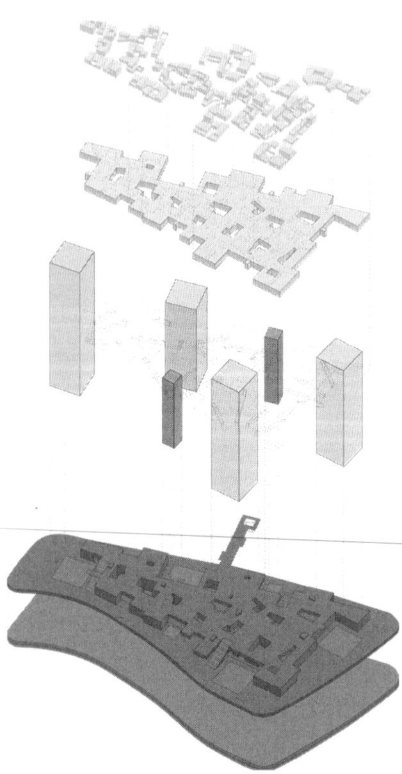

3 Shanghai Bund Finance Center (concept diagram)

LIFTING

We're always asked when we design a building in China if it is Chinese enough. So in this case, the client gave us a painting. "I love this painting," he said. What is this painting about? There are rocks, some gardens and bridges that bring you up to the top. There are waterfalls, there are pavilions in it. "Can you make a building like that for me?" Well of course we can. Remember, we started the talk today referencing Disney-ism. But how to do that in Shanghai, a place where the corporate business approach dominates? We created a sketch to see how we could transform it, using building blocks, office blocks, hotel blocks in a similar manner and fragments of the traditional Shanghai typology, the Lilong, which is the village below, to lift it up. The diagram was a balance between the drawing, Chineseness and corporateness. (fig.3) The project is on an empty plot next to the Bund. For the project, we used office buildings to fragment the city and to make it three-dimensional by connecting different towers at a height of 100 meters and to lend it a kind of composition. One can walk from garden to garden, from village to village; therefore, we were spanning the gap. (fig.4) We were hanging gardens, as kitschy as possible, as strong as possible, in between the corporate towers. The more hanging gardens the better the concept will work. "So, is this abstract enough?" Walt Disney could ask me.

HANGING

The next technique is hanging. You might remember this hanger that we made, the WoZoCos in Amsterdam, which has become a monument in the Netherlands. (fig.5) It was a building for older people with plazas upstairs and downstairs. The cantilevers have big roofs, which move ten centimeters up and ten centimeters down. When I visit it, one woman always runs to the end and says, "Look," and then jumps—all the porcelain doll heads jiggle. This woman is strong for 87. This building was meant for people 55-plus, but it ended up with only 80-year-old residents. I mention this because it had a continuation of what's next and afterwards.

WHAT'S NEXT?

I end with a conclusion. I finished the book; I closed it. After six years, I got rid of *KM3* as a reference, except for one thing. I ended the book with the word evolutionary. That's what it was all about: how to imagine evolution? Not revolution but evolution. How can we imagine the next steps in that way, how can we choreograph it? We imagine the future in such a way that our planning bureaus are not hidden in these castles on the Ringstraße but are open environments where you can activate and change your city. How to keep that promise?

That is what the research project The Why Factory is about. That is the next answer, the next step. Let's broach the issue of the Future City project. We made a pamphlet for The Why Factory and The Future City and we are working with the Dutch government. We made a book about disasters, imagining how many disasters the Netherlands can expect and how to act and react. Do we have to prepare bigger dikes, higher dikes or other kinds of clay? Or do we train ourselves like the Japanese do? That is, how to act when it happens. To gain more flexibility both techniques are explored. We made a book about visions in order to imagine different agendas. Can we call on visionaries again, and how?

I will give a few examples of what sets the tone for The Why Factory at the moment. Individualism is here and it is bringing on a clear change in the public realm. Urbanism is dead according to my former master. I do not agree with him on this. It is the moment for it to reappear. Finally, as everything is done on the Internet, as we spend more than a full day a week on our screens, do we need architecture anymore?

Another demand for visionaries is the Miniature. I love this one. A collection of recent productions of architecture has two things in common: they are bigger than 100,000 square meters; and secondly, they were never published in Wallpaper magazine. Instead, Wallpaper and other magazines only show buildings that are smaller than 500 square meters. And they are beautiful and cute and happy. (fig.6) But what do they say? Cuteness deserves an answer. How can we give this happy [Wolf] Prix a wider agenda so that

4 Shanghai Bund Finance Center (rendering)

5 WoZoCo Apartments, 1997, Amsterdam, the Netherlands

6 Didden Village, 2002–2006, Rotterdam, Netherlands

he can compete with these super big monsters? We have to be confident, and I think the blue houses in Rotterdam are trying to do that.

The third episode is Iconic. The word Iconic is taboo. It was your generation [reference Wolf D. Prix] that coined the word "icon." And it's funny to see that over the last years, our colleagues have created an enormous number of icons all over the world and they all look the same. All the mayors want to have a bridge and say, "I want a Calatrava in my municipality." We behave like curators of a contemporary art museum where you get not a Kiefer but a Calatrava instead, or a Frank Gehry. It's stunning to see. It is important to note the differences. How different are these buildings and what do they contribute? Again, how many of these do we need in our cities? It's fantastic what they did. They put architecture on the agenda but the issue remains. Can we make objects that say something about the world? That give the word "icon" a meaning again? What is the content of the word "icon"? Can we create some kind of criteria for that? Where are the critics? Can you help with this?

Next on the agenda is the poor. I think this is a very clear issue. How to deal with this balance in a moment when some of our colleagues relate to the vanity of that superstar generation in which buildings, the so-called icons, cost so much money? In regard to this discussion, I can only relate to social housing these days. I think the issue of money and the social factor is a fantastic one. I'm happy to see that some of our colleagues made a piece at the last Venice Biennale to make that real. Everything helps with this matter.

Another taboo in the battle of the visionaries is the word "re-." I don't want to hear this word anymore. It's horrible what happens in the Netherlands these days. This is super Dutch. Because of the crisis people are afraid that if they build contemporary architecture it will have less value. Due to the question" How can I get a mortgage?" only mundane architecture is realized. Fear leads to the killing of curiosity. The good thing is that it becomes apocalyptic. There are so many of these buildings that we get bored with them and their value is dropping at the same time. I try to imagine a world without the word re-. No revolution but evolution. No rethinking—as some of the thinkers like to say—but just thinking. No re-imagination but imagination. That's construction. That's a contradiction of course because we have to base the nextness on the layer of history. So yes, the past will always be in it, in any reference, but the re- factor kills any innovation.

The Why Factory research was examining how much we have spent on the future in the gaming and film industry. Why is Steven Spielberg still making shitty decors? Why do they look and feel like ancient cities, not like new ones? Why is the Matrix—even though it is a beautiful abstraction—still not leading to a new kind of hope?

WHAT'S NEXT

We made a book on Mr. Green because he is everywhere, dominating our practice. The most important conclusion is apparently that green buildings are ugly—extremely ugly. That is a strong point. But why is that an issue? About 60 percent of the recent production—greenness representing about 25 percent of the budget, depending on the country—is leading to add-ons. It doesn't matter, you just add and you're green and you get a platinum award. No architectural component here. There is nothing about space and there is no integration at all.

At the moment I am trying to beat Avatar with a sun collector project. I am trying to make a project so green and so beautiful that you can't deny or resist it anymore. In a way we behave like perfectionists and very Walt Disney-like, imagining to accelerate the discussion on greenness. If you speed it up then we don't have to talk about greenness after a while. What are the challenges when greenness is over? What is the next agenda for the visionary city book? Green is done. So can we again ask that question? What's next?

THE TRANSFORMER

This is so small—programmable sand. We worked with a nano group in Delft to give these

7 *Transformer* (rendering)

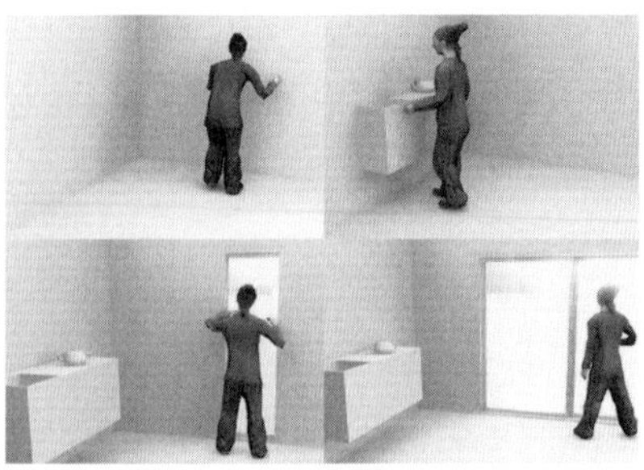

8 *Transformer* (rendering)

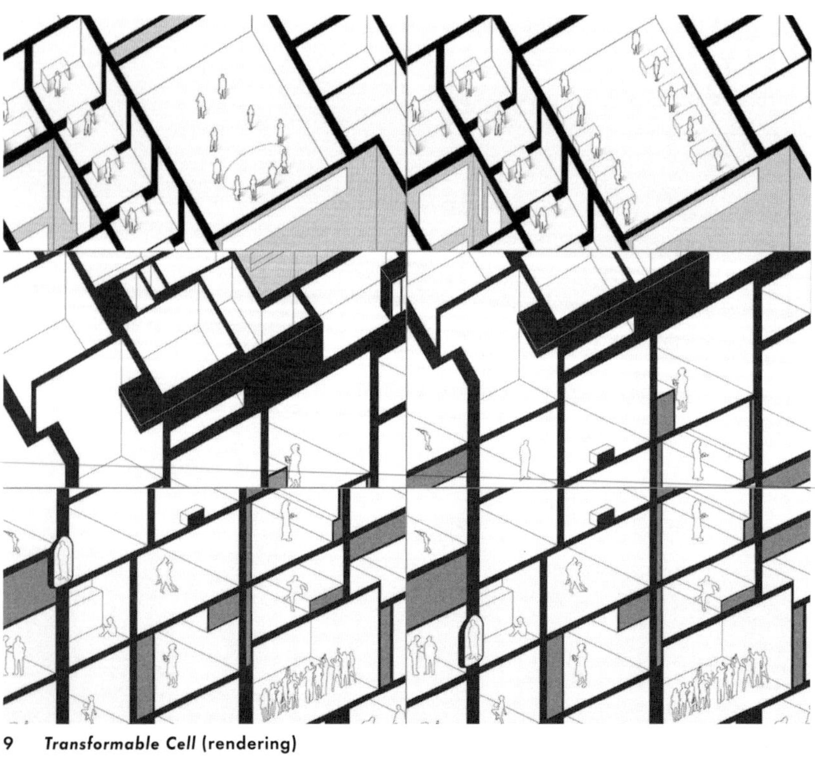

9 *Transformable Cell* (rendering)

transformable cells more character. It's very small. This is architecture. It is a laminate and it contains different messages. (fig.7) It can contain structure, it can contain water, electricity ... and it has a deformation factor that is very important. With a certain kind of input—electricity, water, heat—I can start to steer its direction. Imagine I put this together like in the bubble play area at Ikea. I have an enormous amount of elements. It is sensitive to different forces: to pressure of course, to sound, which is an interesting one. It is sensitive to light—I love that one. It is detachable. You can reprogram it in such a way that it opens itself. I don't need doors anymore. I can program it to open itself. It has an illuminating capacity and it brings light to wherever you want it to glow. Water can go through walls. In addition, I can push the wall in any direction. I can open a shelf and at the moment I open the shelf a neighbor gets another shelf. I can program water to come out. The sink is there and I can wash the dishes, and then it's a wall again. I can throw it away. I can throw a bottle at the wall and it takes it away. If I want to have light and a view, I can do it. Or a book—I can get it and it's away again. You can make it and bring it together to a table. All the desires, all our current loungey desires can then mate with this material. Not only on that small scale. Of course I can take a shower, I can go away and the room disappears because I don't need it. I can watch television with my friend and afterwards it shrinks. I can go to bed with someone I meet from another part of the wall. I can go away and the cell moves. You walk and your cell moves with you. Your gathering space is coordinated by this method. (fig.8, 9) It's a bit like Saint-Exupéry and how he thought about the elephant and the skin that surrounds it.

This is Superstudio in its ultimate form. This is how a technological answer could be imagined for this changing environment. Is it beautiful? Yes, it is fantastic! Is it scary? Honestly, no. The entire planet is only caoutchouc and rubber where you have to find your niche. It's only based on energy. Is it nihilism then? No, it is an adventure to form your own energy within it. With that notion I make the most flexible environment I can imagine. That technology—and I hope to have that building next year, to have it on the campus—this reminds me of what I started the lecture with today, the building as a mattress. And with that I don't know what to say, what's next? Because then it is only energy that I have to give you. We have followed a certain hypothesis, implemented it and it immediately opens up another opportunity, a next step that you didn't incorporate without the knowledge given to you. That again wakens the next step of curiosity that I think is so important for architecture and our society.

Thank you very much.

Brett Steele

Life and Death of Architecture Schools

Edited by Robert Neumayr

I would like to introduce Brett Steele. Every student should know him. He is an architect, a critic, a writer, a lecturer, a reviewer and as his name says: "Steel." He is the dean of the AA. And you need to be made of steel in order to run a school like the AA. If you want to be an architect who knows more than just how to build a house, then there are only a few architecture schools where you can get what you need. Good schools nowadays are points in a network; where new thinking is developed, teaching students to think in concepts rather than in details.

Some architecture schools are putting loads on the shoulders of their students and some schools are giving their students rocket belts. I think the AA—led by Brett Steele—is one of those schools that give students rocket belts for the future of architecture.

Please welcome the dean of the AA. Which means Architectural Association and not Anonymous Angewandte. Please welcome Brett Steele!
—Introduction by Wolf D. Prix

It is a great pleasure to be back. We were chatting last winter and I asked Wolf [D. Prix] on what I could give a talk on and he suggested that I could speak about—what became this topic this evening—architecture schools and their peculiar modern lives and histories.

Which provides a kind of context to rethink what a school might be today. I think architecture is going through a spectacular way of change to the discipline and to the way architects learn. One of the key institutions of architectural culture is what we call an architecture school, which I take to be absolutely and fundamentally the core technology of all of architectural thinking. It's the place where we all learn to think as architects, for architects and like architects.

What I have put together for this evening—it looks at the history of what we think of as the modern architecture school, which you all know—starts with a peculiarly European project in Paris called the *École des Beaux-Arts* in the 1870s, and which evolves over the next 150 years into the kind of setting that I operate in London today. My school with 550 to 600 students is almost exactly the size of the *École des Beaux-Arts* in the 1870s. Like other technologies, schools have gone through a staggering transformation in how they organize space and information. And what I'm really interested in is the new way in which a new wave of media and technology will profoundly change the way we think of an architecture school, and how we all inhabit it as we all teach and learn within the school.

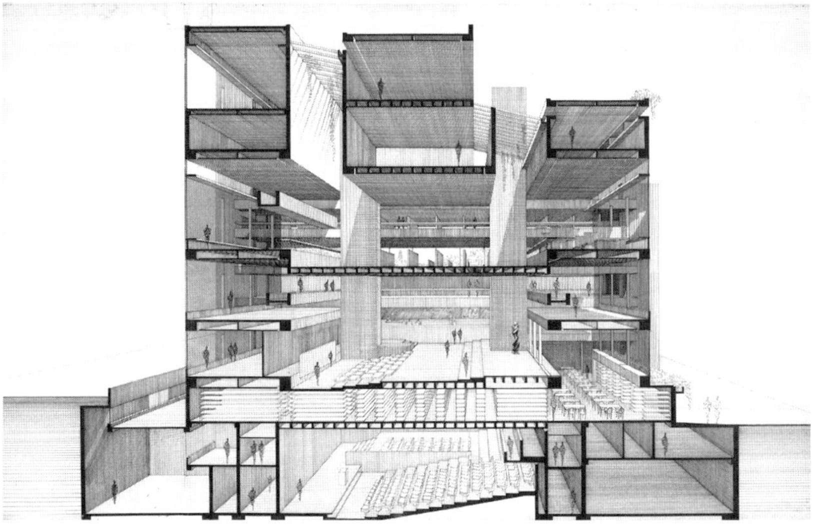

1 Art + Architecture Building (section perspective drawing), Paul Rudolph, 1959–1963

BIRTH

I think you can point to many different dates of birth of what we call the modern or the experimental architecture school. Surely one of the great episodes in that history is the invention of the *Bauhaus* in the 1900s by Walter Gropius, having stolen the idea from Henry van de Velde and others in Amsterdam, who created the idea of a workshop-based experimental school. Gropius imports it into Germany and by 1919, looking very much like a bank manager in the suburbs of Dessau, is operating a machine that's really trying to challenge the traditional academy.

DEATH

What I'm going to sketch through tonight is an evolution of what happens to Gropius's diagram over the years. And that evolution of course leads to death in various ways. The modern architecture school is eventually institutionalized in the 1960s by people like Paul Rudolph, who designs one of the pinnacles of modern architectural education: Yale School of Architecture in New Haven, which brings to an end a first great wave of industrialization within the school. (fig.1)

This coincides roughly with the conversion of Robinson Hall at Harvard in the 1970s, which was a very cheap and low-cost copy of the *Beaux-Arts* in Paris. Converted in 1972 by John Andrews into a peer information space with an open plan floor, the activity of the architects shifts from staring at classical details to the continual conversation between classmates and teachers that creates more architectural opportunities.

CREATIVE DESTRUCTION, AGAIN

I think what we are witnessing today is really a transformation of a classical model of teaching which endured all the way up to the 1980s when I was a student at the AA. This is one of my juries, my critics: in the upper left corner Peter Cook, Cedric Price and others, staring at student drawings and offering commentary, which lies at the center of any architecture school worldwide today.

What I became interested in a few years ago when I came back to the school to teach is that in fact those figures are no longer present in the studio. I took this picture of my students in the studio and what interested me was that there is not a teacher in sight. There isn't a teacher, there isn't a critic, there is just a student and his laptop who had discovered how to do something and suddenly that's where all the attention lies in the studio. It is very much upsetting and overturning the classical and modern assumption of what a teacher-student relationship is like in a classroom. And it is of course upsetting in serious ways—particularly the organization of studio space—that Mies and others installed within the heart of architectural culture in the twentieth century.

This of course is one of the classic photographs of the twentieth century: this is Crown Hall with its Fordist production of young Mies architects where all students literally have the same pose, the same drawing table. (fig.2) All tables are aligned in columns and aisles and rows and Mies's factory for the production of more Mies, which it was the perfect machine for.

This of course eventually evolves into the kind of information and communication spaces that we all in a strange way still inhabit today. But I think there is a breakdown of that model that we're going through whether we want to admit it or not.

WHY SCHOOLS MUST BE DISRUPTERS (AGAIN)

Before I go into the core part of the talk I would like to give you a little preamble, which sets up the center part of the presentation tonight, which is that architecture, architectural schools as technologies, are most interesting when they become that one kind of technology we're all interested

2 Crown Hall, Mies van der Rohe, 1950–1956, Chicago

in today more than any other, which is of course disruptive technologies. Technologies that have the ability to turn upside down the relationships between institutions, academies, teaching regimes, work regimes, concepts, philosophies—all of which are being upset profoundly by technologies which allow us to communicate, talk and think in new and unexpected ways.

The twentieth century project of professionalizing architectural culture is now in place. A century ago it was an idea: that architects would go to a vocational academy, they would train to become qualified professionals and they would work to the standards of the service industries throughout their lives. That was the idea in the 1920s. By the 1940s countries like the United Kingdom and the US bring that into law and create architecture as a regulated profession, which in the 1960s a counterculture can react to. But it nonetheless continues throughout the twentieth century worldwide to the point today that architecture and architecture culture as we know it is a highly standardized, highly regimented profession and that schools have become vocational centers for equipping and training of students to enter that profession.

OK is the world's most known English language word and it is the only word said more often than *Coke*. Coke is a product that exists in more spaces, in more countries, than a representative of the United Nations. Nature has been extended into that kind of endless selling regime. And even when we die and are buried in cemeteries of course, we have things being sold to us in a neverending cycle of exchange.

As alien as many architects tend to treat that kind of reality, one of its most interesting features is that like modern advertising which literally evolved alongside modern architecture from the early twentieth century forward, the exchange space of the city is already deeply embedded within the culture of urbanism and architectural design.

Just to finish this part of the preamble and to suggest that there is a way in which schools can enter into this situation today, I pulled out a couple of images from the deep past of the *AA* which interest me because they go back to the very founding of a school like the *AA* in the mid-nineteenth century. This is the monogram and logo still used by our school today and its peculiar motto. The idea that you use beauty and truth to battle the world today almost seems naive to the point of failure.

But one of the interesting things about it is that it was penned originally by figures like John Ruskin who came to the *AA* in the 1850s. And one of the things that Ruskin does with his followers, including Walter Crane who designs the emblem for the *AA*, is to create for the first time in Europe a generation of artists and critics who take as their task the resistance to the first great wave of industrialization which was rolling across England. Ruskin famously attacks the acceleration of the industry that he thinks destroys the countryside and to a large part the cities of England in the latter half of the nineteenth century. He invents the idea that architects and artists have a role, a social responsibility to not enter into those forms of exchange but to actually stand back, question and interrogate the kind of things that were leading to what was called the railroadification of England and Europe.

Cities like Manchester are turned into production factories in a first wave of industrialization, which I think in many ways creates a kind of model for us to think about what happens when architecture confronts industrialization at the scale of which it is today. Architecture has never confronted a wave of industrialization that had worked itself into the very design systems that we all work with as architects. Today the design market is dominated by about six software packages owned and operated worldwide that become for us the common language, the shared basis for exchange that now organizes not only architecture and architectural culture but of course all of the other design industries and creative industries that work with that very same set of tools.

In the early twentieth century there was the first great wave of industrialization around building materials like glass and steel, which created for modern architects the need for a new model for architectural education. That was the force that created for van de Velde, for Gropius and others an argument, that architects need to learn and think differently. And with that they created the idea of the experimental school. A school where one would sit in workshops, instead of sitting in the École and staring at rocks and paintings, and literally work with the materials of the industrialized age, and out of that develop the principles of architecture.

And I think a century later—it is nearly a century since van de Velde's academy was formed in 1910 in Amsterdam—architects today confront a very similar condition where the demand upon us now is in fact to create a new model of architectural school.

In the mid-twentieth century figures like Le Corbusier thought the architect's body was so stable you could literally put dimensions to it and it became a model for how you organize space with the famous universal Modulor. (fig.3) By the 1970s John Travolta gives you a spectacular critique of Le Corbusier's view of the body. By the 1970s, what Travolta of course realizes is that it's a body in space and a body in motion that matters much more than its physical dimension. Which, you could say, becomes the model of how architects have worked for the last twenty or thirty years.

What architects today confront of course in the next step of that evolution is that our bodies are no longer purely organic in their arrangement, which is exactly the kind of body you are looking at here as I sit in front of a laptop and dependent on the inorganic materials that become a part of the design process and design platform that we all work with. And you can create not only new kinds of materials but new kinds of immaterial systems that we all now negotiate with when we think of what we call design projects or design platforms.

This is one of my design teams a few years ago mapping

over an average work week the file formats that they were passing a project through to try get it to the point of presenting models by the end of the week. Of course what architects are evolving are tools that have not to do with any particular system or file format but with the ability to control how material ideas flow across all of those formats.

The intelligence in working with this kind of system lies in the overview and not in the hyper specialization of any part of it. To overspecialize is to become a technician, which is the fate that many architects face today. And one of the challenges that schools have is to find ways in which students and staff can stand back and not get too close to any of those domains and to fall into the world of technicians.

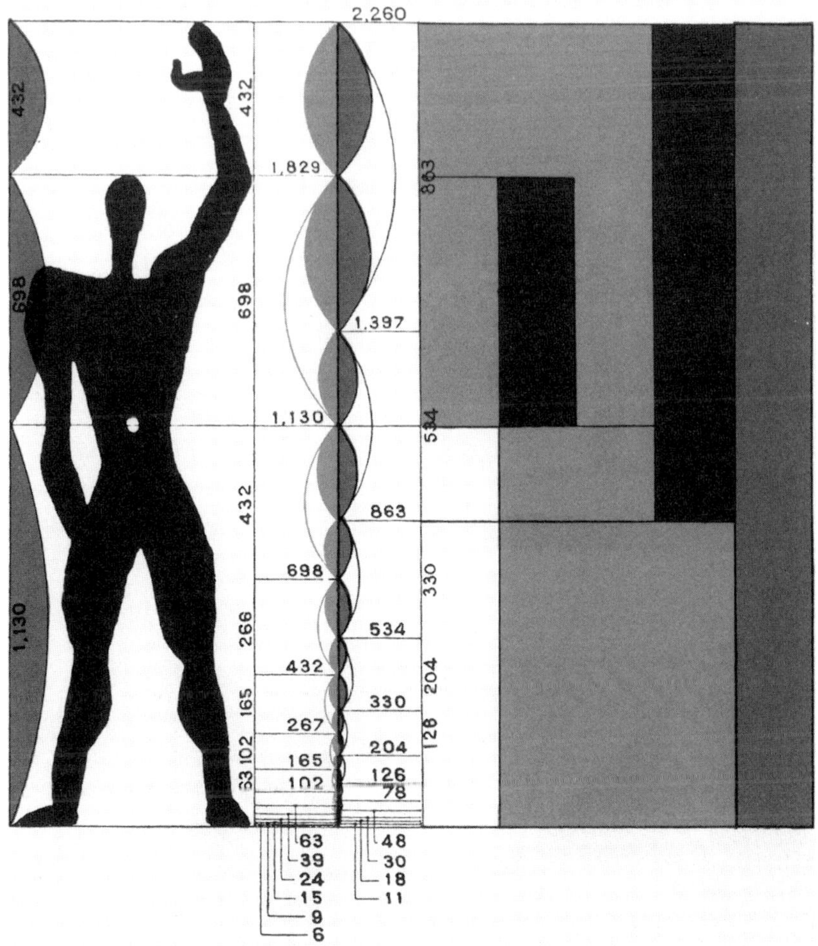

3 *Modulor*, Le Corbusier

7 POINTS TOWARDS A NEW KIND OF SCHOOL

The third and last part of the talk is really just going through a few points about what might become the basis for a new model of an architecture school today. And they're very straightforward points. In fact they are kind of self-evident, certainly not controversial.

1. SCHOOLS MUST AGAIN BECOME DISRUPTIVE TECHNOLOGIES

I have already said the first point and I'll just say it again: the idea of disruptive technologies. Technologies that don't sit within the school but the idea of the school as a piece of a very particular kind of technology whose job it is to open up our understanding of what a school should be. The very idea of the experimental schools in Europe was created in the early twentieth century around that kind of idea. And what they were attacking of course was the academy, which had institutionalized itself by the end of the nineteenth century but which offered no form of learning that would allow individuals to confront the new realities of the twentieth century.

If you look at the history of experimental schools like the Bauhaus one of the most interesting features is the performance space of the students, which absolutely confounds the pedagogical assumptions of people like Gropius and others. Which is certainly one of the lessons for me as a head of a school: students are the ones that determine how a school ought to operate. These are the students that voted Gropius out of office in 1926. He made it seven years in the Bauhaus before students kicked him out. And they kicked him out for a very interesting reason: he refused to teach architectural history, and that drove the students of the Bauhaus crazy for some reason.

Disruptive technologies are products, but they are also the basis for upending a whole series of social and industrial relationships today which are quite deep and profound—Napster of course being an early example of this. A simple product created by a 22-year-old college student had the ability to bring down the music industry in three years' time, before he too was brought down for making the mistake of putting all of the songs and files in one server instead of distributing it over the Internet.

These become models I think for the kind of challenges that schools face today. The same thing is happening in printing publication, the dominant form of communication and architectural culture, the printed book or monograph that circulated the work of architects worldwide. In the early twenty-first century that has become the basis for an entirely self-contained counterfeit industry of book publication that operates out of China. Any book that you know in the architectural world, whether you get it as a hard copy or as DVD. Ten years of *El Croquis* for five dollars delivered to your hotel room that evening with an instruction that if you want the hard copy he'll get it to you by 9 a.m. These become the kind of challenges that schools today in very real ways face as they negotiate all the learning space that we think all schools have been built around.

2. SCHOOLS MUST AGAIN BECOME PROTOTYPES, NOT BUILDING TYPES

The institutionalization of architecture schools evolved and modified what we think of as the building type of the architectural school. One of our deep interests back in London is not to treat a school as a building type but rather as a kind of working prototype in which the space of the school is not neutral and undifferentiated but the actual medium for reconfiguring the teaching and learning within it. The idea of course is that the material of the school becomes the material for learning. An experimental school is based on the premise that you learn by doing something. The best medium an architecture school can have for that is of course its own space and structure. So we spend a fair amount of time every year tearing out walls, floors, ceilings, canopies.

You'll find this embedded in experimental schools, that the prototype becomes much more influential as a teaching model than the repetition of known types, where architects literally learn by just building increasingly large-scale installations. A school like the AA [Architectural Association] took it upon itself to operate that way to allow those individuals, those teams, those collaborators to experiment, learn something and propel an idea forward.

There is a very interesting and deep history of prototyping within the culture of modern architecture. Frei Otto does something very similar in architecture in the 1970s. This is a model of his proposal for the Munich Stadium, which is a very interesting structural model. He's putting loads on that structural net to work out where the deflection and bending is and in effect letting the prototype do the design work instead of creating a model to sell a project. The model becomes part of the work. The prototype becomes part of the design itself, which is where the secret history of prototyping lies within modern architectural experimentation. Architects do a series of projects, test installations, learn something and move to the next project. Even in as late as the 1970s—to make Frank Gehry relevant again for architects today—what's so interesting about his career is that almost by instinct he is completely reinventing his identity, goes out and buys piles and piles of the cheapest material possible—sheet metal, chain link fence, plywood cardboard—and literally starts out prototyping and testing ideas that would create that identity that we all know today.

That's the kind of cultural context that the thinking of a school as a prototype might sit within today. It's not new and I think if you look back at the birth of what we think is the modern architectural project you'll find the very same sentiment at the core. A very young Le Corbusier in 1917 with no clear expertise of concrete at all undertakes a house for a couple in Switzerland, but that very same year draws a diagram that distills the lessons in that, which becomes one of the dominant diagrams in twentieth century architectural culture. The building of the house was not a mastery of construction. It was a learning exercise which allowed him to then communicate the imperative that the structural concrete system that he was working with set out for today.

3. SCHOOLS MUST CONFIGURE THEMSELVES AS MOBILE NETWORKS, NOT IMMOVABLE OBJECTS

Most certainly the idea of a school would be a school as a network and not as an object. Networks are unlike objects in very interesting ways. The idea of the *École des Beaux-Arts* where you and I would stand for five years in front of dead rocks and stare at these rocks to learn architecture has been completely supplanted by the model of the school as a network that gives information across servers, archives and hubs, and allows communication to work in a fundamentally new way.

The school in London becomes in fact only one of a series of hubs around the world which we operate. I have about 700 students enrolled in London this year, and about 1,000 students in about two dozen programs around the world, which lets us of course send students from London out into the world to actually engage with these conditions and settings and hopefully bring things back: ideas, experiences, accidents, souvenirs or whatever it might be that might have an effect on what goes on in London the following year. A school becomes a kind of planetary system in which unexpected overlaps and occurrences might happen. It has been called by some a missionary or imperialist model of inhabitation. I'm not sure that's the case.

In a world like ours today where people travel the way they do I think one of the most interesting things that kind of activity does is that it upends a kind of normal expectation of the relation between the studio and the site.

What we're interested in doing is basically reversing the kind of travel we've had to a city like London for many years. About 90 percent of our students come from overseas, which is a very strange feature of the school there. But of course what we began realizing a few years ago is this diagram only becomes interesting if you can think of it as a form of two-way exchange. So this sort of visiting school model that we are experimenting with now is just thinking about ways in which London can be connected back out to the world in unexpected ways.

To a great degree a school today is nothing but a network of moving bodies. One of the models I like to use to describe schools is to think of them as airports and not destinations. This is the most heavily inhabited building in human history. It is about 20 miles from the AA at Heathrow Airport. About 65 million to 70 million people per year pass through this amazing space for another few years until Beijing surpasses the UK. But it becomes a model to a certain degree for how you might think a school could operate. You don't come to school as a destination. You come for a momentary transition in your life that will propel out you to new and unexpected places.

4. SCHOOLS MUST FOCUS ON THE INVENTION OF AUDIENCES, NOT ARCHITECTS

One of the great mistakes most of the schools make is that they think they invent architects. It's like the worst mistake if you think of it. It's a horrible mistake. If you think that way then you'll end up like Crown Hall. You'll end up with a factory whose job is to produce architects as you already know them. In fact what makes schools most interesting is when they focus on the creation of audiences that they can then embed their students within, and with that create sensibilities and ideas that eventually evolve into the architectural personalities you know. Graduates of the AA—all very different figures and personalities—weren't nurtured as talents within a school that made them. They were individuals who grew in a setting that had wrapped around them hundreds and hundreds of conversations, ideas, debates, discussions that eventually formed their identities in some way, that created the kind of professional identities that their careers eventually define.

That for me is the activity of a school. Within the formal coursework of the AA, the stuff that interests me most is what we call the public program where all the publications, lectures, symposia, conferences, competitions, installations, prototypes that create audiences—where people come together and present their work for discussion or disagreement.

In some way schools become broadcasters. That's what institutions do. Academic institutions communicate ideas; they store them to then be able to be communicated to larger audiences.

All the paperwork we produce over 32 weeks, we sort of bundle it together into a box and send it out to audiences and in a way enter into this interesting and deep history of how institutions have been doing that continuously since the birth of what we think of as the modern architecture school. It's a form we love playing with where posters—the production of posters—becomes a natural extension of the studio.

We have studios that take that on as their design task for the year, others producing magazines and books. And of course merging that into what we think of as the exhibition space as a natural and straightforward activity. And again I think this is just a reiteration of this impulse that modern architecture has long had embedded in it, which is publication and publicity space is architectural space in some way.

5. ARCHITECTS ARE NO LONGER SINGULAR IN THEIR ORGANIZATION.

It is one of our peculiarities that we tend to think of ourselves as individuals. The discipline, like the profession, is entirely distributed in its organization, orientation and definition. The tools that architects use—even in the early twentieth century—have evolved and are now absolutely distributed and collaborative in their imperative and design.

That kind of tool that Frank Lloyd Wright famously used every day in the morning when he sharpened his pencil, went around and marked up everybody's drawings—that kind of a tool no longer exists. That tool has been replaced by a tool that is being used by everybody in the room at the same time.

This is the most famous architecture student of the twentieth century: a middle aged Philip Johnson at Harvard in the 1940s, learning to dress and look like every other student, being trained to compete with every other individual in the room or as a collective to gather around the acknowledged master. That model has been absolutely upended by a world in which identity is today constructed and fluid in its definition. The architect is a composite figure of those people whom he or she works with.

Obviously the figures we think of as the architects are then multiplying. From SOM, who perfected the corporate model, to Superstudio: design thinking in the middle of the twentieth century evolves out of the individual mind and tool to smart groups who have shared purpose and collective interest but operate beyond singular figures.

I put together a show a couple of years ago of a great generation in the 1960s who came of age as the great masters are dying off, with Frank Lloyd Wright in 1959, Le Corbusier in 1965, Mies in 1969. As that generation falls away a generation steps up on the stage who is most interesting for adopting a kind of rock'n'roll model in which people start working together in groups.

It becomes a very dominant model. And Wolf, every time I've seen you lecture, you would mention the Rolling Stones at some point in the lecture. I think that collaborative impulse, the performative impulse of that generation, really takes hold within the discipline. You could maybe say it starts to wane at about this moment for me: when Bono meets the Pope and begins dressing like the Pope you know that the collaborative model as it was formerly defined is starting to undergo some serious change.

But that collaborative impulse is another definition really of how schools operate in the construction of audiences. Architecture is a spectacularly socialized form of knowledge. Architecture is what we all treat as architecture. And to test that thesis you need to be in rooms amongst people for the discussion and debate to take place.

This becomes what the model in the twenty-first century operates as: a kind of crowd-like phenomena. The individual not just works alongside other individuals in a collaborative team. He or she works amongst a larger landscape of technology, platforms and media, all of which operate with all of the peculiarity of crowds much more than rational or understandable individuals.

6. SCHOOLS ARE AN ATMOSPHERE (AND SHOULD NEVER BE A DIAGRAM)

The most interesting thing about schools is to make them an atmosphere, not a diagram, and never have a teaching plan for schools. Just make schools into places where people want to be. This includes that the classrooms are a distraction, the attention is elsewhere. The great problem of most schools is they look like classrooms, they act like classrooms and they have rules. And that makes nobody happy.

Let the performance of the students in the school become the center of the school. And let them begin to rehearse the idea that they will evolve their understanding, their experience and their ideas of architecture in relation to some kind of audience. Which eventually—if everything goes right—will evolve into a group of people that includes those who will support you and make possible these strange ideas that you have. Again, well tested in things like the art world: literally 50 years ago, when the studio as we know it was converted by Andy Warhol into a pure performance space. As he said that the last thing he would do with a studio in New York is actually make sculpture or painting. He hired people to do that across the river and to not bother him. The point of being an artist is to get people together to exchange the ideas and assumptions about what art or architecture might be at any one time.

7. SCHOOLS MUST BECOME (AGAIN) CULTURAL SPACES, NOT VOCATIONAL CENTERS

I've already made the point earlier: the idea of architectural schools today as a culture space, not as a vocational center. The coursework takes care of itself. You all do the work, you do the projects and you have great teachers. The interesting thing becomes then how you wrap that thing around the unexpected installation, the performance, event space, discussion, conversation with an audience, that brings unexpected people together in new and unexpected ways.

I introduced Rem Koolhaas and Peter Eisenman as being collectively 147 years old to the AA audience. They had never shared a stage together. In 2006, when we put them together we had a fantastic conversation about what might constitute a critical project today within architecture. They have as you all know very different opinions of what that is. But this is the purpose of a school today: to engage these kinds of minds with committed audiences to absolutely challenge our expectations or understanding about what architecture might be today.

I think that is actually what architecture schools do best. It's the thing architecture schools can teach other universities extremely well. No other faculties do it the way we do it. In fact it's the one thing we all take for granted.

We live in a world today in which media now distributes agency to the audience, not to the producer, not to the author, not to the artist. Interestingly, because of social media, agency now lies with you. The question is how schools can harness that agency, so that those who use that media can see it as a legitimate form of learning and experience and not as a form of passive game playing and distraction.

END: TODAY'S SCHOOL IS INCREASINGLY INVISIBLE

Maybe the end stage of this evolution, that I find so interesting, is of course that as the school continues to evolve in this form, the school itself begins to disappear. These technologies have the capacities to take learning well outside the boundaries of this building or the building that I inhabit back in London.

Too often, architecture schools imagine they're going to be around forever. They are nineteenth century institutions and they are facing the same challenges as any other nineteenth-century institution, the ultimate threat is what happened to the *New York Times*. As people learn to think, communicate and learn things differently, they can become irrelevant.

The very same year that the *New York Times* opens their grand new building in Manhattan—they wouldn't disclose the actual construction price, it was rumored to be a billion dollars but it was several hundred million for sure—their share price is tanking as we all stop reading the newspaper. Because we all start looking at the news on mobile phones and on computers. In 2009 the company of the *New York Times* is worth less than the Sunday edition of the *New York Times*. Their share price fell below four dollars, which means it is cheaper to buy the company than the actual newspaper.

This is the final issue of the *New York Times*, which has been prepared and laid out for several years by the *Times*. They know they're going to stop printing at some point. They don't know when. They hope that you all have bought recently into their new subscription service online. The challenge really for schools is very similar as learning spaces and communication centers evolve out of the studio, as schools and institutions evolve out of singular places. The great challenge for schools is how they possibly reinvent themselves to become relevant to audiences like you who rightly want to be elsewhere most of the time.

And I'll stop here. Thanks!

Hani Rashid

Circuit Training

Edited by Kristy Balliet

I would like to welcome everyone. Good evening! It is overwhelming to again have such a large audience. Now let me shortly introduce today's speaker Hani Rashid, although he is not unknown here. He, together with his partner Lise Anne Couture, co-founded Asymptote in 1988. Asymptote's projects range from spatial experimentations and installations to urban design to computer-generated environments and architecture realized in the US, Europe and Asia. It is a good opportunity today not only to welcome him as today's speaker but also to announce him as the new professor of architectural design at the University of Applied Arts beginning next semester, Fall 2012.
— Introduction by Gerald Bast

I'm never speechless, but now I'm speechless. I am extremely happy and excited to come to this school. You sometimes wonder, if you were able to design a school or a place where one studies architecture, what would it be like? This school is in fact a ready-made, magnificent place to teach and learn architecture and other related disciplines.

I call this talk circuit training. Partially because I was thinking about what we as architects do and why do we do it and also how we do it in terms of our discipline and other disciplines, but also what's similar with other disciplines. I think in teaching and practicing as an architect there is a constant form of circuit training. We are constantly going back and forth, and delving into conceptual thinking. Then we come out of that, run the circuit and go back and train again.

I thought, well, let's just run through some of the architectural things we've done and try to tie together an idea, which is in fact what happens in our discipline: it's a constant return, a constant spiraling back to the origins and back out again into the space of making architecture. We did an installation for the Guggenheim a few years ago for a show called "Moving Pictures." It was an interesting commission. They asked us to design the interior of Frank Lloyd Wright's Guggenheim. It's difficult because you don't want to play around too much with that building but we had to find

a way to intervene in a spatial way, to make sense of the place.
We carried all the work off the surfaces of the museum and we produced this strange spiral condition, which continues to move down through the building's architectural anatomy. There are many theories about this building but the one I found interesting was the one that suggests it is in fact a screw being put into Manhattan's Central Park. It was Frank Lloyd Wright's attempt to produce an infinite circuit of viewing art and to embed this thing into the city fabric. (fig.1) We continued that and we found when we built this very innocuous little thing that it became a place for people to sit, for people to think and engage with their bodies in the spiral of the Guggenheim.

I was driving through Seoul, Korea, not too long ago in a taxi and I stopped and saw a sign. It was a Jeff Koons sculpture produced as an advertisement for a department store with a woman saddled on Jeff Koons's piece. And I thought, art has really come a long way. It has become this kind of commercial pop condition and in fact in many ways it can now be applied wholesale to any kind of marketing ploy.

In the spirit of that—and this was a little bit before I saw this piece—we were asked to do an intervention for the Guggenheim in Abu Dhabi on Saadiyat Island. We produced galleries that would start to work with the development of Frank Gehry's building and with Jean Nouvel's building. It started as this kind of cell division. The idea was that we would build two enigmatic art-like pavilions to house art but in and of themselves be fetishized objects. We produced a scaffolding-like structural system and then thought about them as perverse objects for themselves. They would sit in the Abu Dhabi desert onsite as these strange, enigmatic UFO-like chrome shells, and these would contain contemporary art and all kinds of other things. (fig.2) In a strange way this speaks to a kind of interesting space that exists in between architectural work and art production. Now you find many artists working as architects doing remarkable things and you have architects who in fact are bridging over into other realms. So the idea of producing art galleries—and in fact these were kinetic—that can be seen as both functional objects but at the same time as fetishized objects of desire sitting in the Abu Dhabi desert were really key to us for the design of this project. The idea was really to produce a kind of instrument in that environment.

In terms of Abu Dhabi, the environment is an unbelievably powerful situation. You have bright sunlight, the extremes of culture and the meeting of the East and

1 Moving Pictures Exhibition, 2002, Guggenheim Musuem, New York

2 Guggenheim Pavilion at Saadiyat Island, 2006, Abu Dhabi

West. For us the chance to build a large project in the Abu Dhabi context—in this case the YAS Hotel—was an interesting opportunity not just to build another five-star hotel, another addition to that environment, but to work in this enigmatic space between art and architecture, between desire and function.

There is a grid shell, and the grid shell in and of itself is a kind of field sculpture. (fig.3) The shells, the grid shells, the different sized panels and the little LED lights resembling hairs or spikes produce a very strange object in the Abu Dhabi context—an object that somehow feels like veils and clothing but at the same time has an animal-like quality. From an architectural point of view it was, pure and simple, about creating a phenomenological architecture in desert conditions. (fig.4) To create some kind of fascinating object, a fascinating surface, is what really drove this project. It was important for us to discover, as our environmental engineer pointed out in the middle of the design process, that we had in fact created by virtue of the stack effect an updraft, a naturally ventilated condition around the building—much like a desert creature that has spikes and scales to keep its body cool. The building is always windy and always ventilated even though the desert is still and stable. This idea of the cooling body was a nice plus to the architectural desire to build a surface.

One aspect that is not often talked about in terms of what you see in the building is the optical interference between the structure, the glass and the actual cars racing on the Formula One track that runs through the building. It's a very beautiful and almost hypnotic situation where the cars and the building interface. In a strange way what we discovered was that we had created a building that has its own views. The interiors were designed so that there was an interplay between typical spaces and artistic interventions that would do similar things with light, space and form or furniture and very simple accoutrements,

3 YAS Hotel, 2007–2009, Abu Dhabi

textures and devices to make the spaces clean in a severe way. (fig.5) This building is in fact two buildings: the bridge over the track and an arena with a stage on the ground. The building was not so much about its material presence and physicality, although it is very muscular and physical. It also becomes a place for various events. The building plays a sensual game with the landscape, with the territory it occupies and maneuvers around like a kind of bodysuit around the physical world. The building changes in the night: it has an integrated LED system. It becomes this fascinating place, a dematerialized building that in fact exists as a kind of blur during events. It is captured always as this kind of field condition behind these spectacular fast-moving cars. (fig.6)

I will switch gears a bit to the projects that are becoming more our focus: urbanism and cities, new cities, new ideas of how we build cities, how we build cities from scratch, how we built cities in the past and how do we interpret cities?

We completed a piece, a video installation at the Documenta 2002 in Kassel. We took skyscrapers from Hong Kong, Tokyo, New York and other cities and mapped them into a very primitive animation system where we could run them like a scroll over an object—which was a kind of metamorphosis of an automobile body—and see if we could in fact make this object read the city as digital data. (fig.7) The idea was to understand city space not so much in the way we had traditionally understood it but more taking off from Yona Friedman's Constant and produce a kind of space that is reading the city in terms of its digital data, its phenomenological situation and its reality as a kind of place or circumstance. When you walked into the space you saw the physical body, which was morphed on the building, and the city would start to run on the surface. Wanting to understand what the sonic data was like in these places, the soundtrack was derived from receiving elevator conversations in these cities from friends around the world.

Our project in Busan, South Korea, just started again. The visions of the actual tower went through a number of permutations and more and more gravitated to a single tower. We were really determined to use this triad tower. (fig.8) How we could bundle and bind it became very important, how we could contain the core and have it rise 680 meters in Busan. It still contains the DNA of the tri-prong or triad condition.

For a port terminal, the idea was to create a spirit of these symbiotic buildings that work in a kind of circuit condition with each other—the ship and the building here become a unified agent, a possibility for assembly. The building is in fact the next generation of what we were doing on the YAS building. The circuitry and the lines determining architectural maneuvers are based on the idea that ships dock next to this building, that the terminal is elevated to allow an urban space to take hold and to allow night markets and interventions to be a part of this building merging with the city. (fig.9) With our engineers we worked on a perforated condition. In this case we produced a system that in fact contains a series

4 YAS Hotel, 2007–2009, Abu Dhabi

5 YAS Hotel, 2007–2009, Abu Dhabi

6 YAS Hotel, 2007–2009, Abu Dhabi

7 Documenta Video Installation, 2002, Kassel

8 World Business Center Solomon Tower, 2007 (ongoing), Busan, South Korea

9 Kaohsiung Marine Gateway (rendering), 2010 (ongoing), Kaohsiung, Taiwan

10 Kaohsiung Marine Gateway (interior rendering), 2010 (ongoing), Kaohsiung, Taiwan

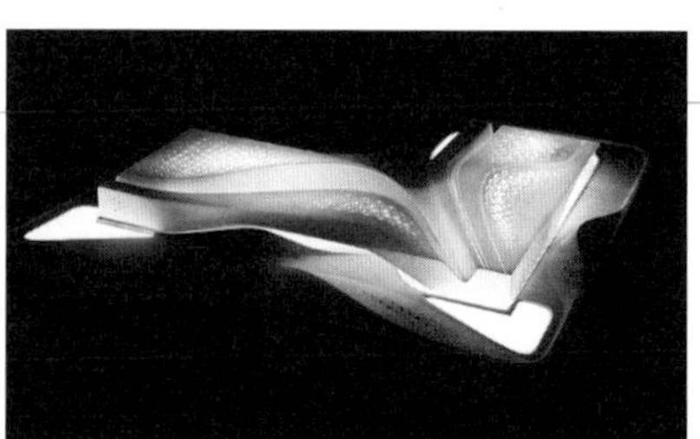

11 Beukenhof Crematorium and Auditorium, 2011 (ongoing), Schiedam, the Netherlands

of birdlike kites above. They actually adjust to light by virtue of computer programming and fold and change according to different light and heat conditions. Back to the idea of the virtual: it's a nice functional piece but at the end of the day it's really a beautiful sky that will be in a constant state of animation and change. (fig.10) It's a building that is in constant spatial dialogue with the city, the ships, and the activities that take place here. I think it's very important that like the hotel in Abu Dhabi, the building gains a presence and power by virtue of marrying urbanism to function. It becomes a place of wonder, a place of magic in a way, for the city.

The last project I want to show is starting construction in the Netherlands. Our client Peter Sanders will be turning 99 in September. He is a patron of the arts and is very important in the Dutch context. I was touched by this commission. Mr. Sanders asked for a crematorium and auditorium in Schiedam near Rotterdam, as a gift to the city. (fig.11) It's an interesting project because in Peter's infinite wisdom and amazing generosity he doesn't see it as a crematorium for any particular religion or even for himself necessarily but rather as a multi-denominational place. There are actually 12 religions more or less that share this neighborhood of Schiedam. The idea is to build a place where people can go to commemorate the loss of a loved one or do other things like performance art and so on in the building. It would function for all the various religions. For us it was key to come up with a scheme that would speak to each particular culture, and each culture would find within the building a kind of importance for their own set of beliefs. It could not become a church, a mosque, a synagogue, a temple, a Buddhist temple. It had to really be a crossover.

In the original sketches a kind of circuit of the building was evolving. It quickly became apparent to us that we would have to find a way to impregnate the building with this character of culture and life. So the various halls were tattooed at first and eventually penetrated the drawings. We started by putting together various windows and mathematical designs from various religions into a single perforation pattern that would actually allow for the building to have a kind of meaning. (fig.12) The halls are planned such that they could have various funerals and situations taking place at the same time. The building exists in many ways as a sort of flower-like form. There are a series of channels on the roof, which run water constantly through the building. There will be the constant sound of water running into waterfalls, across the ceiling and across the spaces. (fig.13) The light comes through perforated openings and produces a very important and sacred light for all religions.

Ultimately, the idea to produce a beautiful, somewhat enigmatic, somewhat powerful architectural statement within the spirit of a person like that makes it a very important piece of work—not only in the art historical context but in realizing how his friendships in life are essential. I think the most important aspect of his character is his unbelievable optimism about everything. Through art and people he has galvanized very important friendships throughout his entire life that he relies on.

What is so unbelievably important is the idea of friends in architecture, and not just as connections or help but really this idea that we have this powerful relationship to the work we do and it is important that our human relationships work at the same level as our love affair with architecture.

Okay, that's my talk. Thank you very much!

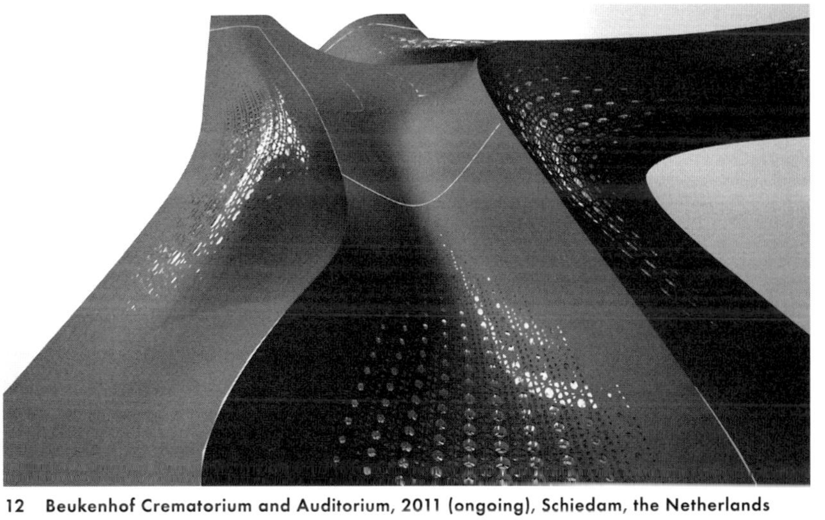

12 Beukenhof Crematorium and Auditorium, 2011 (ongoing), Schiedam, the Netherlands

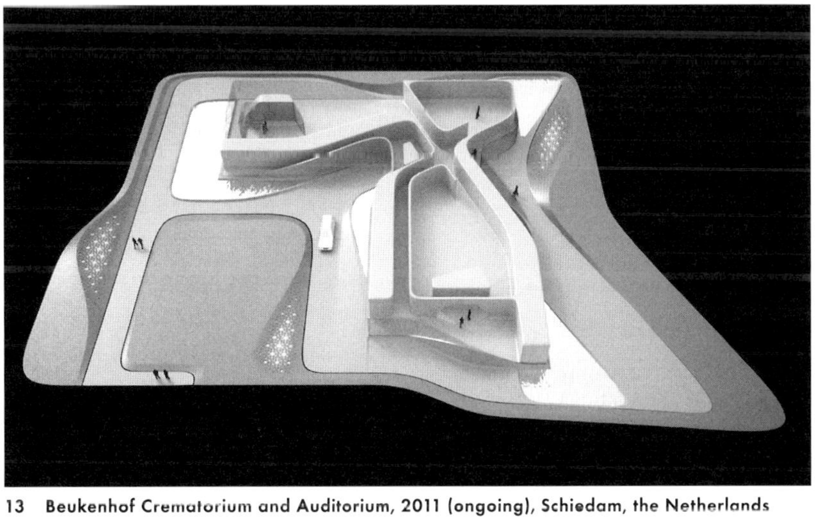

13 Beukenhof Crematorium and Auditorium, 2011 (ongoing), Schiedam, the Netherlands

Michael Rotondi

Hybrid of Extremes

Edited by Guvenc Özel

Our guest tonight is Michael Rotondi. Michael Rotondi is not his real name because we know him as Roto. He doesn't look like an LA guy, he looks like a mixture between a Japanese, Chinese and an "Indisch" guy. This also charcterizes his work, I would say. He has a mind that is open to all cultures, open to all architectural terms and, most importantly, he is the most open-minded teacher I know. The first time I was in LA I went to his office. Zaha told me, "You should visit a team, a young architectural team called Morphosis. The entrance is on Stone Avenue somewhere in LA." I found out where Stone Avenue was, I liked the name because it reminded me of the Rolling Stones. And I expected the architecture of Morphosis to be like the Rolling Stones. But when I came to the office, a garage of course, Michael said, "I will show you some pieces, architectural pieces." And the first project he showed me was a building by Eric Owen Moss. And I thought, this would never ever happen in Vienna. If you visit Vienna and go to Hollein's office, he will never first show you a project by someone else, like Domenig or Himmelb(l)au. This was my first impression of Michael. The second was when he said, "Okay, I'm going to be the dean of SCI-Arc, would you like to come teach at our school?" This was the beginning of my career as a teacher. Michael Roto is, of course, much better: he is of course an architect. He is of course a teacher. I think the most important thing is, and I hope we can see it today, his understanding of different things, which is more than just architecture. Let's welcome RoTo.
— Introduction by Wolf D. Prix

It's unusual to think of an institution as a teacher, but in the very beginning when we started SCI-Arc, being a positive outgrowth of the sixties, there were certain values and strategies that served as a framework for our concepts of how we would organize our new community and engage each other. We left the university because of profound differences, but instead of being angry and "blowing things up," figuratively speaking, we decided to construct the world that we imagined instead of trying to change the one that already existed. Intentionally, we had no structure in the very beginning. We didn't even define ourselves as teachers and students. There was no framework or predetermined rules of engagement. Conflicts were negotiated in the here and now and became creative interactions. This was one great lesson. What we also learned was that we had to take responsibility for our lives, which we thought conceptually we could do, but we had never learned how to do that. So it can be said that the school was truly a self-organizing system and that over the years it organized into a society. We had a common ground, which was for the school to survive, for us to survive and to push architecture to the next level. It was always about being very open-minded about architecture, bringing everything into architecture without narrowing the scope. I have stayed openminded for a whole variety of reasons, and my interests have been very broad.

What I've realized after so many years of both practicing architecture and teaching is that I feel I'm a natural born teacher. And it happens not only in the classroom. I see teaching as a theory of economy, that whatever you know you basically give it away. The economy that we grew up with in America is one that you acquire, you store and you spend strategically, in order to acquire more. Any ideas that you have you keep to yourself. They are intellectual property, trade. Right now in America, I think there is innovation, but not true inventions. The greatest period of invention in America was a couple hundred years ago. Benjamin Franklin, who was one of the founders of the country, had many inventions. He did not patent anything. His belief was that anything anybody invents should be put out into the public realm, so that other people can learn as quickly as possible to take it to the next place. SCI-Arc was predicated on that. It was and still is about cooperation first and competition second. We cooperate with each other and compete against the standard that is set.

So I'm a teacher who practices architecture. Teaching and architecture, as you will see, are integrated into one thing. And maybe it will be coherent. If not then I say, "If you're a cook, whatever the recipe, if you burn the chicken you call it Cajun (blackened)." You come up with a new concept that redefines the situation.

The following are some thoughts that are embedded in my broader worldview, and serve as my *frames of reference. Cooperation is a biological necessity. Teaching and learning are fundamental to evolution.* And coming from a very large family I realized, *everyone is right from their own point of view*. The difficulty begins when we fail to negotiate. The middle is where the truth lies. *The observer is the observed*, which means who I am and what I manifest in the world is me. It's a mirror world. The universe is a continual symmetric operation: osmosis, homeostasis, reciprocal action and karma. *Don't let facts get in the way of imagination.*
To do so I suspend disbelief to believe that anything imaginable is possible. *Humans are inherently good.* This is evident when we create the conditions for others to make others feel safe.

Architecture is a window into a wonderland. Every moment is potentially a pedagogical moment. If we see the world filled with wonder, like a child does as if for the first time, then we always see something new that redefines what we thought we already knew. This is the beginner's mind. As Suzuki Roshi wrote, "In the beginner's mind we see many possibilities and in the expert's we see few."

This has been a way to constantly learn about people and the inherent meaning within projects. I search for simplicity on the other side of complexity, not by reduction but rather distillation. What I learned from the American Indian: *Look twice in order to see once*. This defines the relationship between inevitability and invisibility. *I like to make things, I love people*, which is most important of all.

Equilibrium: everything is always coming back to a state of rest, or zero, before it begins again, like a pendulum. This is another example of a symmetrical operation. Symmetry is not merely a vision; symmetry is conservation of energy—again, *Osmosis*—in the body's cell, equalizing pressure on both sides of the membrane. *Homeostasis*: the body always comes back to a state of rest. In *Physics*, the third law of motion or reciprocal action is action-reaction. And then in spiritual traditions, it is *karma*. What goes around comes around.

One of the biggest problems each of us faces, individually and collectively, is a world moving faster than thought and conscience. The problem is speed and fluency, and the question arises: is it possible to have a long-term vision in a short-cycle world?

Context has become very important in my mind. The world we create in turn recreates us. What we are creating is scripting us right now. I think we need to be aware and reverse this trend or we will be captured in the matrix. Order lies within everything. Even what we think is random has order within it. It regulates everything, at all scales, simultaneously. *Pattern* is the way we read that order. It's an index of things that have already happened. *Light*: what's fascinating about light is that you don't see it, unless it bounces off something. I think that's quite extraordinary because light and water are the source of life. Light triggers life and it is what brings things into existence. *Scale*: shifting scale as architects is a matter of fact, words into image into object and event into meaning. Symbolic language is the format for analogy and metaphor, which is the basis for creative conversion. Scale shift is how the mind moves through time and space as it creates in a matter of seconds. We have a natural capacity to do this because we are learning organisms, both individually and collectively. Creative dialogue can be defined as an infinite game.

I was on a plane recently from China and I had a conversation with a scientist who is doing really interesting research in nanotechnology. He is pulling apart the DNA molecule and then putting it back together, not because he is interested in genetics but rather because he said that the memory of the DNA molecule is so intense that no other part of the body has that kind of memory and he wanted to experiment. He pulls apart two strands, puts together four strands and then he starts connecting the four strands and he goes from a two-dimensional plane to a volume, making a gel out of it. He takes the gel, he puts it into a mold and then he puts it into water. He takes it out of the water, he puts it into another mold, it takes another shape, and then another shape and another shape, he puts it back into the water, it goes back to its original shape. So I ask him, "Is the memory in the gel or is it in the water?" He replies, "I don't know." And I said, "It's a mystery." He said, "No, there is no mystery in science." We spent three hours discussing whether mystery has a place in science. This made me start to think about what was lost or gained when alchemy became chemistry. That was when we went from the age of faith into the age of reason. And then I continued—the nineteenth century, the age of society and technology, and then the twentieth century, the age of economy and wealth and everything goes haywire, as we all know. Now I'm very optimistic, so I believe that this is the beginning of a process of coming back together. We are now moving into the age of humanity, and perhaps a new Axial Age as Karl Jaspers defined it. The current generation of students will take us there. My generation messed up, except for some great things that a few have done. In an age of reason when everything must have a metric to be considered, what is lost is wisdom.

The city we know best has an impact on our psyche. Los Angeles is my city. I know it like a second nature, its places and spaces and its people, 135 different languages and ethnicities. I also know all of its orders. The city grid, the linear and curvilinear freeways, the streets formed by the hilly terrain, and the invisible order of the communications systems, all in our body, in our intelligence and in our psyche. They become integrated in our subconscious, but how do they manifest in our actions? Los Angeles, because of the different types of ordering systems, has definitely had an impact on my psyche. The spatial and movement system of course is the grid. I mapped all the places that I've lived. I have never moved more than two miles from where I was born. This was depressing for a moment, but then again I travel so much it can be reassuring. In the neighborhood where I have always lived is the area where Frank Lloyd Wright first came, then Schindler and then Neutra and then the second and third generations after that. This has always been an inspiring area of the city to live, Silver Lake District.

1 Carlson-Regis House, 1992–1996, Los Angeles

2 Warehouse C, 1997, Nagasaki

I'll show you images of a few projects that I've completed, beginning with a house for my family that I decided to design and build extemporaneously, with no preconception or design drawings, just a model built in real time at full scale without an eraser. (fig.1)

Here is a project in Nagasaki, a 200-meter-long warehouse, the length of cargo ships. The bottom half is the warehouse and it was built by a land builder, and the top half was made by the largest shipbuilders in the world.

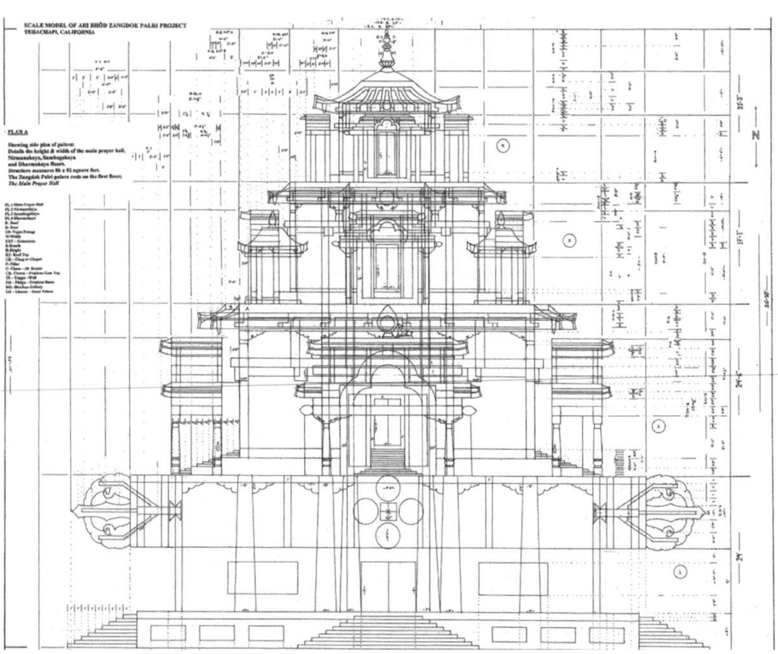

3 Construction Drawing of Ari Bhod Temple – Tibetan Buddhist in California

When I was doing this project in Nagasaki, I was fascinated by shipbuilding technology and the compound shapes that were possible. When I visited the shipyards and saw the way ships were built I knew I wanted to work with these builders. When I saw the ships close up, especially the ones with four steel spheres 30 meters in diameter that hold compressed gas, I thought, "I want one of those." The shipbuilder replied, "What are you going to do with it?" And I said, "I don't know." So I put it on top of a building. (fig.2) I got a call from the governor's office because everybody thought it was going to blow up in the city. He requested that I come to Nagasaki to attend a news conference. It was very formal in Japan, you know. So I'm very nervous when the questions begin.

They begin by asking about the colors of the building, green steel plate skin, orange sphere, blue structure and white rocks. They ask, "Why green?"
And I say, "Like mountain."
And they ask, "Why blue?"
And I say, "Like sky."
And then they ask, "Why orange?"

And I say, after a long pause ...
"Like orange!"
And they say, "Hai Rotondi-san!"

A great project for me is on 500 acres in the mountains of California. It is a monastery for a Tibetan Buddhist community that has a vision to sustain their culture as they let it grow and transform, to make a place for others to come and practice meditation. They are interested in both conservation and change. We completed a master plan and schematics for a mandala temple to Guru Rinpoche, and places for staff and visitors to learn about meditation in peaceful surroundings. (fig.3) This is a project where you have to recede. You have to become very transparent because it's not about me expressing my will. It is about preserving their language and culture.

And now to a building on Hollywood Boulevard that we just finished. It is essentially a public space—the building is a black box, but it is accessible to the public on the ground and on the roof. (fig.4) Projects like this beg the question, "Is it possible to integrate into intellectual practice, which is primarily architecture, and spiritual practice?" When I say spiritual I don't mean religion. It means matters of mind and matters of heart. There are certain projects that allow me to continue with the practice while I'm doing architecture. I have to immerse myself not only in the culture but in their practices. When I want to know what meditation is like I have to go for two weeks inside to meditate before I know what it's like and how hard it is for the mind to be quiet and for your body to be still.

And the architecture has to be the same because the more focused you become in higher states of concentration, the more perceptive we are and the density of detail in the outer world converts into visual noise. When this is eliminated information is flowing from within us.

In a house project in New Jersey, the objective was simply to figure out how complex we could make something and still make it coherent. (fig.5) We set up a system of rules that were manifested geometrically and materially. And then if it's drawn two-dimensionally, it's conceived as a three-dimensional system.

The school of architecture came from working with the students on music. (fig.6) I asked them to draw their favorite piece of music and the drawing had to be as long as a body. They had to do a melodic line and then a rhythmic beat, and I was surprised at the diversity of music that they came up with, and then we basically pulled it all into one drawing.

In the rainforest in Costa Rica we designed a school and it surprised me that everything is food

4 Madame Tussauds, 2006–2011, Hollywood

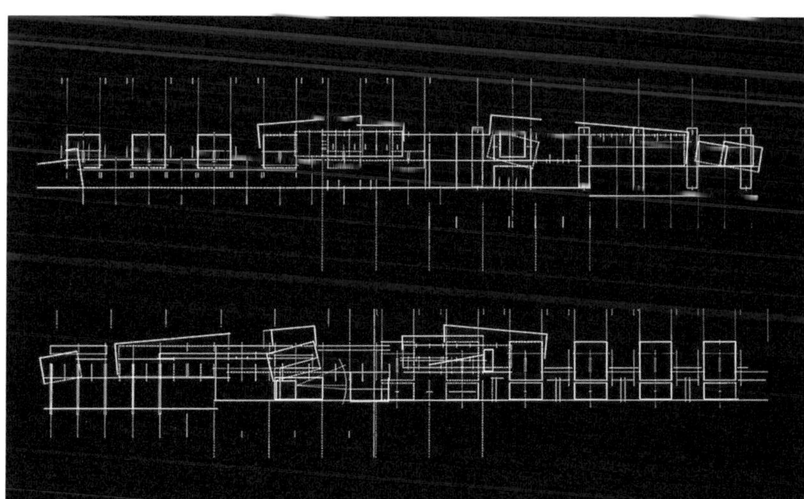

5 New Jersey House (section drawing), 1990–1996

for everything else. This is my model for understanding how everything can coexist simultaneously and benefit everything. There is an utter stillness in the dynamic processes in the forest. It is a steady state, utterly still and quiet.

Another project of cultural sustainability is for Native Americans in the center of America. I learned more than I could have imagined about the hybrid of extreme. The American Indians defined relationships as mutually beneficial and the basis of meaning. Everything in their world was simultaneously practical and profound. So when they mapped the sky, it was for their spiritual journey, and for geography. It was basically their GPS system to navigate as their bodies were moving through space and their spirit. The building was also conceived as an instrument for reading the dynamics of the sky. (fig.7) The building on a reservation is situated to allow the summer solstice and winter solstice to come through.

6 Architecture and Art Building, Prairie View, 2003–2005, Texas A&M University, College Station

7 Sinte Gleska University, 1994–1998, Rosebud Reservation

In the desert of central California we restored a motel and converted it into a retreat. (fig.8) It is a place that sits atop a naturally hot aquifer. Next winter when it will get really cold, imagine the naturally hot mineral water. You need to make your reservation fast.

This is a road to the Second Mesa, which is the oldest human settlement in the United States. (fig.9) This is Hopi; it's been there for a couple thousand years. This is actually a great road, especially at night when there is no light, when it's completely dark. You turn off your headlights and you take your hands off your steering wheel. It's better to do it when your loved ones are not in the car. They get scared. But it's also great to do in the desert. When you drive your car out into the desert, the car moves very slowly by itself without your foot on the accelerator. You can get out of the car while it's moving and walk around in the desert and get back in the car. It is such a liberating feeling. You keep on getting out, you walk ... maybe, you know, have some water, some juice and you get back in the car. So I'm always experimenting, in a variety of ways, always experimenting.

Communal life—is it possible for us to work in ways that remind us that we are interdependent and a part of something grand? This is why societies create reasons to gather until we achieve something together that gives meaning to our relationships and to our lives. Historically the farmers would gather to build their neighbor's barn. The barn was important, but the collective action even more so, and that's why we continually do this. (fig.10) I think this is the way we work in schools of architecture. The creative moment is a very intimate moment, and a very private moment, but then whatever you discover becomes public and it is presented and shared with everyone else. And that's the important thing. The bees and the ants, the termites and the wasps have known this. They are first and foremost altruistic, which means generous towards each other. This is how they survive in sum total as a living organism; if they become individualistic they get kicked out.

What I've realized and seen in Los Angeles—especially in each of the four seasons in Los Angeles, as we say: the fire, the rain, mudslides and the earthquakes—is how everybody becomes altruistic. Everybody cooperates and cares for each other. Is it possible to be altruistic in the best of times, not just the worst of times?

CONCLUSION

Human civilization has endured for millennia, fostered by its most fundamental biological imprint—survival. In the last few years I have visited remote villages in America, China and Iran that are still vital, having endured for 3000 to 6000 years, evidence that the human enterprise is a great wonder, and the most complex of all life forms. It is responsive, adaptive and innovative to any and all forces that challenge its integrity.

- transgressions within the species
- the speed of change that challenges the depth of our memory
- global interactions that challenge our local identities
- the needs of people living in societies being confronted by the autonomous logic of ...
- human institutional structures, and their concepts of power, politics, and money
- forces of nature that are scales beyond real comprehension, let alone preparation

All of these issues and the potential problems that arise are hugely difficult ones, and possibly cannot be overcome in the long term, so why should we try, one might ask? Because it is the right thing to do, and because creative people like big problems. The bigger the problem, the bigger the motivation, the bigger the smile. It is a gift to be an architect, it is definitely a gift to be a teacher and now I can say after so many years, it is truly a gift to have so many friends and comrades, like all of you. I am blessed. Love to you all tonight.

8 Miracle Manor Retreat, 1997–2011, Desert Hot Springs, California

9 View Towards the Second Mesa

10 Communal Life

Carme Pinós

From the Context

Edited by Justin Diles

1 University of Economics (rendering), 2011, Vienna, Austria

Carme Pinós is an architect and teacher from Barcelona. She creates wonderful buildings. I especially recommend visiting her tower in Guadalajara, Mexico. After seeing this project you will understand what she is always saying about architecture. Namely, that it must be much more than just building. When I visited her office not so long ago, Carme showed me the most beautiful models I've ever seen. But they were very, very tiny. If an architectural model is bigger than a matchbox, Carme might say it's too large. Of course architecture is much more than building models, architecture is thinking. Tonight you will see that the work of Carme Pinós is incredibly thoughtful.
— Introduction by Wolf D. Prix

I will start my lecture with a building that is under construction here in Vienna and then present three towers, three projects that are a reflection on the question: What is a tower? I'll conclude with an exhibition building for Zaragoza, Spain.

VIENNA UNIVERSITY OF ECONOMICS

The first project is for the new Vienna University of Economics campus in the Prater Park. The pretension of the master plan, which is not our design, is to make the campus more urban. It keeps the idea of the street instead of putting buildings in a garden as is often done in America. Ironically, the university is in the middle of a huge garden, but the campus architect wanted to create a more urban piece. We won the competition to do a project for one department. It's one department but the master plan calls for two buildings. So a condition was to make a street between two pieces, but because the program is for a single department we have to connect them.
I didn't want to do this simply by connecting two buildings with bridges. I wanted to create a complexity—a building with the complexity that you find in cities. My strategy is to have one building hide the other building. (fig.1) If the goal of the master plan is to create an urban space then my project will work like an urban building.

In a way, the program is very abnormal: offices and offices and offices. The ground floor has classrooms but no auditorium, nothing that can structure a building. Only offices, the corridor and the library, nothing more. I first used small massing models to work through the problem. While designing I try to transform my ideas very quickly into small conceptual models. The first move was to slide things apart to allow light into the corridor. I made more room, made the corridor bigger and connected one piece to the rest of the building, making it possible to pass under the street. The entrance is raised 1.5 meters and from here you will have a view, a perspective, to the library. You enter the building from the center, but it's completely transparent in all directions. After these decisions, I worked to refine the shape, playing a game of moving and changing the heights of the buildings. There is still the question of the façade. How to manage an enormous façade with only small, narrow windows? The original design was a brise soleil over cubic windows, but it was too expensive. So this is taking a lot of time and is still being developed, but the windows are now working from the interior of the offices. When you are sitting you have an impression of the exterior looking down. When standing you see out from different perspectives. This reinforces how the building works as a piece of the city and as an urban building.

THREE TOWERS

Now I will jump to another topic: the three towers—a sustained reflection on what it means to make a tower with one thought leading to the next. The first one is the *Torre Cube* in Guadalajara, Mexico. (fig.2) This is the best project I have done thus far in the second period of my career, though I now have a new project in Zaragoza that is on the same level. Normally a tower design begins with a central core. The building grows up around this core, which is solid for structure and to support circulation. I wanted to challenge this logic by placing a courtyard at the center of a tower. So I took the typical core and cracked it into three pieces that work for structure and also work for circulation. It's the same central core function broken down into three pieces, leaving the center empty. This move permits both circulation and views. Offices

2 *Torre Cube*, 2004–2005, Guadalajara, Mexico

3 *Torre Cube* (study models), 2004–2005, Guadalajara, Mexico

4 *Torre Cube* (model), 2004–2005

can now face the exterior and the interior. They are always in contact with the outside. In a tower the only contact with the exterior is the façade—the envelope. But there is no spatial experience anywhere else. I wanted to offer more spatial experience, more architecture. Spatial experience, this is architecture, no? So instead of thinking of the tower as a question of shape or of skin, I wanted to approach the tower as a spatial experience.

When we arrived the site was completely empty, and now it is full of towers. I like to work in relation to the context but at this moment there was nothing and I was sure that it would change. So I looked for a rule to structure the building. Here are the first small models; I made more than 12. Each was playing with rules of structure. (fig.3) To follow a rule is important, and these must also respond to the program and to an intention. Once I have the rules, a project can proceed to the finish.

The final model really is very small. Before winning the commission I traveled to Mexico to speak with the client, and I brought the model with me in a box. I thought it was better to explain things step by step and not show the model immediately. I started by showing him drawings but he didn't understand anything. And so he asked me, "What's in the box?" I said, "My hamster!" He didn't get it and said, "But the hamster must be hot?" So I opened the box and showed him the small model. (fig.4) The client said, "Wow, I understand now!" And the building contractor said, "It's easy; it's very easy." I received the commission in this moment. (fig.5)

The second tower design is from an invited competition for the bank la Caixa Galicia. I was very close to winning but unfortunately

5 *Torre Cube*, 2004–2005, Guadalajara Mexico

6 Caixa Galicia (rendering), 2008, Coruna

7 *Torre Cube 2* (model)

my design won't be built. I broke the core of the first tower into three pieces to create a courtyard. My idea for the second tower was to break a courtyard into four pieces. The site in La Coruña was very narrow so I first placed sets of parallel shear walls spaced 2.5 meters apart. These walls create four courtyards that divide the tower into four pieces. I then worked to find structural rules that permitted me to shape the massing. (fig.6) Placing a single pillar at the corner of each tower piece allows for vertical movement in the form. I can make the corner pillars however I want and this allows me to experiment with the shape. Multiple shapes are possible but the structural rules are always satisfied. How to meet the ground? Only two of the four pieces come all the way down. One enters the building diagonally, facing the garden. From any point in the interior, you always see through one of the small courtyards. The other pieces of the building are always visible, and you can look through these pieces out to the city. This interior experience is always a spatial experience.

The third tower *Torre Cube 2* is also in Guadalajara and currently under construction. My site is in the middle of a development of terrible towers, real horrors. The client liked my Galicia proposal but because of the surrounding

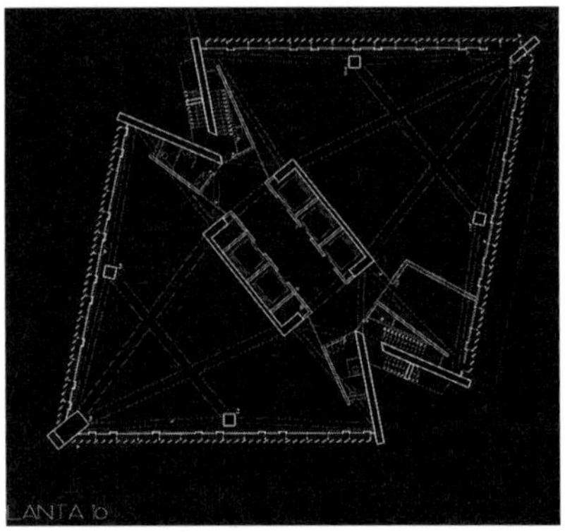

8 *Torre Cube* 2 (plan)

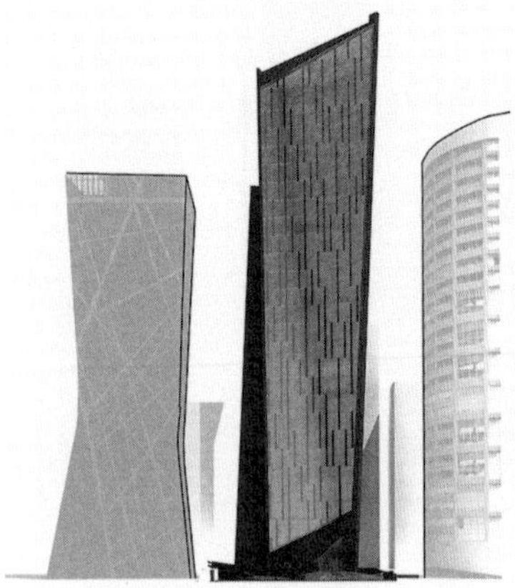

9 *Torre Cube* 2 (rendering)

buildings I decided to make the design more simple and strong. The massing is broken into two pieces, one higher than the other. (fig.7) The client was originally worried about the proportion of circulation to rentable space so I decidedto make the elevator and stair in the optimal way while also enhancing the spatial experience. (fig.8) Notice how the staircase is half inside and half outside—you are inside the building then you move up and are suspended outside. The exterior is clad with a brise soleil. (fig.9)

CAIXAFORUM ZARAGOZA

This is the project that for me is at the level of the *Torre Cube*. It's not a museum but an exhibition building for CaixaForum in Zaragoza. Herzog & de Meuron did a similar project for la Caixa in Madrid, and the brief for my building is the same architectural problem. The problem is actually very simple: two big rooms, one 800 square meters and the other 400 square meters. Surrounding these rooms is an auditorium, a bar, some offices and storage, but it's really all very simple. In a way the entire program is just two big rooms. Our site is in a new park on the periphery of the old city. I decided to elevate the two rooms, permitting one to pass underneath the building. (fig.10) The goal is to connect the periphery to the old city through the park and through the building. So this was the first move, elevating the rooms and intersecting them at the center for circulation. My first sketch also included a structural rule. Two large walls create the primary structure and the rooms are suspended from large beams. The idea of suspension was also present in Herzog & de Meuron's building in Madrid. I liked this but didn't like that they put one room over the other, so in my project I intersect the two rooms. If you go out of the lower one you immediately see the underside of the large room above and the staircase connecting them. You feel a sensation of compression.

The overall massing works with the structure and is derived from the shape of the beams. I wanted to give a sensation of fragility—to show that there are only trusses at the top and that the rooms are suspended from cables without any additional triangulation. For this reason I made a large window at the corner of one of the exhibition rooms showing that there is no heavy structure within the walls. On the exterior, both rooms are clad in aluminum with a leaf-like pattern stamped into the metal. This pattern will be very subtle during the day but at night it will be illuminated. The building will glow and offer light to the park.

10 CaixaForum (model), 2008–2013, Zaragoza, Spain

11 CaixaForum (model), 2008–2013, Zaragoza, Spain

Wolf D. Prix

(Not) The Last Waltz

Edited by Anja Jonkhans and Caroline Ecker
(This lecture was loosely accompanied by a series of images. No direct references were made by the speaker.)

To my students:
The lecture series was very exciting, very intense.
"Selected friends and enemies."
Everyone wanted to be an enemy.
Seems like it is much easier to be an enemy to me than a friend.

There were 24 lectures: different points of departures, different standpoints, different positions.

It was very interesting to listen to the artists—different approaches to art.

It was very interesting to listen to the theorists—very different points of view.

It was great to see all of my favorite colleagues.

Of course it is not the last waltz. This is the last lecture in this series and my last lecture as a teaching professor at this school, but it is not the last lecture forever, certainly!

What does "school" mean to us—to the teachers and to the students?

We announced our upcoming master's program with the topic "We master the future." We do not presume to define the future, but we do have the approach to introduce our students to tools and knowledge in order to master what's coming up. Our school, as well as my teaching, was inspired by the following quote from Antoine de Saint-Exupéry: "If you want to build a ship don't drum up men to gather wood and to distribute the work, but teach them the longing for the wide open sea." That means, don't instruct the students what exactly they have to do. Don't teach them just rules and regulations. In other words, exemplify to them the desire and passion for architecture.

The symbol for our institute could be the open hand. In no way a fist, an open hand. It's an icon created by Le Corbusier, an icon for an open society. There is a deeper meaning as well: Leakey, the anthropologist, insisted that mankind has an opposable thumb in contradiction to monkeys. As a result, monkeys are just able

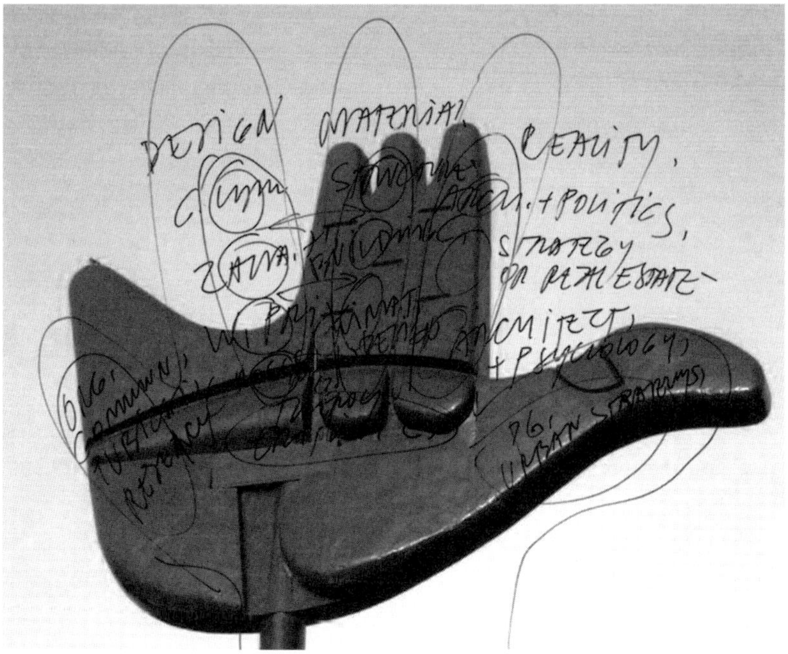

1 *The 5 Fingers of the IoA (Institute of Architecture)*, Wolf D. Prix

to make a fist, whereas man is able to form a pinch grip as well. Sometimes a little movement starts a whole development.

I can describe the development of our school by the following three points: First, we have always tried to create an open platform for investigation, discussion and invention. Second, the interna-tional network supports the students during their studies and allows them to exchange and discuss their ideas in a broader field. The third key is mentorship. We are on the way to creating an alumni community with the goal of supporting and encouraging graduated students.

A long time ago in 1991, when I started to teach here, the studio was like an empire with one emperor on top. When I tried to introduce the word "review," the students replied: "We don't know the word 'review,' we only know the word 'correction.'" I was trained to be a teacher in the USA. "Review" is the way students are taught in the United States. So I went to the former rector and said: "I need to invite people in order to have profound discussions with the students." He answered: "Here, only appointed teachers shall teach students." Finally I did invite guests, willing to bear the costs out of my own pocket. But a lot of people then also came without asking for payment.

After having spent 21 years at the Angewandte it is time to retire. The older an architect gets, the more bad experiences he accumulates. If one shares these bad experiences with students, they might give up their studies. Therefore, a younger teacher should come in—share his passion, his enthusiasm—and the older teacher should move into strategic positions.

A school's reputation can be measured by their graduates' successes. In these 21 years we supervised 250 diplomas. Some examples of the most renowned are: Hannes Stiefel, who just finished his first

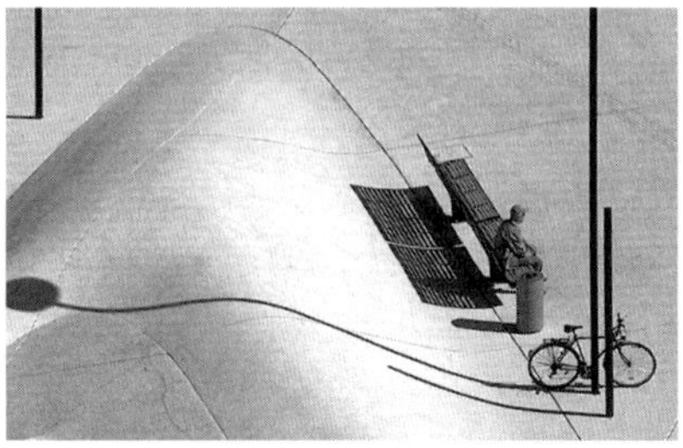

2 Stiefel & Company Architects / LAAC Architects, Landhausplatz, Innsbruck, Austria, 2011

3 Klaus Stattmann, Fluc & Fluc_Wanne, Praterstern 5, Vienna, Austria

4 the next ENTERprise architects: Marie-Therese Harnoncourt, Ernst Fuchs, Wolkenturm, Freiluftbühne Grafenegg, Austria

5 SOMA - Kristina Schinegger, Stefan Rutzinger, Martin Oberascher, Thematic Pavilion, EXPO 2012 Yeosu, South Korea

6 Urs Bette, Design of an Artist-in-Residence Studio for the Australian Experimental Art Foundation, Adelaide, Australia, 2010

project in Innsbruck. Klaus Stattmann, who realized a famous building at the entrance of the Wiener Prater—the Fluc. Next ENTERprise built a fabulous cloud tower as an acoustic tool for a concert area. SOMA recently won a competition in South Korea. Urs Bette, teaching nowadays in Australia, did an experimental living quarters for artists. And I would like to mention all those former students and graduates who are in main positions in our office. These are Luzie Giencke, Andrea Graser, Sophie Grell, Thomas Hindelang, Ivana Jug, Karin Miesenberger, Quirin Krumbholz, Alexander Ott and Guilio Polita.

Bob Dylan: I really like his texts and know many of his texts by heart—sometimes it's a real pleasure to communicate via Bob Dylan songs, preferably with my friend Eric Owen Moss. In connection with our school I want to cite the following quote: "You don't need a weatherman to know which way the wind blows." Think about it. Or: "Don't follow leaders, watch the parking meters."

AN ARCHITECT MUST HAVE 7 LIVES—LIKE A CAT—IN ORDER TO SURVIVE:

FIRST: ENOUGH IS NOT ENOUGH. WE NEED TO DESIRE MORE.
Imagine Che Guevara announcing the "Burning Wing." When visiting a market in Havana, I noticed a table full of books. There were seven books with the title "Che Guevara talks to students about the architecture of the revolution." Che Guevara was a minister back then. Did you ever see a minister here in school talking to us about the architecture of the future? Have you ever seen the chancellor here? So why shouldn't I praise Che Guevara for talking about architecture?

SECOND: ARCHITECTURE IS NOT SURFACE. IT'S CONTENT.
Lady Gaga. Do you know one single song of hers? Of course you know her appearance, her fancy dresses, her masquerade, her glamorous shell—but can you remember the content? Maybe not, because there is no content at all. So I would like to transfer this phenomenon in pop culture to architecture. Architecture is the three-dimensional imprint of our culture on a meta-level. In our current digitized world, which mainly addresses our short-term memory, we need buildings that are readable, writable ... memorable. We must set signs that overcome anonymity. Otherwise we will lose our identity in the anonymity of the random noise of digital images.

THIRD: ARCHITECTURE IS THE SYNERGY BETWEEN CONTENT AND FORM.
As a consequence, content is related to surface.

FOURTH: YOU ARE THE BEST, BUT ARCHITECTURE IS A TEAM GAME.
According to a soccer game, there are different positions, which are constantly changing, and there is a key player who has to perform the task of providing the right player at the right time with the ingenious pass for a goal. In the fields of architecture, Le Corbusier

is the only one I can accept as a singularity without a team.

FIFTH: COMPLEXITY: PLAN = SECTION = VIEW = DETAIL
Complexity only exists if plan equals section and if plan equals view and detail equals ground plan. We started to experiment by appropriating methods from the fine arts, philosophy and education, and produced drawings that were no longer architectural drawings in the traditional sense. They came about automatically, as psychographs of the feelings that the buildings would have when built. We read the plan as outline, as section, as detail. This amounts to freeing the space from the ground plan. And complex problems require complex solutions. Yet it is very difficult to understand complex solutions. They take their time. Simple solutions are easily understood, but unlike simple solutions, complex solutions are always new.

SIXTH: REMEMBER: WHEN THE GRID VANISHES, GESTALT—NOT FORM BUT GESTALT—STILL REMAINS.

LAST BUT NOT LEAST, SEVENTH: TAKE YOUR TIME BUT NOT TOO LONG.

OPEN SYSTEMS AND SELF-DETERMINATION:
We are building for an open society, a society which is connected to everyone, but which is not listening to everyone even though or because everyone is connected to everyone. Closed societies with their rules and regulations prohibit free personal development. Our ego society replaces emotions in architecture with programs, rules and regulations. At this point my second quote of Bob Dylan: "... Oh Mama, is this really the end? To be stuck inside of Mobile with the Memphis blues again." Try to exchange the words "Mobile" and "Memphis" with client and architecture.

7 Architecture is not surface. It is content

8 ... architecture is a team game. COOP HIMMELB(L)AU presented by Erwin Wurm

9 Piedra Movediza de Tandil, Argentina

10 Iceberg, photomontage: Ralph A. Clevenger, 1999

Jan Philipp Reemtsma, a German writer, insisted that nowadays a person who finds a plane in an airport at the right time, which brings him to the right spot, is a complex person compared to a Stone Age hunter who follows the tracks of a deer. If we talk about architecture nowadays, we are only talking about the peak of an iceberg. Usually we do not talk about the submerged, the invisible architecture. Architecture nowadays is managed by clients who are not clients anymore. There are committees managed by lawyers, project managers who self-proclaimed seem to know everything about architecture, about society, about aesthetics. There are project managers who have no clue about the intention, but a smug opinion of how to calculate and therefore judge a building. So this is about politics: Architecture is heavy. Weight costs time and money. Time and money is politics.

In former times—20 years ago—we compared the process of designing with a leaping whale because *entwerfen* is a very complex procedure and it's related to the subconscious and to reality, like a leaping whale. This leaping whale actually—in the moment when the paradigms change, from subconscious to consciousness—architecture or the whale can fly.

STRATEGY:
I would like to exemplify my conclusions on the basis of the game strategy of the soccer club FC Barcelona. There is one remarkable fact in a soccer game: based on the amount of passes, usually, you can tell who the winner is. A soccer game nowadays, similar to playing chess, means every player knows exactly what to do, like the figures on a chess field. It's a so-called regulated game. A game about "knowing:" knowing when to pass, knowing who is running left or right sided, knowing everything. There is an interesting reflection on this while analyzing the FC Barcelona's play: Two parameters are breaking the rule. They are called Xavi and Messi. Two players, who are following the non-rules of "Straßenfußball"—street soccer. Intentionally they break the rules and create—against all odds—more chances than all the other players. Therefore, sometimes breaking the rules in order to create new things is better than

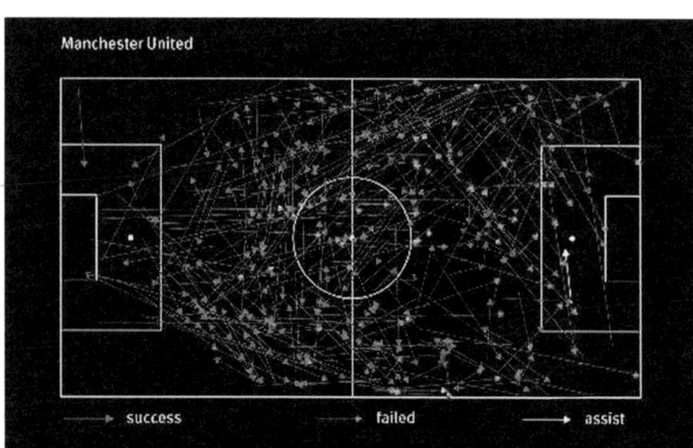

11 Game Strategy FC Barcelona

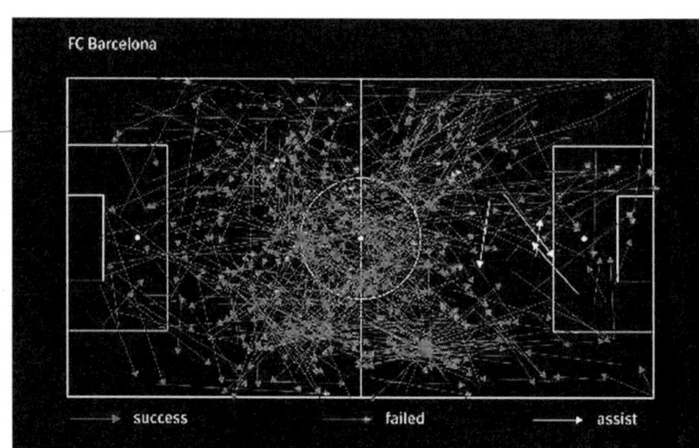

12 Game Strategy Manchester United

13 Constantin Brancusi, *Muse endormie II*, ca. 1925

14 *Cloud #9*, 1995, UNO Genf, Geneva, Switzerland

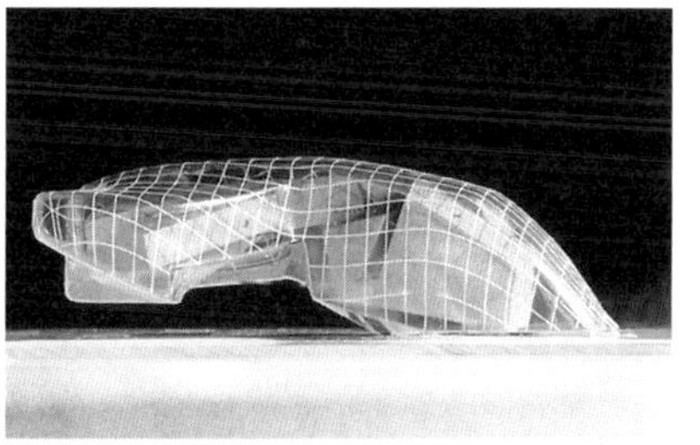

15 *Cloud #9*, 1995, UNO Genf, Geneva, Switzerland

following the rules. "Don't follow the leaders, watch the parking meters."

FORM:

Open and closed forms. Computer generated, closed forms. That means one plus one is two. Brancusi and a lot of other artists created open shapes. These open forms converge to the term "Gestalt." We always tried to introduce random into a strict procedure.

In 1995, by means of a project for the UNO Geneva, we started with experimenting to include randomness as a parameter into our work. Of course, form as well as tools are changing through time. For example, our project for a Chess Academy in Baku, Azerbaijan: In order to introduce "conscious failures," forms which are generated with the help of the computer get remodeled by hand. Or we think about how a dolphin becomes architecture: a sculpture in the middle of two museums under one roof, developed for a project in China. The dolphin is inspired from the image of the moon Phobos and its characteristic strictly "wrong" way of circulating around Mars.

RECENTLY, WE HAVE FIVE PROJECTS ONSITE:

The first is the European Central Bank in Frankfurt. Only with my friend and colleague Klaus Bollinger we were able to define a structure like this. At all times mankind tried to overcome gravity—the Gothic Cathedral acts as a role model for structure meaning to overcome gravity in order to liberate space—like the challenge of the structure and the deformation of the structure of the European Central Bank. We won the competition for the Musée des Confluences in Lyon in 2001, the same time as the BMW Welt and Akron Art Museum. Politics were very hard to overcome, so it took us more than 10 years to get onsite.

16 *Cloud #9*, 1995, UNO Genf, Geneva, Switzerland

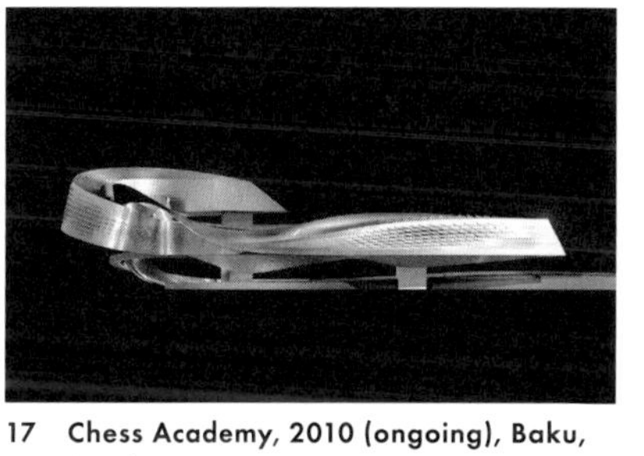

17 Chess Academy, 2010 (ongoing), Baku, Azerbaijan

18 Phoebus circulating around Mars

19 Museum of Contemporary Art & Planning Exhibition, 2007–2015, Shenzhen, China

20 Museum of Contemporary Art & Planning Exhibition, 2007–2015, Shenzhen, China

21 Museum of Contemporary Art & Planning Exhibition, 2007–2015, Shenzhen, China

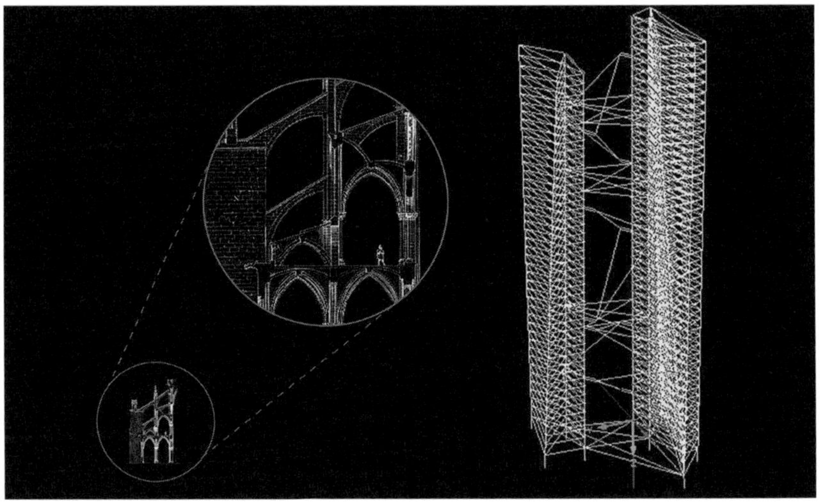

22 European Central Bank (ECB), 2003–2014, Frankfurt/M., Germany

23 European Central Bank (ECB), 2003–2014, Frankfurt/M., Germany

I believe that the realization of thoughts, especially in architecture, is a very important part of the work.

Remember: Only through radical strategies can one really become successful in realizing radical ideas. Otherwise your ideas remain dead paper. And nowadays only ideas which are realized can prove the power of the original idea; in reverse, only realizable ideas are worth thinking of. Therefore, I like the point of departure, the point of breaking the ground, the moment when an idea turns into reality.

24 Musée des Confluences, 2001/2010–2014, Lyon, France

Another project is the Busan Cinema Center in South Korea. It's a building for the Asian Movie Festival. The roof has the largest cantilever in the world, decorated with the Guinness World Record in 2011. It's only held in place by the double cone. The cantilevered part measures 85 meters. When the roof was ready onsite to get fixed, we were confronted with the issue that due to climate change the wind speeds are increasing. So we were supposed to recalculate the wind loads and probably even redesign and rebuild the whole roof. Our solution was to introduce two hydraulic columns hidden in the ground. If the wind is stronger than 200 miles per hour the columns will ascend and hold the roof in place.

Coop Himmelb(l)au, however, has always felt a strong obligation to the roof. It was Corbusier and Niemeyer who liberated the roof from its solely protective function, redefining and adding new meanings to it. Whilst Corbusier created roof landscapes, Oscar Niemeyer, whose roof of the House Canoas in Brazil no longer followed the floor plan of the house, spanned

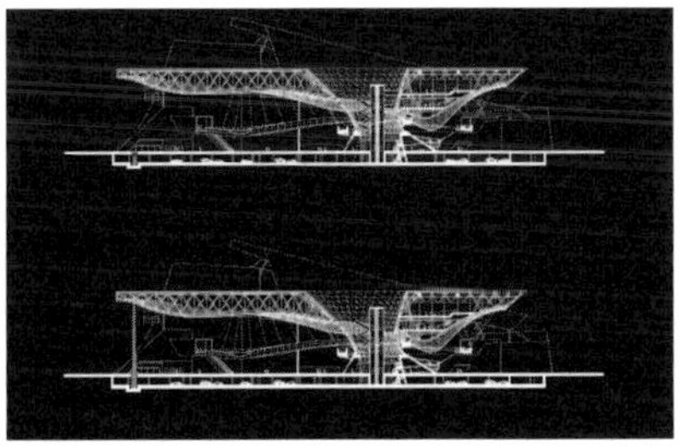

25/26/27 Busan Cinema Center—Busan International Film Festival, 2005–2012, Busan, Korea

28 Oscar Niemeyer: *Casa das Canoas*, 1954, Rio de Janeiro

29 Le Corbusier: Unité d'Habitation, 1946–1952, Marseille

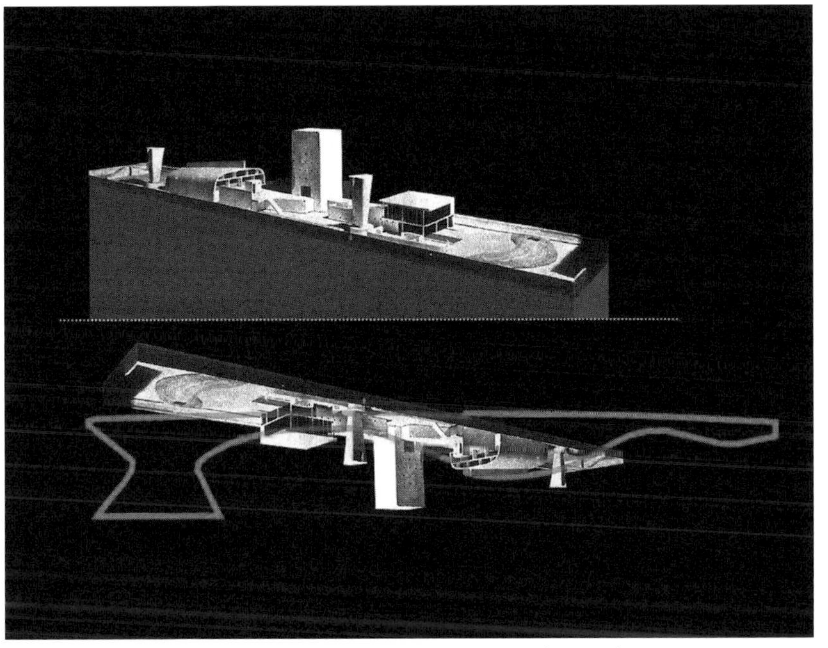

30 Roof Comparison: Unité d'Habitation, Marseille—BMW Welt, Munich

a framework for nature views. The roof has ever since lost its solely protective function and gained added value—one of the things that fascinates us most.

The roof's function shifted from being purely protective to bundling building functions, until it finally developed into a functional sculpture—such as was done at the BMW World in Munich: as a reference to Le Corbusier we turned the roof landscape upside down, in order to differentiate space.

Our building in Dalian, China, is a conference and cultural center, situated west of Beijing at the Chinese Sea. Beautiful site, beautiful size. A long time ago we introduced this idea of "The feeling of the inside stretches the skin of the outside," and is de-forming it. The program: 35 conference halls surrounding an opera, exhibition spaces and galleries—all connected by bridges and ramps. Our interpretation of an urban structuring of space. The skin serves the climate concept. The whole building is designed to offer natural light. For us this was very important. Usually conference centers only have artificial light, which is not only tiring but also wastes energy.

Due to the Chinese client's request to present conventional European Opera as well as entertainment shows or even conferences, the different needs for the "multifunctional" opera were rather complex to design. The overall acoustic concept follows the issue of having the best acoustical conditions for all these performances. The structure uses the amount of steel, equaling the weight of 40 tanks. The façade of the building is very complex and highly differentiated. In opposition to a black box it's a glass box with louvers. The louvers are following the rules of the energy concept: They save 30 percent energy, more than the code requires. Shading on the one hand, creating passages for the wind in order to provide natural circulation on the other hand. And, they confer a lively visual appearance to the building.

Parts of the structure are built in a shipyard. As Le Corbusier said, you have to build a building like a ship. Corbusier promised it, we hold the promise. A lot of our structures were built in shipyards because of amongst other things their special knowledge of bending huge twisted parts.

The last project I want to introduce is our smallest one. Sometimes it can be very refreshing, after having all these big-scale projects with lots of people and partner companies involved, to have a small project where things can be investigated and some ideas get clarified. The new church is located in Hainburg/Donau, my hometown. The roof was built in a German shipyard, brought to site and set on top of the building by a crane. The main idea for the roof was taken very intentionally from Le Corbusier: catching light in tubes. In our building the roof of his church in Ronchamp and the tubes of La Tourette are cited, combined and further developed. I would describe this project as "conscious random": a lot of things we invented did not consider the liturgy of the church, but the people of the church interpreted it as very intentional. For example, the theme of the table: the roof is sitting on a table-like structure. In turn, the table is one of the most important liturgy tools in the Protestant church. And of course we chose three tubes, three light snakes. As we know, three is a holy number. The façade has the surface of a desert sand dune so therefore it got interpreted as a liturgical approach—Jesus in the desert—but it wasn't. It was just

31 Dalian International Conference Center, 2008–2012, Dalian, China

32 Dalian International Conference Center, 2008–2012, Dalian, China

33 Dalian International Conference Center, 2008–2012, Dalian, China

34 Martin Luther Church, 2008–2011, Hainburg, Austria

35 Martin Luther Church, 2008–2011, Hainburg, Austria

36 Martin Luther Church, 2008–2011, Hainburg, Austria

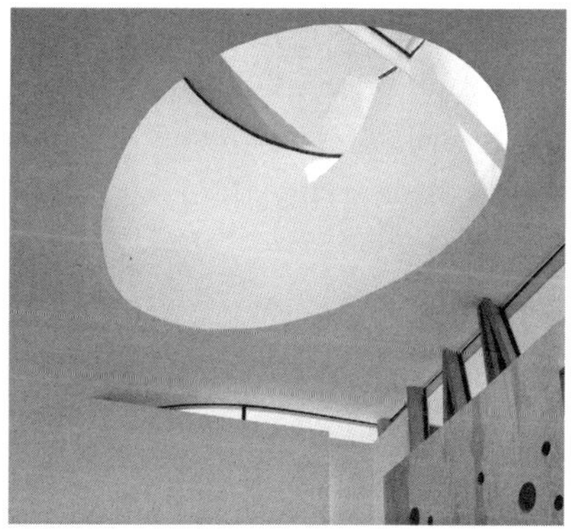

37 Martin Luther Church, 2008–2011, Hainburg, Austria

our intention to do a church like we wanted to do a church.

Nearby the site, a Romanesque building from the twelfth century—actually a bone house—is located. We adopted the curve of this ancient roof, calculated and simulated it in the computer and then of course modulated it. The first step was creating a model and afterwards destroying the model to create the curve by hand. Imagine an ancient roof as the forming parameter for light snakes creating a distorted ceiling.

The roof structure itself was built in a very sophisticated shipyard. Finally, when we had to choose the layer for the interior ceiling where the plaster could be applied, we decided to use reed, a very ancient and also traditional material. It was definitely the best way to follow the sculptural shape of the inside of the roof.

Furthermore, we combined two ways to put a roof on a wall. On the one side there is the simple way, like Mies van der Rohe has done it with his Barcelona Pavilion. On the other side there is this very intelligent, sculptural way to lift up the roof, originally also invented by Le Corbusier: a joint out of light. Of course the church is some kind of light experience. From the outside the façade seems to be more a glass curtain than a façade, inside a cross carved in wood. The altar follows the same geometry rules as the roof.

Everybody is right but nothing is correct. Believe me or not. It's up to you. Last but not least I would like to draw a perspective for the future. Before that, I want to express my gratitude to this school for allowing me to teach architecture here, to discuss ideas with my colleagues and to research for the formal, structural and technical requirements of a future society.

The best description of architecture of the future can be read in H. Melville's *Moby-Dick*: "Would now the wind but had a body; but all the things that most exasperate and outrage mortal man, all these things are bodiless, but only bodiless as objects, not as agents." Can you imagine the wind having a body? If yes, then you are an architect.

Therefore the future of architecture is no gravity, no columns and buildings hanging in the sky.

Can you imagine a building built from the song "Gimme Shelter" by the Rolling Stones? The sound of Keith Richard's guitar: If we can do that then the wind will have a body. Structures generated by music are my dream. Sooner or later we will build buildings like the Rolling Stones are playing music.

Thank you very much!

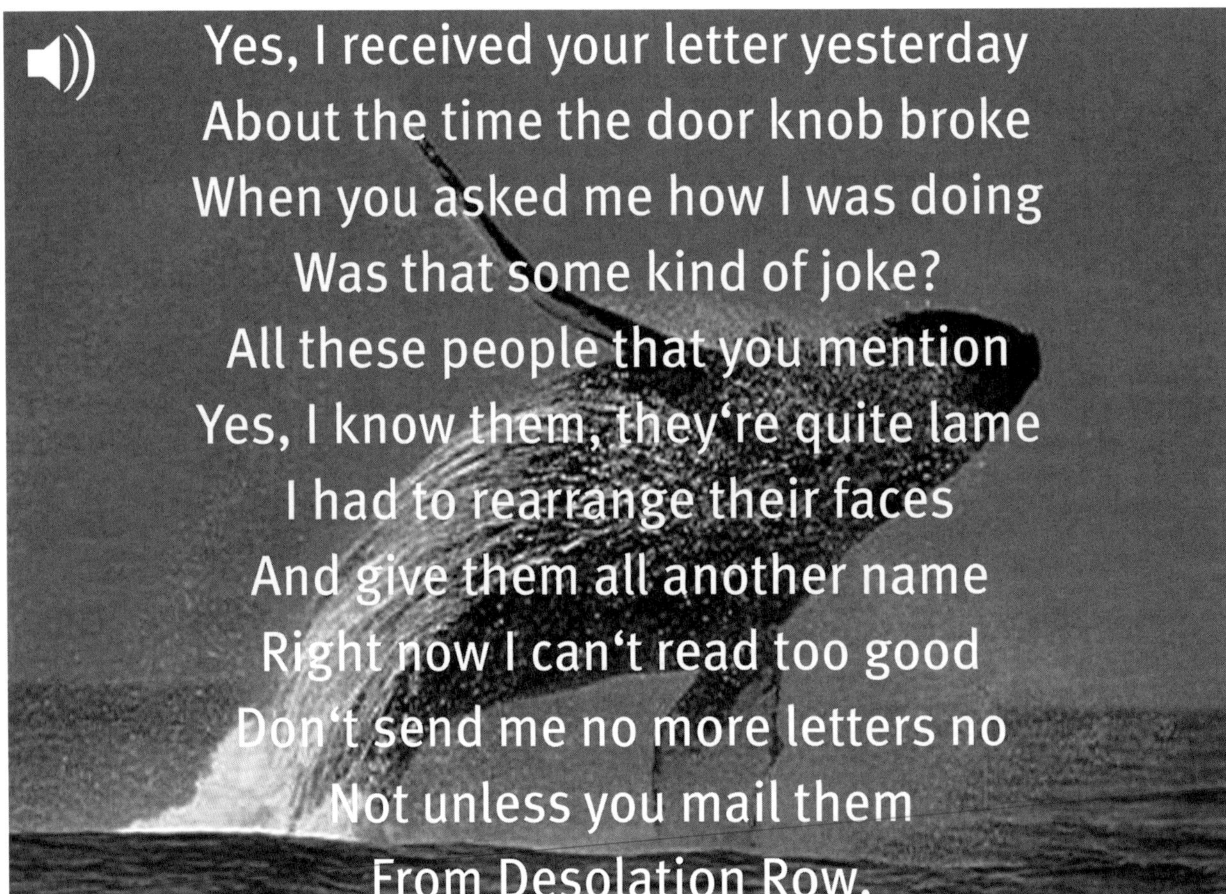

38 "A jumping whale. A whale, a fish, that is not a fish changes from one medium to the next; and in the moment when it moves from water to air, 30 tons fly."

Field Relationships

Afterword by Kristy Balliet

"It's complicated". A common status for both personal and professional relationships. A discipline is defined by relationships, alliances and intense associations—we define each other. A lecture series is a means to "set up" relationships. Encounters that are charged by opposition, sparked by admiration and embody nuanced perspectives. The lecture series *Massive Attack: Selected Friends and Enemies* was developed as a prolonged encounter, a retrospective—of sorts—marking the retirement of Professor Wolf D. Prix from the University of Applied Arts Vienna. Invitations were extended to a diverse set of characters, representing a range of connections—from the flourishing to the strained. This publication is an edited* collection of such perspectives, the description of relationships, anecdotes on the past and predictions for the future.

Vienna has often fostered the avant-garde. It has at times enjoyed the liberation associated with its peripheral status, a non-center. The *SLIVER* series developed precisely as a means to cultivate the palpable mood of the fringe, to take advantage of the status of outlier. When people are removed from the obligations of the center they loosen up, take risks and let you in—if only a little. As an outsider in Vienna, I had a heightened awareness of the profound differences this institution embodied. The series took advantage of the confluence of guests that had relationships with the university and their willingness to experiment socially and pedagogically. This publication offers an opportunity to look at what this constellation of events says about relationships at a particular moment in time. In a city known for the response to any inquiry that probes beyond the status quo as *nicht möglich*—not possible—this was a time when everything was possible!

The quantity of lectures, 24 in a single semester, was Massive. The density of lectures, at times three per week, contributed to the "attack" quality. The intensity and proximity of lectures allowed them to flow one from the other, from the hall to the bar. The audience grew. It was a giant conversation that had multiple entry points. For the students it was a first date, for others it was complicated. The influence and impact of our peers is one of the most critical components that assist in defining an architect's agenda.

Peers challenge our motives and support agendas. We push off of, stand on the shoulders of and in the best of cases launch from the one to many in a linked network. The lectures range from hotel pillow talk, first exposures, childhood memories and chance encounters. It was a game of charades. Full of pretense, chatter, drama, the division of teams and entertaining conviction.

You find yourself in the narratives. The series and indeed this publication is two-fold, an opportunity to highlight intimate relationships critical to the field of architecture and to draw others into the affair.

* The lectures have been transcribed and edited for length and clarity.

Hitoshi Abe is an architect, professor and the Chair of UCLA's Department of Architecture and Urban Design. He is the principal of Atelier Hitoshi Abe, founded in 1993 in Sendai, Japan and in Los Angeles. Known for architecture that is spatially complex and structurally innovative, the work of Atelier Hitoshi Abe has been published internationally and received numerous awards.
www.a-slash.net

Kristy Balliet is an assistant professor at The Ohio State University's Knowlton School of Architecture. She is a co-founder of the Possible Mediums Project, a series of events showcasing design investigations based in speculative architectural mediums. From 2006-2011, Balliet was an assistant professor at the University of Applied Arts Vienna in Studio Greg Lynn. She was the co-creator of the SLIVER series and editor of the *Visual Catalog: Greg Lynn's Studio*.
www.kristyballiet.com

Aaron Betsky is a prolific writer and editor with a dozen books and articles to his credit. Mr. Betsky is a former professor with the School of Architecture and Interior Design (now DAAP) at the University of Cincinnati, and he continues teaching and lecturing in the United States and abroad. He was the Director of the Cincinnati Art Museum. He is currently the dean at the Frank Lloyd Wright School of Architecture at Taliesin and Taliesin West.

Brennan Buck is principal of FreelandBuck in New York and Los Angeles and a critic at the Yale School of Architecture. His work and writing focus on technology within the discipline and its associated aesthetic culture.
www.freelandbuck.com

Sir Peter Cook, founder of Archigram, former Director of the Institute of Contemporary Arts, London, and the Bartlett School of Architecture at University College London, has been a pivotal figure within the global architectural world for over half a century. In addition to his roles at the ICA and UCL, Peter has been director of Art Net in London and curator of the British Pavilion at the Venice Architecture Biennale. He practices with Gavin Robotham as CRAB (Cook Robotham ArchitecturalBureau).
www.crab-studio.com

Kristin Feireiss is an author, art historian and the co-founder (with Helga Retzer †1984) of the Aedes Architecture Forum in Berlin, founded in 1980 as the first private architecture gallery worldwide. Since 1994 she partnered with Hans-Jürgen Commerell. K. Feireiss was director of the Netherlands Architecture Institute (NAi) in Rotterdam from 1996 until 2001, commissioner of the Dutch Pavilion of the Architecture Biennale in Venice in 1997 and 2001, was awarded with Dr. h.c. by the University of Braunschweig in 2007 and has been a jury member for the Pritzker Prize since 2013.
www.aedes-arc.de

Zaha Hadid is the founder of Zaha Hadid Architects and was awarded the Pritzker Architecture Prize in 2004. She is internationally known for both her theoretical and academic work. Each of her dynamic and innovative projects builds on over 30 years of revolutionary exploration and research in the interrelated fields of urbanism, architecture and design.
www.zaha-hadid.com

Marie-Therese Harnoncourt is an architect based in Vienna. She graduated from the University of Applied Arts Vienna, Studio Wolf D. Prix. With her partner, Ernst J. Fuchs, she founded the next ENTERprise–architects in 2000. From the beginning, tnE have operated in a field that ranges from experimental installations to architectural practice, treating both approaches as equal and mutually influential.
www.thenextenterprise.at

Hans Hollein was an architect, designer and exhibition curator. Hans Hollein attended the Akademie der bildenden Künste in Vienna before going on to study architecture and urban planning at the Illinois Institute of Technology in Chicago and the University of California, Berkeley. In 1964 Hans Hollein opened an architecture practice in Vienna and soon made a name for himself worldwide as a leading exponent of postmodernism.
www.hollein.com

Sylvia Lavin is a critic, historian and curator whose work explores the limits of architecture across a wide spectrum of historical periods. Some of her books include *Form Follows Libido: Architecture and Richard Neutra in a Psychoanalytic Culture*, *Flash in the Pan*, *Kissing Architecture and Everything Loose Will Land*. She is Professor at UCLA and has taught at many schools, including Princeton, Harvard and the MAK and is currently working on her next exhibition, *The New Creativity*, which explores transformations in architectural creativity since the advent of computing. (Photo © Richard Schulman)

Greg Lynn is a professor at the University of Applied Arts Vienna. He is the founder of Greg Lynn FORM where in addition to award winning buildings he has designed industrial objects in production with Swarovski, Alessi and Vitra. He won the Golden Lion and represented the United States at Venice Biennales of Architecture, is a fellow of United States Artists and received the American Academy of Arts & Letters Architecture Award. He is the author of eight books. He is founder and chief creative officer of Piaggio Fast Forward and the design advisor for Curbside.
www.glform.com, www.shopcurbside.com, www.piaggiofastforward.com

Winy Maas is one of the co-founding directors of the architecture and urban planning firm MVRDV based in Rotterdam, known for projects such as the Expo 2000 and the vision for greater Paris, Grand Paris Plus Petit. He is a professor and director of The Why Factory, a research institute for the future city, at the Delft University of Technology.
www.mvrdv.nl, www.thewhyfactory.com

Gerhard Matzig is a journalist based in Munich. He studied political science and architecture in Munich and Passau. Working as a freelance journalist, Gerhard became the editor of the feuilleton section of the Süddeutsche Zeitung in 1997. Since 2009 he is the head of the SZ Wochenende.

Thom Mayne is an architect and professor. He founded Morphosis in 1972. As design director and thought leader of Morphosis, Mayne provides overall vision, project leadership and direction to the firm. He is also committed to the education of young designers and currently holds a tenured faculty position at the UCLA School of Arts and Architecture, Los Angeles.
www.morphosis.com

Eric Owen Moss is an architect and the director of SCI-Arc. He is the principal and lead designer of Eric Owen Moss Architects (EOMA). EOMA has built a wide array of award-winning buildings, and has helped shape the discourse of architecture internationally. Eric Owen Moss has held teaching positions at major universities around the world including Harvard, Yale, Columbia, University of Applied Arts Vienna and the Royal Academy in Copenhagen. He was honored as the 2006 AIA/LA Educator of the Year.
www.ericowenmoss.com

Peter Noever is a designer, curator and exhibition designer. From 1986 to 2011 he was Artistic Director and CEO of the MAK (Austrian Museum of Applied Arts / Contemporary Art), Vienna and Los Angeles. He has edited and authored numerous books, magazines and other publications on art, media, design and architecture.
www.noever-design.com

Nicolai Ouroussoff was named the architecture critic of the New York Times in 2004, where he was a finalist for the Pulitzer Prize in 2006. Before that, from 1996 to 2004, he was the architecture critic of the Los Angeles Times, where he was a finalist for the Pulitzer Prize in 2003 and 2004. He is currently writing a book on architecture in the twentieth century for Farrar, Straus and Giroux.

Carme Pinós is an architect based in Barcelona. After reaching professional recognition together with Enric Miralles she established her own practice in 1991. She has combined her career as an architect with teaching, participating in seminars, courses and workshops. She has also been guest professor at universities including Columbia University in New York (1999), the École Polytechnique Fédérale in Lausanne (2001–2002), the Harvard University Graduate School of Design (2003), the Accademia di Architettura di Mendrisio in Switzerland (2005–2006) and the Università di Roma Tre (2007–2008).
www.cpinos.com

Wolf D. Prix co-founded COOP HIMMELB(L)AU in 1968. After teaching abroad he responded to a call as professor of the University of Applied Arts Vienna in 1993 where he served as vice-rector until 2011 and head of the Institute of Architecture until 2012.
www.coop-himmelblau.at

Hani Rashid co-founded the New York-based collaboration Asymptote Architecture with Lise Anne Couture in 1989. The practice has been situated on the forefront of technological innovation in the field of architecture, having received numerous awards and recognition for visionary projects ranging in scale from art installations to building design to master planning. Currently he leads a studio at the University of Applied Arts in Vienna Austria.
www.asymptote.net

Michael Rotondi, FAIA, was a founder and partner of Morphosis (1975–1991) and RoTo Architects (1991 until present). He was a founder—and from 1987 until 1997 the second director—of SCI-Arc. His research and work as a trans-disciplinary educator-practitioner has given him an open-minded approach, which has given him opportunities to work with a diverse range of people, investors, educators, cultural, civic and government leaders, conservationists, Native Americans and Buddhist lamas. The projects are as unique as the personal or working relationships.
www.rotoark.com

Eva Schlegel is an artist who lives and works in Vienna. She attended the University of Applied Arts Vienna with Oswald Oberhuber. From 1997 to 2006, she held a professorship of Art and Photography at the Academy of Fine Arts Vienna. In 2011 she was the commissioner of the Austrian Pavilion at the Venice Biennale.
www.evaschlegel.com

Patrik Schumacher is a partner at Zaha Hadid Architects and founding director at the AA Design Research Lab. Since 2004 Patrik Schumacher has been a tenured professor at the Institute for Experimental Architecture, Innsbruck University. Currently he is a guest professor at the University of Applied Arts Vienna.
www.patrikschumacher.com

Kivi Sotamaa is an international architect and designer based in Helsinki. He is the principal of Ateljé Sotamaa, and founder of ADD Aalto University Digital Design Laboratory. Previously he held professorships at UCLA, the Ohio State University and the Institute of Architecture at the University of Applied Arts Vienna. Sotamaa is one of the most well-respected practitioners from his wave of new digital design, and his work has been particularly significant in exploring innovative lines of communication between digital design technologies and the material realities of construction and manufacturing.
www.sotamaa.net

Brett Steele, AA Dipl, Hon FRIBA, is the Director of the Architectural Association School of Architecture, including the AA Public Programme and AA Publications. In 2008 he founded the AA Visiting School, an international program of global design workshops that have enrolled over 1000 visiting students all over the world. He is partner of desArchLab, an architectural office in London, and has taught and lectured at schools throughout the world.
www.aaschool.ac.uk

Erwin Wurm is an artist currently living in Vienna. His work is primarily sculptural. It is based on objects, installations, drawings, videos, photographs, dust objects and the "One Minute Sculptures." From 2002 to 2011 he was a professor of sculpture and multimedia at the Institute of Fine Arts and a professor of media art at the University of Applied Arts Vienna.
www.erwinwurm.at

ILLUSTRATION CREDITS

Hans Hollein

All images courtesy of Atelier Hollein unless stated otherwise

1 Tomb of Eurysaces the Baker, Rome, 1960
2 Baker's Tomb Inspired Sketch, Hans Hollein, 1960
3 Cantilever Building Sketch, 1958
4 Skyscraper Sketch, Chicago, from left to right: 1958, 1959, 1960
5 Skyscraper Sketches, Chicago, 1958
6 *Potjomkin* Sculpture, University of California Berkeley, 1960; © Hans Hollein
7 Collage Over Vienna, 1960, Collection Centre Georges Pompidou, Paris
8 Aircraft Carrier in the Landscape, 1964, Collection MoMA Museum of Modern Art, New York, Philip Johnson Fund, 1967
9 Rolls Royce Grill on Wallstreet, 1966
10 Retti Candle Shop, Vienna, 1964–1965; photo Franz Hubmann
11 Städtisches Museum Abteiberg Mönchengladbach, 1972–1982; photo Sigfried Mayske
12 Museum of Glass and Ceramics Tehran, 1977–1978; photo Jerzy Surwillo
13 Mobile Office, 1969; photo Gino Molin-Pradel
14 Hans Hollein, Non-Physical Environment Pill, 1969
15 *Strada Novissima, The Presence of the Past*, 1980, Venice Biennale, 1980; photo Atelier Hollein/Franz Madl
16 Vulcania, European Center of Volcanism, St. Ours-les-Roches, France, 1994–2002; photo Atelier Hollein/Sina Baniahmad
17 Vulcania Museum Sketch, 1994, Hans Hollein, Archive
18 SBF Tower Shenzen, China (rendering), 2009

Eva Schlegel

All images courtesy of Atelier Eva Schlegel unless stated otherwise

1 Untitled, 1985, Super8 film on ventilator, diameter 60 cm
2 Untitled, 1985, graphite on plaster, pigment on plaster, 30 × 20 cm each
3 Untitled, 1989, graphite on plaster, silkscreen on lead, 140 × 100 cm
4 Untitled, 1991, Installation view Kunsthaus Aarau, graphite on plaster, silkscreen on lead, 140 × 100 cm each
5 Untitled, 1993, silkscreen on glass, 180 × 113.5 cm texts, 17 × 10 cm
6 Untitled, 1993, 1,000 books with blurred texts, 17 × 10 cm each
7 Untitled, 2010, installation view MAK, Vienna, video projection on rotors, 380 cm
8 Untitled, 2007, silkscreen on lead, 30 × 40 cm
9 Untitled, 2010, installation view MAK, Vienna, 500 balloons

Kivi Sotamaa

All images courtesy of Sotamaa Design unless stated otherwise

1 *Spanish Dancer*, 21st Century Museum of Contemporary Art, 2004, Kanazawa, Japan
2 *Extraterrain*
3 *Orca*
4 *aDrift*, New York Times Capsule Competition, 1999
5 Töölö Stadium, Helsinki Finland
6 *Mantaray*
7 *Ahead*
8 *TerraCultura*, 1997, Jyväskylä
9 *Intencities*, 2000, Helsinki, Finland
10 *Frozen*
11 *Flowers*, PS1/MoMA, 2006
12 *Sirocco*, 2010, Helsinki, Finland

Erwin Wurm

All images courtesy of Studio Wurm unless stated otherwise

1 *Untitled*, 1997, oil paint
2 *59 positions*, 1992, c-print
3 Gasteiger+Reiter, 2011; photo Elfie Semotan/Wallpaper
4 Untitled, 1989, coat, wood
5 Untitled, 1989, coat, wood
6 *One Minute Sculpture*, 1997, c-print
7 Erwin Wurm, One Minute Sculpture, 1997, c-print
8 *Geste mobil*, 2008, mixed media; courtesy MAK/Museum of Applied Arts Vienna
9 *Fat House*, 2011, iron, wood, polystyrene, aluminium, electric installation, video on DVD; courtesy Galerie Thaddaeus Ropac Paris, France
10 *Fat Convertible*, 2005, mixed media sculpture; courtesy/Image Xavier Hufkens Gallery, Brussels, Belgium
11 *Mies van der Rohe—melting*, 2005, resin, paint
12 *Guggenheim—melting*, 2005, resin, paint; courtesy Galerie Thaddaeus Ropac Paris, France
13 *Butterbrot II*, 2005, aluminium, paint; photo Lisa Rastl
14 *Telekinetically bent VW-Van*, 2006, mixed media, e-mail correspondence; courtesy/Image Städtische Galerie im Lenbachhaus, München, Germany
15 *Mentally Yellow (Apex of the Sun)*, 2008, canvas, wool
16 *House Attack*, 2006, c-print; photo Lisa Rastl
17 *Adorno as Oliver Hardy In the Bohemian Girl (1936) and the burden of desperation*, 2006, acrylic
18 *Fountain for Arthur Rimbaud*, 2007, concrete, water pump; courtesy Xavier Hufkens Gallery, Brussels, Belgium
19 *Big Gulp, Series: Philisophers*, 2009, bronze, patina; courtesy/image Xavier Hufkens Gallery, Brussels, Belgium
20 *Narrow House*, 2010, mixed media; courtesy Galerie Thaddaeus Ropac Paris, France; Xavier Hufkens Gallery, Brussels, Belgium

Aaron Betsky

1 W Hotel Room, Midtown Atlanta; image courtesy of ICRAVE (www.icrave.com)
2 W Hotel Lobby, Midtown Atlanta; image courtesy of ICRAVE (www.icrave.com)
3 Alice Tully Hall, Diller Scofidio + Renfro, 2009, New York; photo Donna Pallotta
4 Alice Tully Hall, Diller Scofidio + Renfro, 2009, New York; photo Iwan Baan
5 Toy Furniture, Greg Lynn, 2008, Venice Biennale; image courtesy Greg Lynn Form
6 Blob Wall Pavilion, Greg Lynn, 2008, SCI-Arc Gallery; image courtesy Greg Lynn Form
7 *The Manhattan Transcripts*, Bernard Tschumi, 1976–1981; image courtesy of Bernard Tschumi Architects
8 *Icebergs*, Lebbeus Woods, 1991; image courtesy of Lebbeus Woods
9 *Underground Berlin*, Lebbeus Woods; image courtesy of Lebbeus Woods
10 *Die Freiheit wird jetzt einfach gesponsert, aus der Portokasse*, 1990 *(Freedom is Now Simply Going to Be Sponsored – Out of Petty Cash)*. © Hans Haacke / VG-Bild Kunst; courtesy Paula Cooper Gallery, New York, photo Werner Zellien

Zaha Hadid

All images courtesy of Zaha Hadid

1 *The Peak Leisure Club*, 1982–1983, Hong Kong
2 Qatar Museum (model)
3 MAXXI National Museum of the 21st Century Arts (spatial diagram), 1998–2009, Rome, Italy
4 MAXXI National Museum of the 21st Century Arts, 1998–2009, Rome, Italy
5 Guangzhou Opera House (exterior rendering), 2003–2010, Guangzhou, China
6 Guangzhou Opera House (interior rendering), 2003–2010, Guangzhou, China

Sir Peter Cook

All images courtesy of CRAB Studio unless stated otherwise

1 Paradise Restaurant, Gunnar Asplund, 1930; photo Svenskform
2 Taiwan Tower (section)
3 *Hidden City* (drawing), 2009
4 Soak City (rendering)
5 Law Library (rendering), University of Economics, Vienna
6 Soheil Abedian School of Architecture, Bond University (interior rendering), 2011, Gold Coast Australia
7 Soheil Abedian School of Architecture, Bond University (cartoon), 2011, Gold Coast Australia
8 Soheil Abedian School of Architecture, Bond University (cartoon), 2011, Gold Coast Australia

Peter Noever

1 *Solar Tree*, Ross Lovegrove, MAK, 2007; photo courtesy of Gerhard Koller/MAK
2 MAK Plattform, Peter Noever and Michael Embacher, 2009; photo courtesy of Stefan Klein/MAK
3 MAK Terminal Ausschnitt + MAK Terminal, Peter Noever and Michael Embacher, 2009; photo courtesy of Stefan Klein/MAK
4 *Judd Stage Set #22*, Vienna; photo courtesy of Gerald Zugmann/MAK
5 *The City Inside Us*, Vito Acconci, 1993; photo courtesy of Gerald Zugmann/MAK
6 The Domestication of a Pyramid,

Magdalena Jetelová; photo courtesy of M. J. Hannappel/MAK
7 *Shooting into the Corner*, Anish Kapoor, 2009; photo courtesy of Wolfgang Woessner/MAK
8 *Open University of Diversity*, Koen Vanmechelen
9 *Narrow House*, Erwin Wurm, Venice
10 *(Des) Orientation*, Magdalena Jetelová

Hitoshi Abe
1 Shirasagi Bridge, 1993–1994, Shiroishi, Miyagi; photo courtesy of Shunichi Atsumi
2 Setsugetsuka Restaurant, 1997–1999, Sendai, Miyagi; photo courtesy of Shunichi Atsumi
3 Yomiuri Guest House, 1995–1997, Zaou, Miyagi; photo courtesy of Shunichi Atsumi
4 Aoba-tei, 2004, Sendai, Miyagi; photo courtesy of Daici Ano
5 Reihoku Town Hall, 2000–2002; photo courtesy of Daici Ano
6 Kanono Museum, 2003–2005, Shiogama, Miyagi; photo courtesy of Daici Ano

Thom Mayne
1 Cooper Union, 2006–2009, New York City; photo Iwan Baan
2 Cooper Union (nterior), 2006–2009, New York City; photo Iwan Baan
3 Phare Tower (rendering), 2006 (ongoing), Paris; image courtesy of Morphosis
4 Phare Tower (optimized skin rendering), 2006 (ongoing), Paris; image courtesy of Morphosis
5 Olympic Village, 2012, New York; image courtesy of Morphosis
6 *YONKXI.*; image courtesy of Michael Powers
7 *YONKXI.* (detail); image courtesy of Michael Powers

Eric Owen Moss
1 *Medusa*; photo Eric Own Moss
2 Trajan over Nero
3 Angkor Wat
4 *The Helmet*, Henry Moore, 1939–1940, Scottish National Gallery of Modern Art; purchased with help from the National Heritage Memorial Fund, the Art Fund (Scottish Fund) and the Henry Moore Foundation 1992
5 *The Desperate Man*, Gustave Courbet, 1843–1845
6 *US-Mexican Border*, 2006; image courtesy of EOMA
7 *Make It New*

Marie-Therese Harnoncourt
1 Zirl House, 1997, Zirl, Austria; photo Lukas Schaller
2 *Blindgänger*, 2000, Austria; photo courtesy of next ENTERprise
3 Lido Bath (collage), 2006, Caldaro/Kaltern, Austria; photo Lukas Schaller
4 Lido Bath, aquarium, 2006, Caldaro/Kaltern, Austria; photo Lukas Schaller
5 Lido Bath, 2006, Caldaro/Kaltern, Austria; photo Lukas Schaller
6 *Ice Storm*, 2003, MAK; photo courtesy of Andorfer
7 Warmbad, 2006, Villach, Austria; photo courtesy of Lukas Schaller
8 Cloud Tower, Grafenegg, Austria; photo courtesy of Lukas Schaller
9 Archaeological Center Mainz (model); photo courtesy of next ENTERprise
10 Archaeological Center Mainz (rendering); photo courtesy of next ENTERprise

Greg Lynn
All images courtesy of Greg Lynn FORM unless stated otherwise
1 Port Authority (rendering), 1995, New York
2 Korean Presbyterian Church, 1999, New York; photo Jan Staller
3 Korean Presbyterian Church, 1999, New York; photo Ari Marcopoulos
4 7th Venice Architecture Biennale, 2000
5 The Predator, 2001, Wexner Center Columbus Ohio.
6 Visionaire, 2001
7 Vitra Ravioli Chair, 2003–2006; photo courtesy of Vitra
8 Sciarra Lantern, 2008
9 Sciarra Lantern, 2008
10 56′ Suncat (rendering)
11 Trimaran (rendering)
12 Bloom House, 2010, Los Angeles; photo Richard Powers
13 Bloom House, 2010, Los Angeles
14 *Triton Fountain*, Gianlorenzo Bernini, Rome
15 *Fountain*, 2010, Hammer Museum Los Angeles; photo courtesy of Brian Forrest

Brennen Buck
All images courtesy of FreelandBuck unless stated otherwise
1 Three Geometries
2 *Technicolor Bloom* (drawing), 2008
3 *Technicolor Bloom*, 2008, Vienna; photo Christof Gaggl
4 *Technicolor Bloom*, 2008, Vienna; photo Christof Gaggl
5 *Surface Poché* (diagrams)
6 Exhibition mockups, 2011, WUHO Gallery
7 Woodlot House Diagram, 2010, Portland Maine
8 Woodlot House (massing), 2010, Portland Maine
9 Woodlot House (rendering) 2010, Portland Maine
10 Detroit Super Division, 2009, Detroit
11 Detroit Super Division, 2009, Detroit

Winy Maas
All images courtesy of MVRDV unless stated otherwise
1 Busan Cinema Complex (diagram), 2005, Busan, South Korea
2 Busan Cinema Complex (rendering), 2005, Busan, South Korea
3 Shanghai Bund Finance Center (concept diagram)
4 Shanghai Bund Finance Center (rendering)
5 WoZoCo Apartments, 1997, Amsterdam, Netherlands; photo Rob 't Hart
6 Didden Village, 2002–2006, Rotterdam, Netherlands; photo courtesy of Rob 't Hart
7 *Transformer* (rendering)
8 *Transformer* (rendering)
9 *Transformable Cell* (rendering); image courtesy The Why Factory

Brett Steele
1 Art + Architecture Building (section perspective drawing), Paul Rudolph, 1959–1963, Image Courtesy of School of Architecture, Yale University, Records Concerning Events and Exhibitions, 1970–2008 (inclusive). Manuscripts & Archives, Yale University
2 Crown Hall, Mies van der Rohe, 1950–1956, Chicago; photo Chicago History Museum
3 *Modulor*, Le Corbusier; © FLC/VBK, 2013

Hani Rashid
All images courtesy of Asymptote
1 Moving Pictures Exhibition, 2002, Guggenheim Musuem, New York
2 Guggenheim Pavilion at Saadiyat Island, 2006, Abu Dhabi
3 YAS Hotel, 2007–2009, Abu Dhabi
4 YAS Hotel, 2007–2009, Abu Dhabi
5 YAS Hotel, 2007–2009, Abu Dhabi
6 YAS Hotel, 2007–2009, Abu Dhabi
7 Documenta Video Installation, 2002, Kassel
8 World Business Center Solomon Tower, 2007 (ongoing), Busan, South Korea
9 Kaohsiung Marine Gateway (rendering), 2010 (ongoing), Kaohsiung, Taiwan
10 Kaohsiung Marine Gateway (interior rendering), 2010 (ongoing), Kaohsiung, Taiwan
11 Beukenhof Crematorium and Auditorium, 2011 (ongoing), Schiedam, Netherlands
12 Beukenhof Crematorium and Auditorium, 2011 (ongoing), Schiedam, Netherlands
13 Beukenhof Crematorium and Auditorium, 2011 (ongoing), Schiedam, Netherlands

Michael Rotondi
All images courtesy of RoTo Architects unless stated otherwise
1 Carlson-Regis House, 1992–1996, Los Angeles
2 Warehouse C, 1997, Nagasaki
3 Construction Drawing of Ari Bhod Temple—Tibetan Buddhist in California
4 Madame Tussauds, 2006–2011, Hollywood
5 New Jersey House (section drawing), 1990–1996
6 Architecture and Art Building, Prairie View, 2003–2005, Texas A&M University, College Station; photo Farshid Assassi
7 Sinte Gleska University, 1994–1998, Rosebud Reservation
8 Miracle Manor Retreat, 1997–2011, Desert Hot Springs, California
9 View towards the Second Mesa
10 Communal Life

Carme Pinós
All images courtesy of Estudio Carme Pinós unless stated otherwise

1 University of Economics (rendering), 2011, Vienna, Austria
2 Torre Cube, 2004–2005, Guadalajara, Mexico; photo Lourdes Grobet
3 Torre Cube (study models), 2004-2005, Guadalajara, Mexico
4 Torre Cube (model), 2004–2005
5 Torre Cube, 2004–2005, Guadalajara Mexico; photo courtesy of Lourdes Grobet
6 Caixa Galicia (rendering), 2008, Coruna
7 Torre Cube 2 (model)
8 Torre Cube 2 (plan)
9 Torre Cube 2 (rendering)
10 Caixaforum (model), 2008–2013, Zaragoza, Spain
11 Caixaforum (model), 2008–2013, Zaragoza, Spain

Wolf D. Prix
All images courtesy of COOP HIMMELB(L)AU unless stated otherwise

1 *The 5 Fingers of the IoA (Institute of Architecture)*, Wolf D. Prix
2 Stiefel & Company Architects / LAAC Architects, Landhausplatz, Innsbruck, Austria 2011, photo courtesy of Günter Richard Wett
3 Klaus Stattmann, Fluc & Fluc_Wanne, Praterstern 5, Vienna, Austria, photo courtesy of Michael Nagl
4 the next ENTERprise architects: Marie-Therese Harnoncourt, Ernst Fuchs, Wolkenturm, Freiluftbühne Grafenegg, Austria, photo courtesy Lukas Schaller
5 Soma – Kristina Schinegger, Stefan Rutzinger, Martin Oberascher, Thematic Pavilion, EXPO 2012 Yeosu, South Korea, photo courtesy of Florian Rist
6 Urs Bette, Design of an Artist-in-Residence Studio for the Australian Experimental Art Foundation, Adelaide, Australia, 2010, photo courtesy of Daniel Kerbler
7 Architecture is not surface. It is content
8 ... architecture is a team game. COOP HIMMELB(L)AU presented by Erwin Wurm, photo courtesy of Erwin Wurm
9 Piedra Movediza de Tandil, Argentina, photo courtesy of Samuel Boote, c. 1880
10 Iceberg, photomontage: Ralph A. Clevenger, 1999, photo courtesy Corbis
11 Game Strategy FC Barcelona
12 Game Strategy Manchester United
13 Constantin Brancusi (1876–1957): Muse endormie II, ca. 1925, Bronze polished; 17 × 27 × 17cm, Kunsthaus Zürich, Legat Heinz Keller, © Bildrecht, Vienna, 2015
14 Cloud #9, 1995, UNO Genf, Geneva, Switzerland, photo courtesy of døgl & cherkoori
15 Cloud #9, 1995, UNO Genf, Geneva, Switzerland, photo courtesy of Markus Pillhofer
16 Cloud #9, 1995, UNO Genf, Geneva, Switzerland, photo courtesy of Markus Pillhofer
17 Chess Academy, 2010 (ongoing), Baku, Azerbaijan
18 Phoebus circulating around Mars
19 Museum of Contemporary Art & Planning Exhibition, 2007–2015, Shenzhen, China, photo courtesy of Markus Pillhofer
20 Museum of Contemporary Art & Planning Exhibition, 2007–2015, Shenzhen, China
21 Museum of Contemporary Art & Planning Exhibition, 2007–2015, Shenzhen, China
22 European Central Bank (ECB), 2003–2014, Frankfurt/M., Germany
23 European Central Bank (ECB), 2003–2014, Frankfurt/M., Germany
24 Musée des Confluences, 2001/2010–2014, Lyon, France, photo courtesy of Hubert Canet, Balloïde Photo
25 Busan Cinema Center—Busan International Film Festival, 2005–2012, Busan, Korea, photo courtesy of Duccio Malagamba
26 Busan Cinema Center—Busan International Film Festival, 2005–2012, Busan, Korea, photo courtesy Markus Pillhofer
27 Busan Cinema Center—Busan International Film Festival, 2005–2012, Busan, Korea, photo courtesy of Nathan Willock
28 Oscar Niemeyer: Casa das Canoas, 1954, Rio de Janeiro
29 Le Corbusier: Unité d'Habitation, 1946–1952, Marseille Roof View, photo courtesy of Lucien Hervé
30 Roof Comparison: Unité d'Habitation, Marseille—BMW Welt, Munich
31 Dalian International Conference Center, 2008–2012, Dalian, China, photo courtesy of Duccio Malagamba
32 Dalian International Conference Center, 2008–2012, Dalian, China, photo courtesy of Duccio Malagamba
33 Dalian International Conference Center, 2008–2012, Dalian, China, photo courtesy of Duccio Malagamba
34 Martin Luther Church, 2008–2011, Hainburg, Austria
35 Martin Luther Church, 2008–2011, Hainburg, Austria
36 Martin Luther Church, 2008–2011, Hainburg, Austria, photo courtesy of Duccio Malagamba
37 Martin Luther Church, 2008–2011, Hainburg, Austria, photo courtesy of Duccio Malagamba
38 "A jumping whale. A whale, a fish, that is not a fish changes from one medium to the next; and in the moment when it moves from water to air, 30 tons fly."

SPECIAL THANKS

The editors would like to thank everybody who contributed to the development and success of the IOA Sliver Lecture Series. The series began with modest means and grand ambitions. The first four years were successful and enjoyable because of you:

Mirta Bilos
Brennan Buck
Eva Diem
Justin Diles
Mihaela Dumitru
Susanna Ernst
Florian Fend
Julcsi Futo
Nora Graw
Florian von Hayek
Niels Jonkhans
Julia Koerner
Csenge Lanszki
Martina Lesjak
Verena Lihl
Oliver Lösser
Greg Lynn
Kriszti Nagy
Maja Ozvaldic
Sabine Peternell
Anna Psenicka
Phillip Reiner
Andrea Sachse
Karl Sekora
Bengt Stiller
Stephan Sobl
Igor Szuba
Siim Tuksam
Markus Willeke
Angelika Zelisko

Video Documentation
Peter Strasser*

*In large part to Peter, most lectures are available to view online at www.i-o-a.at/sliver/2010-friend-and-enemies-massive-attack